– Contents –

Wallace Nutting
(1861 –1941)

By 1917 Wallace Nutting's picture business had become more successful than he had ever dreamed possible. His hand-colored platinotype pictures had caught the attention of an early twentieth century American middle class which purchased literally millions of his interior and exterior scenes. With many day-to-day operations in his profitable picture business turned over to several key employees, Wallace Nutting turned his attention to his true love...early American antiques.

Nutting began actively collecting antiques shortly after moving his picture business to Framingham, Massachusetts, in 1912, and although he began with little practical experience, he soon became a national expert sought out by many of the country's leading (and wealthiest) collectors. Nutting jumped into his newest avocation with a passion. First buying just one antique, and then a few more, his passion grew to where he once purchased the contents of an entire antique shop, just to obtain a few special pieces.

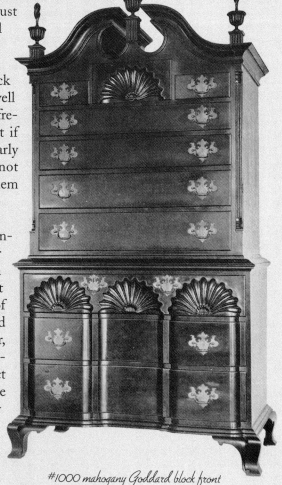

But Nutting certainly wasn't the only person collecting antiques back then. Even as early as 1917 with the colonial revival movement well under way, the finest examples of early American furniture were frequently unobtainable...anywhere. Nutting quickly recognized that if he was having difficulty obtaining the best and rarest forms of early American antiques, so too were other collectors. Many could not afford the finest forms and, quite often, those who could afford them simply could not find them.

Enter the Wallace Nutting furniture reproduction business. Beginning first with Windsor chairs in 1918, Nutting went on to gather some of the finest seventeenth, eighteenth, and early nineteenth century American furniture ever produced. He sought out the best chairs, tables, mirrors, dressers, beds, desks, and literally hundreds of different furniture forms. He would then photograph each piece and document what he saw, analyzing and measuring every leg, stretcher, spindle, and seat, making whatever "improvements" he felt appropriate. He would then reproduce what he perceived to be the perfect piece of furniture...piece-by-piece...turn-for-turn...as close to the original as possible...using many of the same methods employed by eighteenth century furniture makers.

This book is about Wallace Nutting bench-made reproduction furniture. And just so there is no question about how I feel about Wallace Nutting furniture, let me begin this book by stating emphatically, and without reservation, that in my opinion

#1000 mahogany Goddard block front chest-on-chest, from the 1937 furniture catalog

Wallace Nutting produced the finest reproduction furniture of the twentieth century. Better than Margolis. Better than Fineberg. Better than Kittenger. Better than Potthast. Better than Stickley. Better than any of the early twentieth century's best furniture makers.

Wallace Nutting furniture is an area of collecting that has been attracting increased attention in recent years. Until fairly recently it was a closely held secret. Relatively few people, mostly current or former members of the Wallace Nutting Collectors' Club, had been collecting Wallace Nutting furniture since the 1970s with remarkably little competition from the outside world. It was a collecting niche that most of the antiques and collectibles trade pretty much ignored. Occasionally a few speculators jumped into the market hoping to make a quick hit buying and selling Nutting furniture. More often than not they just as quickly jumped out of the market when they realized how little Nutting furniture was available to acquire, and how difficult it was to make a significant profit in this area.

Yet despite all the increased attention that Wallace Nutting collectibles have been receiving in recent years, I'm still amazed at the large number of individuals who still aren't aware that he reproduced furniture. Hopefully this book will change that.

#733 Goddard block front secretary desk, sold by the Weschler Auction Co.

Approximately 10 – 15 years ago I began predicting that Wallace Nutting furniture was ready to skyrocket in price. I had publically stated that Wallace Nutting furniture was the best-of-the-best in early twentieth century furniture and once the word got out, I expected prices to increase exponentially.

Today I will be the first to admit that prices didn't grow quite as quickly as I had anticipated. While Stickley's finest furniture reached $596,500.00 (Christie's — New York, November 1999), Wallace Nutting's finest furniture generally languished below the $5,000.00 level. To my dismay is was not uncommon for certain Wallace Nutting pictures to bring stronger prices at our auctions than Wallace Nutting furniture. What was I missing?

Well, as it turns out...nothing. What I had predicted would take place in the mid 1990s is starting to take place today. It seems that I was just off by a few years.

Back in 1997, Weschler's Auction Co. sold a Wallace Nutting #733 Goddard Block front secretary desk (one of only seven produced by Nutting) for $14,950.00 which set an auction record for a single piece of Wallace Nutting furniture. That may sound like a lot of money to some, but that's really an insignificant amount when talking about quality American furniture. Especially when you are speaking of the best-of-the-best ever produced by the twentieth century's most famous furniture maker.

After that auction record was set our auction company sold a slant front desk for $10,000.00, several other cases pieces for $4,000.00 – 6,000.00, but nothing approaching the $14,950.00 auction record price.

That auction record remained intact until 2002 when another #733 Goddard Block front secretary desk sold for a much stronger $36,750.00, more than doubling the previous auction record set nearly 10 years earlier. Although this didn't even come close to the $596,500.00 Stickley auction record, and although I feel that the ceiling for Wallace Nutting furniture has not ever come close to being reached, at $37,000.00 you're now starting to talk about some serious money.

Introduction

*The 2002 record-setting $36,750.00
#733 Goddard block front secretary desk.
Photo courtesy of the
Sharon & Ken Lacasse collection.*

I published my first book on Wallace Nutting furniture, *The Guide to Wallace Nutting Furniture*, back in 1990. In that book I told the story of Wallace Nutting furniture and provided representative prices on a limited number of pieces that had either sold privately or at auction.

This book goes a great deal further and is actually broken down into two parts. The beginning of the book provides a much more thorough background and history on Wallace Nutting furniture. I have taken the basic story first told in 1990, and updated it based upon 15 additional years of auction experience and 15 additional years of research.

The end of the book, the Price Guide to Wallace Nutting Furniture, is probably the most important part of this book because most people want to know what it's worth, what you should pay, or what you should ask, for a specific piece of Wallace Nutting furniture. This book tries to answer both questions for you by providing actual auction prices, general rules of thumb, and consensus current market values on most Wallace Nutting furniture produced between 1918 and 1937.

On one hand, the price guide was relatively easy for us because The Michael Ivankovich Auction Company is fortunate enough to sell more Wallace Nutting furniture than anyone else in the country. And because of this we probably have better experience pricing Wallace Nutting furniture than anyone.

Yet you would be surprised at the large number of Wallace Nutting furniture designs that have never appeared on the auction or retail market over the past 30+ years. I recently went through the 1932 *Wallace Nutting General Catalog, Supreme Edition*, and ascertained that I had never personally seen, or even heard of anyone owning, 188 of the 330 items pictured in that catalog. This mean that in my 30-year association with Wallace Nutting furniture, I have never seen 57% of the items pictured in that catalog.

So, if no piece has ever surfaced, and if there is no track record of actual sales, how do you reasonably estimate the value of such a piece of furniture? I'll tell you how we did this in An Introduction to Values on page 95.

But as we begin The Wallace Nutting Furniture Story, let's set the stage first with Wallace Nutting pictures, Wallace Nutting books, and Wallace Nutting's quest for early American antiques because each of these three areas played a significant role in the development of Wallace Nutting's reproduction furniture business.

– Chapter 1: Hand-Colored Photographs –

While preparing for the ministry as a Harvard University student in 1886, probably the last thing Wallace Nutting ever envisioned was a career as a photographer, author, publisher, lecturer, collector, or furniture maker, or becoming America's foremost authority on antiques. But that is exactly what life had in store for this versatile and most gifted individual.

Wallace Nutting was born in 1861 in Rockbottom, Massachusetts. Upon his father's death in 1864, during the Civil War, he moved to Maine to live with his grandparents. After working on his grandfather's farm and attending high school there, he entered Exeter Academy in 1880. He attended Harvard University from 1883 to 1886, the Hartford Theological Seminary from 1886 to 1888, and later the Union Seminary in New York.

In 1889, Wallace Nutting was ordained as a Congregational minister at the Park Congregational Church in St. Paul, Minnesota. There was no doubt that he always wanted to become a minister as he was frequently quoted as saying "I would rather preach than anything else on earth." And preach he did. Never willing to accept second best, Wallace Nutting worked unrelentingly at writing the perfect sermon. He would work many days writing each sermon, and would be tired long afterward.

Wallace Nutting, the photographer

Wallace & Mariet Nutting, circa 1938.
Photo courtesy of the Pedro Cacciola collection

While they were living in Providence, Rhode Island, his wife, Mariet Griswold Nutting, had suggested that he take long bicycle rides into the countryside on Mondays, no doubt to relax from the stress he had incurred preparing for his Sunday sermons. He seemed to feel that if he would take his camera along, the trip would become shorter and more fruitful.

As the next several years went by, he began touring the New England countryside while on vacation, either by carriage, car, or train, taking photographs of rural America. Nutting was one of the first to recognize that the American scene was rapidly changing. Industrialization was altering the way America looked and our pure and picturesque country would never look the same again. He seemed to feel it his divine calling to record the beauty of America for future generations.

Perhaps he worked too hard, because his 16 years in the pulpit began to take their toll. Some sources report that he suffered from vertigo. Some say that he suffered a nervous breakdown resulting from the energy he expended preaching. Others speculate that he was simply looking for an excuse to start his new photographic career. Regardless of the cause, Wallace Nutting retired from the ministry in 1904 due to ill health.

Nutting opened his first studio in New York City in 1904, almost immediately after his retirement but apparently the big city atmosphere didn't agree with him. After a lengthy illness, he decided that he needed the fresh air of the country. In 1905 he purchased a pre-revolutionary home in Southbury, Connecticut, which he named Nuttinghame, and opened a much larger photographic studio there.

Hand-Colored Photographs

Honeymoon Stroll,
a typical Nutting exterior scene

Nutting developed a keen eye for composition and he mastered the technical skills of printing high quality pictures on a special platinum paper. He enhanced the beauty of his pictures by having them hand-colored by a small group of colorists he employed in his studio. He placed some of his pictures in several smaller art and gift shops where they readily sold. He then used his early profits to purchase better equipment and to expand the scope of his operations.

Starting first in Vermont, and then eventually traveling throughout the rest of New England, Nutting would photograph country lanes, streams, orchards, lakes, and mountains. Wallace Nutting would take the photograph, assign a title, and instruct his colorists how it should be colored. Each picture that met Nutting's high standards of color, composition, and taste would be affixed to its matting and signed by his employees with the "Wallace Nutting" name. Those pictures that did not meet his strict standards were destroyed.

Beginning first with outdoor scenes in New England, Nutting eventually traveled throughout the United States and Europe, taking photographs in 26 states and 17 foreign countries between 1900 and 1935. Overall, he took more than 50,000 pictures, 10,000 of which he felt met his high standards. The balance were destroyed.

It was around 1905 that Nutting began taking his first interior pictures. Supposedly one day while it was raining outside, Mrs. Nutting suggested that he take a more "personable" picture indoors. So he set up a colonial scene in his Southbury home, had an employee dress up in a colonial fashion, and took several different pictures. These sold relatively easily which encouraged him to expand further into this area.

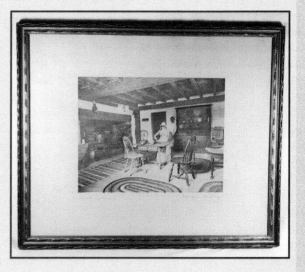

A Stirring Scene,
a typical Nutting interior scene

Nutting interior scenes always featured fine
early American antiques

Working in Southbury, Connecticut, from 1905 to 1912, and then in Framingham, Massachusetts, from 1912 until his death in 1941, Nutting sold literally millions of his hand-colored photographs, each carrying the distinctive "Wallace Nutting" signature. Sold throughout the first portion of the twentieth century, well before the invention of color photography, these pictures initially cost only pennies. His picture market was primarily those middle and lower middle class households which could not afford finer forms of art. Because of their low price, Wallace Nutting pictures were purchased in large numbers and by 1925 hardly an American middle-class household was without one. They were purchased as gifts for weddings, showers, Christmas, birthdays, and just about any other reason imaginable.

Hand-Colored Photographs

The height of Wallace Nutting picture popularity was 1915 – 1925. During this time Nutting employed more than 100 colorists, along with another 100 employees who acted as framers, matters, darkroom printers, salesmen, management, and assorted administrative office personnel.

Let there be no mistake about it — Wallace Nutting Pictures were big business. Shortly before World War I, the business was grossing as much as a thousand dollars a day.

The distinctive Wallace Nutting signature, circa 1915

Summary of Key Points

Wallace Nutting was born in 1861, and his father died during the Civil War.

He was ordained as a Congregational minister in 1889.

After serving several pastorates throughout the country, his final congregation was in Providence, Rhode Island.

He retired from the ministry in 1904 citing personal health reasons, then immediately opened a photography studio in New York City in 1905.

Wallace Nutting worked in Southbury, Connecticut, from 1905 to 1912, and in Framingham, Massachusetts, from 1912 to 1941.

Between 1905 and 1941 Wallace Nutting sold literally millions of his hand-colored interior and exterior scenes.

Wallace Nutting went on to sell more hand-colored photographs than anyone else in history and his research into his colonial interior scenes were partially responsible for his introduction to and love of early American antiques.

Wallace Nutting colorists, circa 1925

Old Mother Hubbard,
Sold at our auction for $8,910.00 in 2002

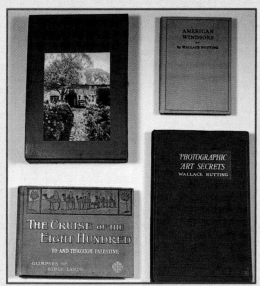

Top row: *England Beautiful; American Windsors*
Bottom row: *Cruise of the 800*
Photographic Art Secrets

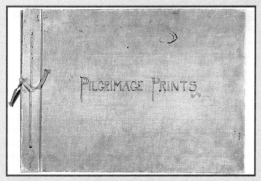

Pilgrimage Prints,
issued in 1905, sold for $7,920.00
at our June 2002 auction.

Up at the Vilas Farm
sold for $8,360.00 at our June 2003 auction

Best known among the general public for his hand-colored pictures, Wallace Nutting was also widely recognized as one of the leading authors of his time. He personally authored 20 books, contributed photographs to several other books, published many picture and furniture catalogs, and wrote numerous magazine articles about antiques and colonial living.

Some of Nutting's earliest photographs were first published in 1905. During the previous year he sailed on a cruise through the Holy Lands along with a large group of ministers, missionaries, and other religious individuals. One result of this trip was the publication of the book *The Cruise of the Eight Hundred to and through Palestine*. Although Wallace Nutting himself didn't write or publish this book, he did contribute many of the pictures included throughout its nearly 400 pages.

Nutting's first attempt at self-publishing occurred in 1905 when he issued *Pilgrimage Prints*. This portfolio included a series of black and white platinotypes taken on his 1904 cruise to the Holy Land. Signed but not titled, this Wallace Nutting rarity even has its cover title written in pen and ink. We are aware of only one remaining complete copy of this book, which last sold at our June 2002 auction for $7,920.00.

Over the years Nutting contributed photographs to several other books authored by others including *Social Life in Old New England* (1914) and *Pathways of the Puritans* (1930).

In 1912, Wallace Nutting put together a leather-bound portfolio book titled *Up at the Vilas Farm* for his friend, Charles Nathaniel Vilas. Apparently Mr. Vilas, a wealthy businessman from Alstead, New Hampshire, commissioned Nutting to photograph a series of pictures throughout his estate, have them hand-colored, and included in a book which Mr. Vilas gave as presentation gifts to several of his friends or clients. *Up at the Vilas Farm* did not include actual text, but it did have a leather cover, and 22 individual pages, each containing a hand-colored photograph, mounted and signed upon an indented, mat-like page. I am aware of only three existing copies of this book and one last sold at our June 2003 auction for $8,360.00.

Up at the Vilas Farm inspired Nutting to publish his first copyrighted book the following year, *Old New England Pictures*. This book was similar to the *Up at the Vilas Farm* portfolio in that it included 32 pages of hand-colored pictures, each mounted upon a signed mat-like page. But taking this endeavor several steps further, Nutting added titles to each of the pictures, and more importantly, he included 32 pages of text on old New England houses.

He was more widely known for his *States Beautiful* travel series. As Wallace Nutting traveled throughout America taking his photographs, he wrote eight books about states that he visited. Each book contained approximately 300 of his pictures which had been photographed throughout the state, and text about the state's key regions and its houses, history, people, and charm.

These *States Beautiful* books had two primary markets. First, the residents of each particular state. Most people like reading about themselves, or at least about something near and dear to them — their home state. As a result, he would sell a considerable number of books to residents of each state that he wrote about. Secondly, this was an era before travel became inexpensive and convenient. Commercial air travel had not yet arrived, transatlantic ocean voyages were lengthy and expensive, and the automobile was still being improved. Books were the easiest way to travel. Libraries were frequent purchasers of his *States Beautiful* books, as well as those individuals interested in learning about new and far-away places.

Wallace Nutting published a total of 10 *States Beautiful* books which included eight U.S. states and two European countries using pictures taken on several of his trips overseas.

Wallace Nutting's States Beautiful Series

Connecticut Beautiful (1923, 1937)
England Beautiful (1928, 1936)
Ireland Beautiful (1925, 1935)
Maine Beautiful (1924, 1935)
Massachusetts Beautiful (1923, 1935)
New Hampshire Beautiful (1923, 1935)
New York Beautiful (1927, 1936)
Pennsylvania Beautiful (1924, 1935)
Vermont Beautiful (1922, 1936)
Virginia Beautiful (1930, 1935)

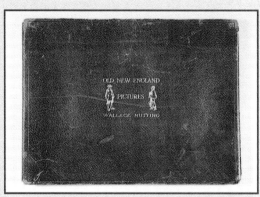

Old New England Pictures
sold for $11,275.00 at our June 1999 auction

Five other *States Beautiful* books were under consideration: Ohio, Colorado, California, New Jersey, and Florida, but none of these were ever published. The dust jacket of the first edition *Connecticut Beautiful* book went so far as to state that *Florida Beautiful* was released in 1924 but that never occurred. Twenty-five pages of the unpublished manuscript were found but no such book was ever published.

Nutting sold tens of thousands of his *States Beautiful* books. Based upon comments in *Wallace Nutting's Biography* (Wallace Nutting wrote and published his autobiography in 1936), approximately 10,000 copies of most first editions (green covers) were sold. Second editions (tan covers) were released in the mid 1930s.

First editions (1922 – 30) had green covers;
Second editions (1935 – 37) had tan covers.

Books

Windsor Chairs (1917). Note the different American Windsors title on the cover in an earlier photo.

The success of the *States Beautiful* books led Nutting to publish several other books on subjects where he possessed significant knowledge: clocks and photography. In 1924, he published one of the most definitive books ever written on the subject of clocks, *The Clock Book*. This book pictured nearly 250 clocks, described in detail many forms and variations of different types of clocks, and compiled the most extensive listing of American clock makers known at that time.

Photographic Art Secrets was published in 1927, and included Nutting's philosophy and knowledge of successful photography. Chapters included such diverse topics as The Tripod, The Shutter, Exposure, Composition, Latitude from the Equator, Animal Pictures, and much more. For serious picture collectors, this book is important because it contains many pictures that were never published in any of his *States Beautiful* books or picture catalogs.

With his numerous publications over the years, Nutting published many of his books through his own publishing company, the Old America Company. Other books were published by Dodd, Mead & Company, and Marshall, Jones and Company. Later editions were published by Garden City Publishing Company, MacMillan Publishing Company, and Bonanza Books, Inc.

If Wallace Nutting became well known for his *States Beautiful* series, he became even more famous for the books he published on his true passion: early American antiques.

Nutting claimed that the search for attractive backgrounds for his interior pictures was responsible for his fascination with antiques. Through the accumulation of antiques for his interior scenes and for several of his homes, Wallace Nutting had the opportunity to see such a diverse assortment and large quantity of antiques that he began to record what he saw through his camera.

In 1917 he published his first book on antique furniture, *American Windsors*. Although other books have been published on the subject, relatively few people are aware that Wallace Nutting wrote the first comprehensive book on Windsor chairs more than 80 years ago. Although the book's cover title was *American Windsors*, the dust jacket called the book *Windsor Chairs*. This book was nearly 200 pages long and was the first serious study into Windsor chairs dating from 1725 to 1825. Picturing nearly 100 different Windsors, this book included an in-depth discussion of Windsor variations, and each chair's merit, dating, and frequency of occurrence.

Nutting's passion for antiques then led to his publication in 1921 of *Furniture of the Pilgrim Century*. This work went beyond the Windsor form to include American chests, desks, tables, non-Windsor chairs, mirrors, clocks, utensils, and hardware.

Nutting felt that World War I stirred a great deal of patriotism and stimulated interest in the work of our forefathers. Some credit him with playing a significant role in the colonial revival movement. More than 500 pages long, and including more than 1,000 photos of items dating between 1620 to 1720, Wallace Nutting tried to include only things made in America of native American woods.

The Furniture of the Pilgrim Century was revised in 1924, eliminating some pieces which had been later determined to be of non-American origin, adding a few new sections, and eliminating a few controversial pages on ironwork. Wallace Nutting took most of the photos used in this book, and wrote all copy. Except for the more serious collectors, this extensive publication was all but forgotten because it was eclipsed by his most important work — *The Furniture Treasury*.

The Furniture Treasury, still available in bookstores today, is really not one book, but three separate volumes. Volumes I and II, published in 1928, contained more than 5,000 photos of American furniture and utensils throughout 1,536 large octavo pages. Somewhat overlapping the *Furniture of the Pilgrim Century*, this work covers 1,650 to the end of the Empire period which according to Nutting, "brings us to the beginning of the degraded styles." Nutting claims to have spent $65,000.00 over 20 years in the research and accumulation of photography that went into these books. In 1930 Nutting was selling (and getting) $25.00 for the standard two-volume set; $26.00 for the library edition, uncut with gilt top; and $40.00 for the three quarter deluxe set where each volume included a hand-colored interior scene. What I find incredible is that you can still purchase *Furniture Treasury* at a book store or on the Internet today, for a price not too much higher than when it was originally released 75 years ago!

Nutting published a third volume of *The Furniture Treasury* in 1933. Intended as a supplement to Volumes I and II, this book supplied additional details concerning styles, dates, construction, and origins of the previous volumes. It also provided a listing of early American clock makers which supplemented the listing in his 1924 publication of *The Clock Book*. Unlike the first two volumes of *The Furniture Treasury*,

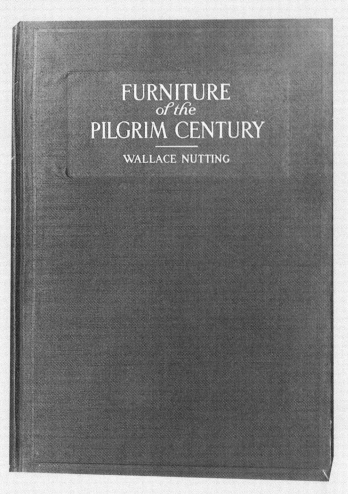

Furniture of the Pilgrim Century (1921)

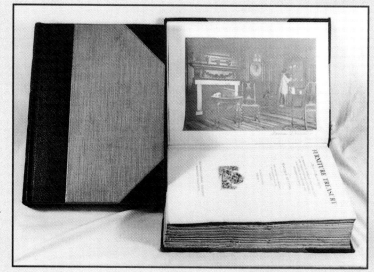

Furniture Treasury, deluxe edition with one hand-colored interior in each book.

Books

Volume III had no photographs. Rather, it was illustrated with hundreds of sketches, mostly drawn by his assistant, Ernest John Donnelly.

After more than 60 years in print, *The Furniture Treasury* still has not been superseded as the finest and most complete visual reference book of early American antiques ever published.

With his picture business successfully up and running, and with interest in the colonial revival movement growing, Nutting started to become more actively involved with antiques. Fortunately for him he began collecting in an era when many fine early pieces were still available if one looked hard enough. With so many great antiques still available and with so much more to learn Wallace Nutting began his lifelong quest for antiques.

Wallace Nutting Bibliography

1904	*Cruise of the Eight Hundred*		1928	*England Beautiful,* First Edition
1905	*Pilgrimage Prints*		1928	*Furniture Treasury, Volume I*
1912	*Up at the Vilas Farm*		1928	*Furniture Treasury, Volume II*
1913	*Old New England Pictures*		1930	*Virginia Beautiful,* First Edition
1914	*Social Life in Old New England*		1930	*Pathways of the Puritans*
1917	*American Windsors*		1933	*Furniture Treasury, Volume III*
1921	*Furniture of the Pilgrim Century,* First Edition		1935	*Ireland Beautiful,* Second Edition
1922	*Vermont Beautiful,* First Edition		1935	*Maine Beautiful,* Second Edition
1923	*Massachusetts Beautiful,* First Edition		1935	*Massachusetts Beautiful,* Second Edition
1923	*Connecticut Beautiful,* First Edition		1935	*New Hampshire Beautiful,* Second Edition
1923	*New Hampshire Beautiful,* First Edition		1935	*Pennsylvania Beautiful,* Second Edition
1924	*Furniture of the Pilgrim Century,* Revised Edition		1935	*Virginia Beautiful,* Second Edition
1924	*Maine Beautiful,* First Edition		1936	*The Clock Book,* Second Edition
1924	*Pennsylvania Beautiful,* First Edition		1936	*England Beautiful,* Second Edition
1924	*The Clock Book,* First Edition		1936	*Wallace Nutting Biography*
1925	*Ireland Beautiful,* First Edition		1936	*New York Beautiful,* Second Edition
1927	*New York Beautiful,* First Edition		1936	*Vermont Beautiful,* Second Edition
1928	*Photographic Art Secrets*		1937	*Connecticut Beautiful,* Second Edition

Summary of Key Points

• Wallace Nutting authored more than 20 different books between 1905 and 1936.

• His *States Beautiful* travel series included books on eight American states
and two foreign countries.

• He published six books on early American antiques.

• His *Furniture Treasury* book has never been surpassed as the finest visual reference
book ever published on early American antiques.

• He published books on clocks and photography as well as his autobiography.

• He issued three portfolios of his hand-colored photographs which are
extremely valuable and collectible today.

• He also contributed photographs that were used in books by other authors and he was
a widely published author in many different national magazines.

• Wallace Nutting's books provided him with valuable experience in the field of
antiques and helped to make him a nationally recognized name.

An Afternoon Tea,
taken at Nuttinghame, Southbury, Connecticut

The Old Homestead,
an outside view of Nuttinghame, Southbury, Connecticut

Although Wallace Nutting began purchasing antiques while in Southbury, Connecticut, he really didn't begin seriously collecting until moving to Framingham, Massachusetts. With the transition from Southbury to Framingham completed in 1912, and with sales of his interior pictures at an all-time high, Nutting began looking for quaint new settings for his colonial interior scenes. Finding the appropriate room with the correct furnishings often proved more difficult than he had anticipated.

He photographed the earliest interior scenes in his Southbury, Connecticut, home (Nuttinghame), and then in his Framingham, Massachusetts, home (Nuttingholme). When he ran out of creative scenes there, he began taking pictures in the homes of his friends. But, as the sale of his interior scenes began to increase, he felt that new and different settings were needed. So over the next several years, he purchased and restored five historic homes throughout New England.

In 1914, he purchased his first home in his colonial chain: the Wentworth-Gardner House (56 Gardner St., Portsmouth, New Hampshire). Built in 1760 by Madam Mark Hunking Wentworth, and later owned by Major Gardner of Revolutionary War fame, the house looked out over the Piscataqua River. One of the most important aspects of this house was its upstairs and downstairs hall, once considered the finest hall in America. Nutting furnished this home with a fine collection of Chippendale mahogany and earlier period furniture worthy of the house. Items included a set of six walnut chairs with rich carvings; a set of fourteen Chippendale chairs, with a three-chair-back settee to match; a specially carved, cabriole-legged, ball and claw bed; a six-leg highboy; rare gate-leg tables; block front desks; pie crust tables; a set of braced-back Windsors; a lounge chaise; and numerous other pieces of high-style furniture.

The Spinet Corner,
taken in Nuttingholme, Framingham, Massachusetts

A postcard view of Nuttingholme,
Nutting's Framingham, Massachusetts, home

This house was built during the period generally considered to be the peak of Georgian style. When Nutting had completed his restoration work, it was furnished just as an American or English gentleman of taste and means would have done during the mid-eighteenth century.

The next home he purchased was the Hazen Garrison House (6-8 Groveland Street, Haverhill, Massachusetts). Built in 1680, this home was the perfect type of brick English manor house, nearly identical to a home in Kent, England. This house was one of the earliest and most perfectly restored Garrison houses in the country. (Note: A Garrison house was a secured house that settlers retreated to during threat of Indian attack.) Furnished with very early pine and oak furniture, this home had several massive fireplaces with double ovens which provided an unusually large provision for cooking. The Hazen Garrison House, first owned by the Revolutionary War's General Hazen, was said to be the first building used as a shoe factory in America, and was well known for its quaintness, daintiness, and harmony of design.

A third house was the Cutler-Bartlet House (32 Green Street, Newburyport, Massachusetts). This was built about 1782 and was the largest home in the colonial chain. Furnished with a variety of Chippendale, Hepplewhite, and Sheraton furniture, individual pieces included secretaries, mahogany tables, sideboards, highboys, lowboys, and a very large collection of Windsor chairs. This particular house was the boyhood home of John Pierrepont, grandfather of the famous J.P. Morgan. This home was also used as a secondary picture studio during the summer months, allowing tourists to watch as colorists tinted the famous Wallace Nutting pictures. Many Wallace Nutting pictures hung throughout the house, displayed beside older historical prints.

The Iron Works House, or Broadhearth (127 Center Street, Saugus, Massachusetts), was purchased in 1916. This was the site of the first working ironworks in the colonies in 1642. It still possessed the bog pits where early iron was dug and had a working foundry where Nutting began a brief business in reproduction ironwork. This house was the oldest in Saugus, one of the oldest in the country, and one of the few early houses where the overhang appeared on the side, showing a strong Gothic influence. The early furniture, with many pieces dating from the 1600s included trestle tables, pilgrim chairs, and oak chests. The house included several massive fireplaces which were said to be some of the largest in the country, and which were featured in many of his interior scenes.

Wayside Inn, Old Tap Room,
taken in the Wayside Inn, Sudbury, Massachusetts

Good Night!, taken in the Wentworth-Gardner House,
Portsmouth, New Hampshire

Colonial Chain of Picture Houses labels, circa 1915

The Webb House, or Hospitality Hall (89 Main Street, Wethersfield, Connecticut), was purchased in 1916, featured Dutch and Chippendale furniture, and was built in 1752. Much of the beauty in the Webb House was centered around rooms with beautifully colored wallpaper.

Wallace Nutting & His Hunt for Antiques

Christmas Gifts,
taken in the Hazen-Garrison House, Haverhill, Massachusetts

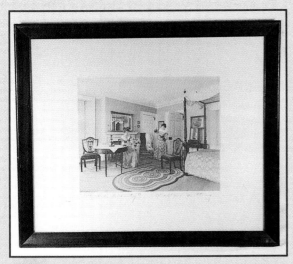

What A Beauty!,
taken in the Cutler-Bartlett House, Newburyport, Massachusetts

Nutting had purchased these five homes because he felt each represented a different period of early American style and architecture. Hoping to capitalize on the growing motor-tourist trade, Nutting completely restored and refurbished the homes, and then opened them to the public for a small admission fee. They came be known as The Wallace Nutting Colonial Chain of Picture Houses.

By 1920, all had been sold. High restoration costs and lower than anticipated attendance due to a decrease in motor-tourist trade resulting from the effects of World War I, both contributed to Nutting's decision to close the colonial chain. Three of the houses (Wentworth-Gardner House, Cutler-Bartlet House, and Webb House), and their entire contents, were sold to John Wanamaker's department store. The antiques were exhibited by Wanamaker's in New York before being publically sold, while the houses were sold in separate transactions. The two remaining homes (Saugus Iron Works and the Hazen-Garrison House) were sold privately, while their contents were sold to an antique dealer, presumably for inventory.

Nutting claims to have made neither a profit nor loss on the sale of his colonial chain of houses. "Some houses were sold at a fraction of cost, others far above cost, but the average was a stalemate." Others report that Nutting actually lost a considerable sum of money in his colonial chain business venture.

But it was in this period, 1914 – 1920, that Wallace Nutting began his close association with antiques. An education in antiques has never been easy to come by, especially in those early days. Compared to today, there were very few reference books in print, and even fewer places to turn for advice. Most of his education was a self-learning process. He read whatever books were available, toured museums and private collections, and visited with individuals more scholarly and knowledgeable than himself. He attended auctions, visited a variety of dealers, and was even known to knock on a stranger's door asking to preview their antiques.

For someone with the high moral fiber of a minister, Nutting was not always totally above-board in trying to achieve his goals and objectives in his pursuit of antiques. According to one researcher, "Nutting was a buccaneer of a collector. Lacking a fortune with which to buy antiques, he wheedled, conspired, sermonized, and all but promised salvation to get the antique that he wanted. He argued that the owner of a fine antique without the means to properly protect or display it had a moral obligation to turn it over to someone who could — namely Wallace Nutting."

One such story centers around his purchase of the famous Prence-Howes court cupboard. Nutting had purchased this court cupboard in 1921 from an Abby Howes, a Danvers, Massachusetts school teacher, for $3,000.00. Apparently this piece had been in her family for generations, once owned by the first governor of the Pilgrim Colony, but Nutting somehow succeeded in convincing Mrs. Howe to sell it to him.

Upon learning that Nutting was going to resell that court cupboard to J. P. Morgan for $20,000.00 as part of his personal antique collection, Mrs. Howe sued to regain her family heirloom, claiming that:

1) Nutting persuaded her that it was her civic duty to sell it to him.
2) He told her he planned to put the cupboard on display at his Framingham studio where others could study and appreciate it.
3) Nutting promised to hire her as his secretary so that she could continue to be close to her cupboard (he never did).
4) He assured her that his offer was a fair one and that the cupboard was worth no more than what he offered.

Nutting's defense was that the court cupboard was indeed worth no more than $3,000.00 when he had purchased it. But his ownership of it, along with the added value now attached to it resulting from its association with the respected Wallace Nutting name, had increased its value to the present level. Nutting testified that he had almost sold his antique collection to Henry Ford, but, after further negotiations, decided to sell his collection to J.P. Morgan. "Morgan didn't know any more about an antique cupboard than a hole in the wall," Nutting testified under oath.

Nutting won the case, and the cupboard is now part of the Wallace Nutting collection residing in the Wadsworth Atheneum in Hartford, Connecticut.

Nutting claims that he experienced three distinct phases in his antique collecting career.

Phase I began with the furnishing of his houses — Nuttinghame, Nuttingholme, and the five houses in his colonial chain. This was his basic learning phase and resulted in many mistakes which undoubtedly added to his overall knowledge. In order to completely furnish these seven houses, Nutting purchased well over a thousand antiques during this phase, and rejected many thousands of others. Initially Nutting only appreciated the earliest forms, that is, Pilgrim, William & Mary, Windsor chairs, and a few other seventeenth and eighteenth century forms. But it was during this period that Nutting first began to appreciate some of the later styles, i.e., Queen Anne, Chippendale, Hepplewhite, and Sheraton. This phase of collecting ended upon the sale of his colonial chain in 1920.

Phase II began shortly after he ceded control of his picture and furniture business in 1921. Upon entering his second "retirement," he began a much more serious period of antique collecting and accumulation. This was his most serious and dedicated phase of collecting during which he was able to accumulate the majority of what eventually came to be known as the Wallace Nutting Collection of early American antiques. This phase ended with the sale of his personal antique collection to J.P. Morgan in 1923.

Phase III was a more informal, low-key collecting phase, consisting of what he termed "odd buying," purchasing items for use in his home, items to copy in his reproduction business, or things that he simply liked and presumed would end up as part of his estate after his death.

Ready for Callers, taken at Broadhearth, or the Iron Works House, Saugus, Massachusetts

Birthday Flowers, taken in the Webb House, Wethersfield, Connecticut

Wallace Nutting & His Hunt for Antiques

During his years of collecting, Nutting developed a series of rules for buying antiques, some of which included:

1) Buy only good things in fair condition. Things repaired are little better, or worse, than new.
2) Buy not for age only, but for beauty, or merit, or use, or rarity.
   Two of these reasons ought always to inhere in the articles.
3) Buy only after taste is cultivated by reading the books on the subject, of course Wallace Nutting books!
4) Buy only with good advice — not a dealer's advice. Are you looking for men to be angels before their time?
5) Buy only for a specific place in the dwelling. Get something you need, not something that is merely a bargain.
6) Do not collect one class of articles, but a variety. They who collect a class should found a museum.
7) Buy mostly American articles because they look well in an American setting .
8) Never collect "fixed up" furniture. That means passing by many shops entirely.
   It is usually impossible for an expert to detect, on a nice piece of work, where the new begins.
9) Collect what you learn to be approved after many years trial as to style. Do not buy merely because you like it.

These guidelines for buying antiques seem nearly as applicable today as they did when Nutting first published them more than 70 years ago.

Nutting's antique education obviously was accelerated due to the incredibly large number of pieces he found. While researching his antique books, he came into contact with well over 20,000 different antiques. The better ones were photographed and included in his books; the remainder were studied for their bad points. Nothing was lost in his quest for knowledge.

Over the years, Nutting's vast experience with antiques led him to become a recognized expert on the subject. Perhaps he wasn't considered the most scholarly or knowledgeable man in his field but he did become one of the most widely known. He contributed numerous articles to such respected publications as *The Magazine Antiques*, *The Saturday Evening Post*, and *Women's World*. He gave lectures, provided slide presentations, and was consulted by some of the top scholars and wealthiest collectors in the country. In what really amounted to only a few years, Nutting became one of the country's leading authorities on antiques.

Being the entrepreneur that he was, he quickly realized that if he was having difficulty obtaining the finest forms of early American antiques, so too were other collectors. Many could not afford the finest forms and, quite often, those who could afford them could not find them.

It was his love of antiques and his uncanny sense of entrepreneurial spirit that led Wallace Nutting to his least profitable, and according to some, most important business venture of all. It was at this point, beginning in 1917, that Wallace Nutting decided to begin reproducing furniture.

Summary of Key Points

• Wallace Nutting purchased a colonial chain of five historic New England houses primarily
to provide him with appropriate background settings for his
colonial interior hand-colored photographs.

• His research into properly furnishing these houses with period antiques provided him with
valuable experience in early American antiques

• Wallace Nutting owned a total of seven historic houses where a large
percentage of his interior scenes were taken:

1) Nuttinghame (Southbury, Connecticut)
2) Nuttingholme (Framingham, Massachusetts)
3) Wentworth-Gardner House (Portsmouth, Massachusetts)
4) Hazen-Garrison House (Haverhill, Massachusetts)
5) Cutler-Bartlett House (Newburyport, Massachusetts)
6) Iron Works House or Broadhearth (Saugus, Massachusetts)
7) Webb House (Wethersfield, Connecticut)

• Wallace Nutting operated his colonial chain of houses between 1914 and 1920.

• Wallace Nutting experienced three distinct phases in his quest for early American antiques.

• Wallace Nutting became one of the most knowledgeable and published experts on
early American antiques of his time.

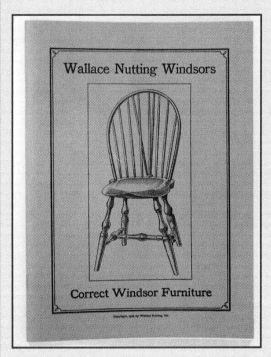

Wallace Nutting Windsors: Correct Windsor Furniture catalog (1918)

#415 knuckle arm comb back Windsor chair. Block brand.

$1,000.00 – 1,500.00

As mentioned earlier, Wallace Nutting completed the first definitive study on Windsor chairs with the publication of *American Windsors* in 1917. In researching this book Nutting sought out the finest Windsor forms he could find, assembling a collection of nearly 150 chairs. Approximately 75% of the chairs photographed for this book were owned by Nutting himself.

It therefore shouldn't come as any surprise that the first furniture Nutting began reproducing was Windsor chairs. Nor is it too surprising that Nutting released his first reproduction furniture catalog, *Wallace Nutting Windsors…Correct Windsor Furniture* in 1918, shortly after the publication of *American Windsors*. After all, timing is everything in business and what better time to begin selling reproduction Windsor chairs than at the same time a new book on Windsor chairs is released. His Windsor chair catalog contained some superb examples that were unavailable except through Wallace Nutting's furniture company.

This chapter will focus upon the production of Windsor chairs and other furniture using the Windsor form. Considerable time will be spent discussing Windsors because it is far and away the most common type of Wallace Nutting furniture you will find. Also, many of the construction techniques and finishing procedures that apply to Windsor chairs were used upon his other types of furniture as well.

We'll focus upon several other forms of Wallace Nutting furniture in subsequent chapters.

Wallace Nutting started reproducing furniture in 1917 at an old woolen mill called the Scott Mill. This site was adjacent to the Saugus Iron Works property which he had just recently purchased and restored as part of his colonial chain.

Nutting had long felt that the Windsor form was one of the finest styles of furniture ever produced in colonial America — and one of the most abused forms as well. Many had tried to reproduce Windsors before him but, in his opinion, no one had yet done it correctly. He seemed to consider it his divine calling to resurrect the Windsor chair. His 1918 Windsor chair catalog begins with this bold statement — "The Redemption of the Windsor Chair: All persons of taste and discernment will be glad that at last someone has had the courage to undertake the redemption of the Windsor Chair."

Since he owned nearly 150 different examples of Windsor chairs, Nutting had ample opportunity to study the best — and worst — examples of Windsor design. Out of his huge collection of Windsors, Nutting claimed to have found only one (his #310) perfect enough to reproduce exactly. By placing such a large grouping of chairs together, Nutting felt that nearly all fell short in some respect of what he perceived to be the "perfect" Windsor chair. If the comb was just right, the legs were too short; if the seat was nearly perfect, the back was not; if the height was correct, the woods were incorrect. Practically no chair he found ever lived up to his concept of the perfect Windsor chair.

With so few original Windsors meeting his high standards, Nutting set out to create the perfect Windsor chair, with every part suggesting grace, strength, harmony, and comfort. If the grandest eighteenth century craftsmen were unable to produce the perfect Windsor chair, then Wallace Nutting would do it himself.

In order to produce the perfect Windsor chair, correct in every detail, Nutting would generally follow a five-step approach:

1) *Observation and Analysis.* The first step in copying a piece of furniture would be to closely study and analyze it. Nutting, with the help of the craftsmen he employed, would visually inspect a chair from all sides. They would look at the piece's overall merit and compare it to other fine Windsors. Where appropriate, photographs were taken. Each dimension was carefully recorded and when necessary, an entire chair would be carefully taken apart, measured inch-for-inch, turn-for-turn, until Nutting understood what made the chair so correct and appealing.

2) *Detailed Sketches and Drawings.* Once a piece was selected for reproduction, many scaled drawings were made: frontal views, side views, rear views, top views, and bottom views. Each drawing would include the exact dimensions of each component part, down to the nearest 1/16 of an inch.

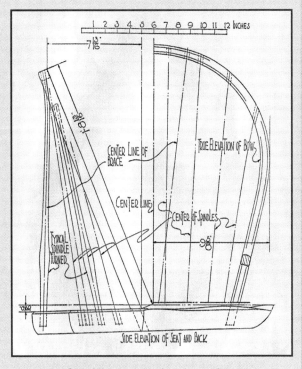

Scaled drawing, Windsor chair, side view, from the **Furniture Treasury**, *Vol. III*

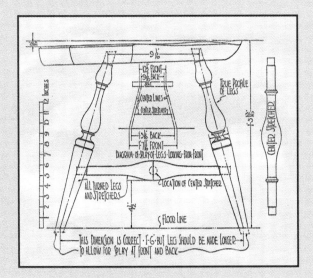

Scaled drawing, Windsor chair, bottom view, from the **Furniture Treasury**, *Vol. III*

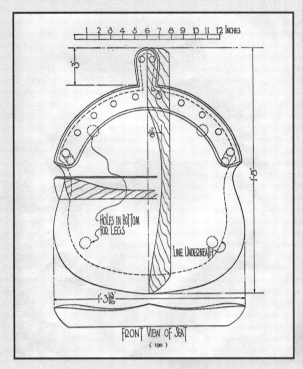

Scaled drawing, Windsor chair, seat view, from the **Furniture Treasury**, *Vol. III*

Windsor Furniture

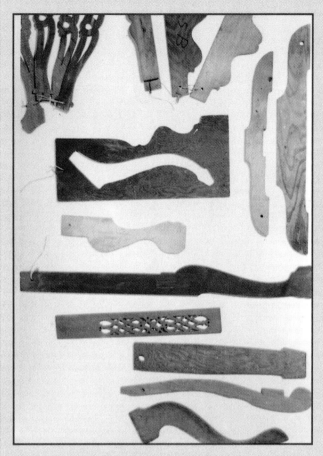

Wallace Nutting wooden furniture templates

Assorted model furniture parts

3) *Adjustments and Improvements.* Since most chairs Nutting selected for reproduction were nearly perfect, most characteristics were already correct. Nutting would focus upon those few aspects that still needed to be corrected in order to make the chair perfect, describing in detail what adjustments were needed to the chair's dimensions, design, turnings, or woods.

4) *Patterns.* Once Nutting's improvements were made and the final scale drawings completed, a chair was nearly ready for production. The next step was to construct paper patterns for each individual component in the chair, with a separate pattern being created for the seat, legs, stretchers, spindles, bows, and arms. For items that were to be reproduced frequently over a longer period of time, wooden or metal patterns were constructed.

5) *Model Pieces of Furniture.* Finally, sample pieces of each individual component were constructed by closely following the patterns. Once these individual model components met with Nutting's approval, an entire chair was assembled using individual model pieces. Once the entire chair was correct, this became the final model chair that was to be followed as closely as possible by the workmen, without deviation.

Windsor Chair Construction

The key to the inherent beauty of any piece of furniture lies in its construction, those special production techniques which are nearly invisible to all but the master craftsmen. Through his close analysis and observation, Nutting took note of those special techniques and included those that he felt necessary to create his perfect Windsor.

Nutting stated he could produce a chair for one-twentieth the cost by machine, but a machine-produced chair nearly as good as one made by hand was a chair "degraded to the capacity of the machines." As a result, his Windsor chairs were created almost entirely by hand.

1) Seats: Each seat was shaped from a single piece of 2" thick country pine. After being cut to the desired shape, the center of the seat was deeply scooped to nearly one-half the thickness (1"), and at the edges the chamfer was shaped above and below to meet in a hairline, giving the impression of a much lighter, thinner, and more delicate seat. Any tailpieces were also hand finished, with a hollow, half-round molding completing the back of the seat.

#408 bent arm, bow back Windsor arm chair.
Block brand. $850.00 – $1,325.00

Windsor chair seats, cut from a piece of country pine 2" thick, then hand carved.

Windsor Furniture

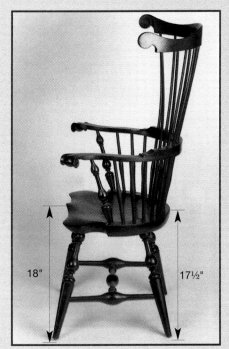

All but two of Nutting's Windsor Chairs were precisely 18" from floor to front seat, and 17½" floor to rear seat.

All Windsor chairs were raked 4" within the 18" height.

2) Legs, Stretchers, and Spindles: Most legs and stretchers were finished on a hand lathe. Although Nutting felt that a machine could produce a decent turning at considerable savings, he believed that machines had to be avoided wherever possible because they could not provide the extremely deep cuts or delicate lines needed for the correct look.

The bulbs were a full 2" and the tapered legs were turned to ¾" or ⅞".

Once the legs were attached to the seat, seats were precisely 18" from seat top-to-floor in the front, and one-half inch shorter (17½") in the rear. Two exceptions to the 18" rule were slipper chairs (15") and child's chairs (10").

All legs were raked 4" within 18" in order to provide the greatest strength and stability.

Wherever the legs entered the thinned portion of the seat, they generally penetrated the seat entirely, wedged from the top in their grooved joint.

All spindles were one piece, running through any arm rails and bows to the top of the chair, penetrating the bow or hoop back, except on the sides. At least three spindles were pinned and all were glued. The bracing spindles were pinned top and bottom.

3) Bows, Combs, and Arms: Bow backs entirely penetrated the seat from above, and were wedged from below the seat. Because of their excessive length, they were carved entirely by hand rather than machine, and were bent using wet steam.

All combs were delicately shaped and thinned from the lower to the upper edge, entirely by hand, giving them an added feel of delicacy and lightness, and bent using wet steam. Combs were pinned in at least three places, and glued to each spindle.

All assembling was done with fox-tail wedges and hot glue.

Arm rails, where ending in a knuckle, were carved entirely by hand, and were ½" nearer the seat in the front than in the back.

Each of these steps contributed to a finer, more correct Windsor chair. None of these procedures were discovered by Nutting. Each step had been known by furniture makers since the eighteenth century, but each additional step takes more time and costs more money. Most furniture makers over the years were willing to cut a few corners, produce each chair just a little faster, thereby shaving their costs as much as possible. The end result was inevitably an inferior chair.

The difference between a Wallace Nutting Windsor chair and Windsor chairs from other furniture makers is that Wallace Nutting didn't cut corners. He produced each chair as well as it could be constructed, regardless of expense.

Windsor Chair Woods

Generally Wallace Nutting Windsors were made of three different woods: rock maple for the legs; country pine for the seats; and hickory for the spindles, bows, bent-arm rails, and combs.

According to Nutting's 1918 Windsor chair catalog: "Maple is the most generally useful of furniture woods. It soon took the place of oak and beech. It was abundant, strong, often very handsome, smooth working, and freer from the worm than most woods. Further there is much fine American sentiment in connection with the rock (what a strong name) maple, otherwise called the sugar maple. A tree which furnished its sweetness for many a year, of a flavor unsurpassed — the natural and uncultivated source of all the sugar needed, was later cut down and worked into furniture and kept on in a useful career. It made the best hot fire. It was the American wood above all."

"Pine was a wonderfully useful wood, rare in parts of the world from which our ancestors came. The great 'pumpkin' pines supplied wall panels up to four feet in width. It cut like cheese, but was very durable and pleasantly aromatic. The merits of unfinished pine, its rich, soft yellow browns have not been felt sufficiently. People hasten to cover it with paint. The seat of a Windsor was made of knotty pine which would not split and was therefore valuable. It went well with maple."

"Hickory became the reliance of the settler for all work requiring toughness and lightness. Spindles and spokes were perfect for this wood."

Turning Variations

The most common turning used in Nutting Windsors was the Northern or New England turning. The most obvious characteristics of this style included the straight tapered leg and the bulbous spindles. Northern or New England turnings account for approximately 85% of the Wallace Nutting Windsor chairs you will find.

The Pennsylvania or Philadelphia Windsor was actually an earlier Windsor form. but is much rarer in Wallace Nutting furniture. The primary characteristic of the Pennsylvania turnings focus upon the cylinder and ball foot legs, and the straight taper spindles.

Whereas the New England spindle had a simple bulbous turning approximately 6" above the seat, flowing into a gradual taper as it entered the bow or comb, the Pennsylvania spindle contained no bulbous turning. Rather, it simply flowed from its thickest point where it left the seat, gradually thinning until it entered the rail and comb.

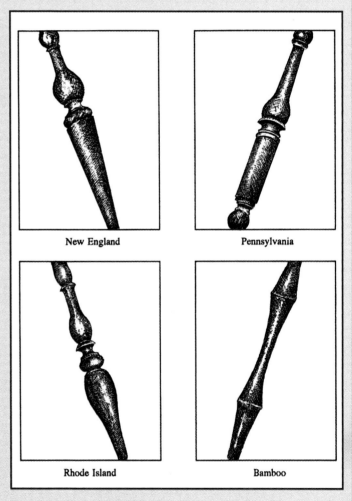

New England   Pennsylvania

Rhode Island   Bamboo

Four types of Wallace Nutting furniture turnings

Windsor Furniture

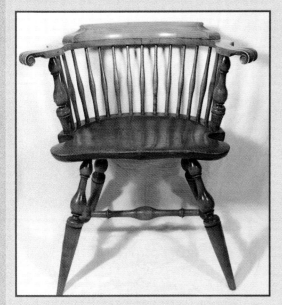

#413 low back Windsor arm chair, with New England leg turnings. Block brand. $800.00 – 1,200.00

#412 Pennsylvania high comb back Windsor arm chair, with Pennsylvania leg turnings. Block brand. $1,000.00 – 1,500.00

Pennsylvania turnings account for approximately 10% of the Wallace Nutting Windsor chairs you will find, making them significantly rarer than the New England variation.

Two additional turnings Nutting produced were the Rhode Island turning and the Bamboo turning. The Rhode Island type had a hollowed tapered foot, slightly bowed at the top of the taper. The latest Windsor form that Nutting copied was the Bamboo turning. Sales on both were quite low, with combined production for both forms accounting for less than 5% of the Wallace Nutting Windsors you will find.

Nutting stopped reproducing Windsor chairs with the Bamboo turning. He felt that Sheraton Windsors, which dated approximately 1800 – 1810, were the beginning of the degraded Windsor form.

Windsor Chair Finishes

The greatest chair, with a mediocre finish, becomes an average piece of furniture. After going to such great lengths to produce such a fine piece of furniture, the detail-oriented Nutting was not about to degrade the end result of his work with a cheap finish. Each part of every chair he produced was finished at least five times by hand, usually with a special shellac finish with hand rubbings between each coat. The cost of Nutting's finishing alone exceeded the total cost of most other manufacturer's reproductions. His refinishers were only able to turn out three chairs per day, on a good day.

Overall, the vast majority of Nutting Windsors, perhaps 98 – 99%, were finished in only two styles, a darker "antique" or mahogany finish, or in a lighter maple, or amber, finish. Of these two styles I would say that the breakdown would be approximately 50 – 50.

Of the darker mahogany finish, Nutting said "It has the merit that a chair so finished will never require doing over. The older it grows the more the natural wear will blend with the finish, and the richer and softer will the surface become."

In all my years of collecting, I have rarely seen a Wallace Nutting chair finished in his original paint. Yet, according to Nutting's sales literature, he did offer several different types of paint. Bottle green, eggshell enamel black, old red, and yellow were all available in 1918.

The rarity of Nutting chairs finished in his original paint can be supported by the sale some years ago of a matched set of eight green-painted Windsors (six braced bow back side chairs and two knuckle arm sack back chairs), selling for a then-Wallace Nutting auction record price of $15,950.00 at Sotheby's.

However, under no circumstances would he sell a chair in white paint. ("In no case will we use white paint, which is an abomination on Windsors, entirely unsuited to their homey, sturdy quality.")

Nor would he sell a Windsor painted with more than one color. ("The earliest Windsors in the period were not so painted. That style came only with the degraded Sheraton backs and the rungs which followed round the legs, abandoning the middle stretcher.")

Markings

Let there be no mistake about it, Wallace Nutting made excellent furniture. And because this furniture was so well made, Nutting wanted it clearly marked so it would unquestionably be identified as Wallace Nutting furniture. The earliest Nutting Windsors were marked with a simple paper label. Later pieces were literally branded with the Wallace Nutting name.

Wallace Nutting furniture markings and identification will be discussed in considerable detail in Identifying and Dating Furniture and the Numbering System page 68. Rather than discussing markings here, the entire subject of identifying Wallace Nutting furniture through its various markings will make much more sense when grouped together into an entire chapter later in this book.

At this point you should simply be aware that Nutting clearly marked most, but not all, of his furniture.

Unmarked Windsor Chairs

According to his 1918 Windsor chair catalog, Nutting refused to sell anything unfinished. "We do not care to have our name associated with the bizarre effects sometimes tried on Windsors, and we therefore do not supply chairs in the white, that is, unfinished."

Apparently he relented on this point in later years because a later advertising piece states that he was selling pieces "in the white," but without guarantee, and with his "name omitted, because of danger of swelling and unsatisfactory finish."

Nutting also offered to begrudgingly sell unsigned pieces in his 1927 – 1928 furniture catalog. On page 3 of that catalog, in a section titled Unfinished Furniture, Nutting writes: "If necessary, but contrary to my advice, pieces not too large will be sold unfinished. But said furniture is liable to sudden swelling. I do not warrant it, and do not care to burn my name on it."

#305 bent rung Windsor side chair, with bamboo leg turnings. Block Island. $700.00 – 950.00

A Rhode Island turning

**WALLACE NUTTING
HIS FURNITURE**

MADE BY HIM, ONLY, AT
46 PARK ST., FRAMINGHAM, MASS.
FINISHES

"In the white" {Sold without guarantee}
no finish whatever. Name omitted,
because of danger of swelling and
unsatisfactory finish.

"Natural" A rarely used finish, clear
white shellac, on curly maple;
used on order only.

"Amber" same as {All maple, oak and pine
"Old Maple" { in this finish, a light
stain followed by many coats of
orange shellac, ending with bee's wax.
Ornaments and molds on oak are
black or maroon.

"Mahogany" Used only on solid
mahogany.

"Walnut" A French walnut used on
walnut. Other woods in
walnut finish, on order.

"Vandyke Brown" Goes well with mahogany. To order on maple and pine.

"Paint" Black on plain turned chairs is
proper, and bottle green, black, old
red and yellow on Windsors.
To order only.

"Oil" Table tops for dining, or refections,
finished in oil regularly, to prevent
discoloration.

All special finishes subject to delay.

Furniture finishes sales piece

Just to make sure you understand the significance of this point: Nutting *did not* put his name on every single piece of furniture that left his factory. He omitted his name from furniture that was not finished according to his strict refinishing standards.

Neither his 1930 nor 1937 furniture catalogs mention the sale of unsigned, unfinished furniture, but it is unclear whether he simply stopped selling furniture "in the white" by this time, or whether he still sold it, but did not advertise it in his catalogs.

Now imagine for a minute what may possibly be sitting in private collections, museums, or circulating through the trade. It's no secret that a good craftsmen or furniture maker can build a brand new piece of furniture, artificially age it, and make it look old. Things are being made today that are good enough to fool many experts, let alone the average collector.

Now consider how many Wallace Nutting Windsor chairs may have been sold unfinished and unmarked more than 75 years ago. Chairs that could have been artificially and prematurely aged, painted by someone else, and now having 75 years of wear and patina added to them. Fifty chairs? One hundred? More? No one really knows because no production records have ever been found.

We do know this:

That in the 1920s, a Nutting child's high chair, originally selling for $19.00 was artificially aged and resold for nearly $1,000.00. It took Wallace Nutting himself, the maker of the furniture, to discover the fraud.

Some years ago it was reported that Winterthur quietly removed from exhibition a supposedly eighteenth century Windsor high chair after it was suspected of having originated in Nutting's shop. Supposedly several other Museums have quietly removed Nutting pieces as well.

I have personally seen dozens of Wallace Nutting Windsors being offered as original at antique shops and shows. How many have I not seen?

In May 1988 the *Maine Antique Digest* reported a story of a criminal case in New Jersey whereby two individuals sold a Windsor chair to a collector for $6,000.00, claiming it to be an original eighteenth century piece. The collector eventually came to believe the chair was not as represented and demanded his money back. When the sellers refused to refund the $6,000.00, a lawsuit and trial developed.

At the trial, three experts were called to testify. Each inspected the chair, and each disagreed.

One expert, a specialist in furniture restoration and handmade American antiques, figured the chair was made about 5 – 10 years prior and was worth about $500.00.

Another expert, a South Jersey auctioneer and appraiser with 22 years experience, thought the chair was worth $3,000.00 – 4,000.00 and estimated that the chair was made between 1830 – 1850, or possibly as late as the 1870s.

The third expert, a Philadelphia Windsor chair collector and author of two books on Windsor chairs, testified that the chair was worth about $1,500.00, was made around 1920 – 1930, and was a Wallace Nutting reproduction.

Although I was not involved in the case and did not personally inspect the chair, based upon the photograph in the *Maine Antique Digest*, there was no doubt in my mind that the chair was a Wallace Nutting #415 comb back knuckle arm chair, and was indeed worth around $1,500.00 at that time.

Anyway, the point is this, if Wallace Nutting reproduction Windsor chairs are good enough to fool experts and museums, how many unsigned, unmarked Wallace Nutting Windsors are still being cherished by unsuspecting collectors today as authentic, period pieces. That's a frightening thought.

Rarity

With Nutting reproducing over 100 different forms of Windsor chairs between 1918 and 1937, what is considered common and what is considered rare? Without any production records, we don't know exactly how many of each form were produced. Nor do we know how many of each form are still in existence today.

Over the past 30+ years I have seen a great deal of Wallace Nutting furniture, ranging from single pieces to entire collections. I receive hundreds of e-mails and letters each year from people asking me to evaluate their furniture, I attend numerous antique shows and auctions, I follow the trade papers religiously, and I've lost count of the number of phone calls I've received from people asking me about their furniture.

As a result of this significant exposure to Wallace Nutting furniture over the years, I feel comfortable offering these following guidelines regarding the rarity of Wallace Nutting Windsor chairs:
- Arm chairs are much rarer than side chairs.
- Pennsylvania turnings are much rarer than New England turnings.
- Rhode Island and Bamboo turnings are rarer than New England and Pennsylvania turnings, but they are also less desirable to most collectors.
- Settees, child's chairs, and baby cribs are quite rare.
- Fan back side chairs are rarer than bow back side chairs.
- Continuous arm chairs are rarer than knuckle arm chairs.
- Windsors with Nutting's original paint are extremely rare.
- The light maple finish and darker mahogany finishe are both fairly common, with the darker finish being somewhat more desirable to collectors.
- Ten-leg settees are rarer than six-leg settees.
- Low back windsor chairs are rarer, but generally less desirable, than high back Windsors.
- Tenoned arm pieces are rare.
- Double combs or imposed combs are quite unusual.
- Writing arm windsors are especially rare.

Remember these are only guidelines. But if I were to present one general rule of thumb regarding rarity, it would be this: *The more difficult a piece was to produce, the higher the original cost. And the higher the original cost, the fewer pieces produced, and the rarer they are today.*

Wallace Nutting

Windsor Furniture

One additional thought I want to leave you with is this: Windsor chairs are the most common type of Wallace Nutting furniture you will find, for five reasons.

1) Wallace Nutting was producing Windsor chairs longer than his other forms of furniture. Starting in 1918, he continued to manufacture Windsor chairs throughout the 1930s. On the other hand, he only produced his more formal, non-Windsor styles from the mid-1920s, which gave him fewer total productive years.

2) He produced more variations of Windsor chairs than his other forms of furniture, offering more than 100 Windsor designs over his 20 year furniture career. All these forms combined account for a very large percentage of his total production when compared to any other single form (e.g., tables) or style (e.g., Chippendale).

3) His Windsor chairs were generally less expensive than his other chairs and furniture, which made them affordable to more people, especially during the 1930s Depression years.

4) Chairs were often produced in sets of four, theoretically making them four times more plentiful than comparable pieces not produced in sets.

5) And finally, the Windsor chair has always been a very popular form. Its simplicity in design has made it one of the most desirable American forms ever produced and its popularity has held true over the years.

Wallace Nutting Windsor chairs were especially popular with professional and business people during the 1920 – 1930s. It was fairly common for banks, doctors, dentists, lawyers, and other professional offices to furnish their waiting rooms and reception areas with Wallace Nutting chairs, thereby contributing to the larger overall production volume. Large corporations and businesses often furnished their executive offices and corporate board rooms with Wallace Nutting Windsors as well.

We are aware of one elderly doctor who furnished his entire waiting room with Wallace Nutting furniture in the 1930s, and used it continually until the 1980s. It was only when he became informed of its current value that he decided to quietly replace it with more contemporary furniture.

In summary, Wallace Nutting really didn't copy any single chair exactly. Rather, he would take the best examples of the various Windsor forms, copy those characteristics he felt were the best, and incorporate any improvements he felt were needed in order to produce a perfect Windsor chair.

No single feature in any chair is false or inaccurate. Each style of chair, from the simplest bow back to the most complex writing arm Windsor, contained those features which were indicative of the finest surviving examples of that particular form.

But it was the incorporation of so many correct and wonderful characteristics into a single chair that almost made Nutting Windsors appear to be somewhat of an exaggeration in form.

I am aware of no other twentieth century furniture makers who produced Windsors nearly as well as Wallace Nutting, on the scale that Nutting accomplished. Certainly there were other good furniture makers in the early twentieth century and yes, some did produce some excellent Windsors, but compared to Nutting, their overall output was minuscule and their impact was minimal.

It was Nutting's initial success in reproducing Windsor chairs, and the early commercial success that followed, that encouraged him to expand into two other endeavors — the reproduction of early American Ironwork and reproducing other non-Windsor forms of antique furniture.

Summary of Key Points

• Wallace Nutting's 1917 *American Windsors* was the first definitive study
ever published on Windsor chairs.

• Wallace Nutting's *Wallace Nutting Windsors: Correct Windsor Furniture* catalog was released in 1918.

• Beginning in 1918 Nutting began reproducing more than 150 different Windsor forms.

• Nutting's objective was to take a very good original Windsor piece, and make whatever corrections
might be necessary in order to make that Windsor piece perfect in
grace, strength, harmony, and design.

• Nutting's furniture construction techniques were designed to make the finest furniture possible
without cutting corners in terms of labor or expense.

• Wallace Nutting Windsors included the finest woods, faithful turnings, and
the highest quality finishes.

• Wallace Nutting Windsors were usually clearly marked with the "Wallace Nutting" name,
but a few were sold unmarked.

• Certain Wallace Nutting Windsors are rarer than others, with rarity and condition being
two primary determinants of value.

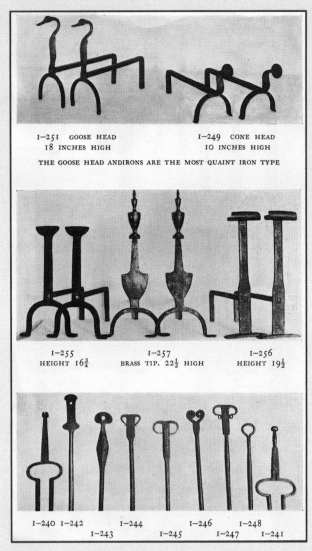

I-251 GOOSE HEAD
18 INCHES HIGH

I-249 CONE HEAD
10 INCHES HIGH

THE GOOSE HEAD ANDIRONS ARE THE MOST QUAINT IRON TYPE

I-255
HEIGHT 16¾

I-257
BRASS TIP. 22½ HIGH

I-256
HEIGHT 19½

I-240 I-242   I-244   I-246   I-248
    I-243   I-245   I-247   I-241

*A page from the ironwork section found in
Nutting's 1930 furniture catalog*

It was in the restoration of his chain of colonial homes that Wallace Nutting first began to understand and appreciate early American ironwork. The earliest American homes had a great need for products made from iron. The hearth, which was the center of home life, needed the most diverse forms: andirons, shovels, and tongs for working with the fire; cranes, pot hooks, skewers, trivets, and forks, for cooking over the fire. Lighting fixtures, door latches, door hinges, and window shutter fasteners were all made from iron. Wrought iron nails were used to hold things together, and iron bolts were used for heavier duty fastening work.

Apparently Nutting had great difficulty in locating a good source for early ironwork that was correct in detail and provided the seventeenth and eighteenth century look and feel that he needed. Nutting wanted every detail in his chain of colonial homes to be as accurate as possible so, when he couldn't locate a source for the iron that he wanted, he decided to produce it himself.

Wallace Nutting had purchased the Saugus Iron Works for two primary reasons. First, he felt this home was architecturally unique. Not only was it one of the oldest houses in the country, but it also contained much of its original seventeenth century iron hardware which he felt gave it the finishing touches of originality.

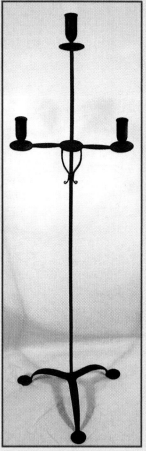

#1-61 Wallace Nutting wrought iron candlestand, the first of only two pieces of Wallace Nutting ironwork that we have ever sold. It sold for $2,970.00, at our November 1998 auction.

Secondly, this house represented the earliest ironworks in America. This had been the residence of America's first successful iron master, Joseph Jenks, the inventor of the long scythe. Jenk's invention had enabled the earliest Americans to harvest their crops three times as quickly as before, thereby symbolizing one of the earliest major improvements to farm productivity in the colonies.

After Nutting refurbished the iron master's home to his satisfaction, he restored the old forge in the rear, hired an iron master, and began reproducing iron, partially to fill his own needs, and partially to satisfy a commercial need he felt existed in the marketplace.

Edward Guy was the iron master who worked for Nutting at the Saugus Iron Works from 1916 to 1921. Production increased fairly rapidly, with Nutting issuing a Wallace Nutting ironwork sales catalog in 1919, similar to his 1918 Windsor chair catalog. This catalog, Early American Ironwork, was copyrighted 1919 by Wallace Nutting Inc. and included a wide variety of iron products that Nutting was commercially reproducing. The catalog was only 24 pages, much smaller than his Windsor chair catalog, but this early American ironwork catalog displayed a much wider array of iron products than most people would have realized. This catalog included sections on fireplace furniture, candlestands, wall sconces, table lights, movable candlesticks, chandeliers, door knockers, door latches, hinges, and even weather vanes.

Each particular piece of iron had a unique catalog number, just as his hand-colored pictures and reproduction furniture had specific catalog numbers. All iron products began with the capital letter "I," followed by a two or three-digit number.

Edward Guy, with Nutting's guidance, produced what were expected to be the bestselling items in advance, stockpiling them for inventory. Those that could not be stockpiled would be made to order. Nutting claimed he was able to furnish the entire hardware for any seventeenth or eighteenth century house, either from designs submitted by the purchaser or from his own personal designs.

The question of whether Nutting ever invented any original iron designs came into question several years after he opened the ironworks. In 1922, the year after Nutting released ***Furniture of the Pilgrim Century***, and one year after Guy had left Nutting's employment, Edward Guy released a letter to bookstores and librarians who may have purchased ***Furniture of the Pilgrim Century***, claiming that some of the iron that Nutting listed as original was actually produced by Guy himself in 1918.

1919 *Early American Ironwork* catalog

IRON PRICE LIST

LATCHES

Number		Price
I-1	Triangle latch, large	$10.00
I-1A	Triangle latch, small	7.00
I-2	Tulip bud, large	15.00
I-2A	Tulip bud, small	11.00
I-3	Crescent and ball	15.00
I-4	Open heart latch	22.00
I-5	Flat ball and spear	16.00
I-6	Heart and point latch	12.00
I-7	Pointed heart latch, large	12.00
I-7A	Pointed heart, small	8.00
I-8	Hampden latch	24.00
I-9	Ball and spear latch	17.00
I-10	Combination knockers	20.00
I-10A	Knocker only	16.00
I-11	Oval, large	7.00
I-11A	Oval, small	6.00

HINGES

I-25	Serpentine L, 37"	$17.00
I-26	Hammered HL hinge, large	12.00
I-27	Tulip bud and blossom	35.00
I-28	Pointed heart 31"	8.00
I-29	Pointed heart 24"	7.00
I-30	Archaic butterfly, large	4.00
I-30A	Archaic butterfly, small	4.50
I-31	Butterfly, large	5.00

Number		Price
I-31A	Butterfly, small	$4.50
I-32	Scrolled H large	5.50
I-32A	Scrolled H small	4.50
I-33	Plain H large	3.50
I-33A	Plain H small	3.00
I-34	Plain HL large	6.00
I-34A	Plain HL small	5.00
I-35	Butterfly and strap	8.00
I-36	Hammered HL small	5.00
I-38	Coxcomb, 3½ x 8¼"	12.00
I-39	Scrolled T, 6 x 9"	6.00
I-119	Moravian scroll	$15 to 25.00
I-127	Chest pins, pair	.50
I-128	Strap chest hinge	4.00

SHUTTER FASTENERS

I-80	Pair, outside	$2.50
I-81	Pair, outside	3.00
I-82	Pair, outside	2.50
I-83	Pair, outside	2.50
I-51	Scrolled fastener	3.00
I-52	Fastener, inside	2.00
I-144	H door fastener	4.50

LIGHTING FIXTURES

I-61	Floor stand, 3 light	$15.00
I-62	Floor stand, 2 light	18.00

[6]

Partial Wallace Nutting ironwork price lists (1926)

IRON PRICE LIST — *Concluded*

Number		Price
I-63	Fine iron and brass, floor	$26.00
I-70	Adjustable, floor	20.00
I-71	Chandelier, wood hub, 6 light	30.00
I-72	Chandelier, all tin, 4 light	15.00
I-220	Tin candle sconce, sunburst	5.00
I-221	Tin candle sconce, narrow	2.00
I-222	Tin candle sconce, narrow, hand painted	4.00
I-232	Corner sconce, plain	6.00
I-233	Corner sconce, decorated	8.00
I-235	Oval, decorated, sconce	4.00
I-236	Oval with mirror, sconce	6.00
I-237	Single branch, sconce	9.00
I-238	Double branch, sconce	12.00

FIREPLACE FURNITURE

I-249	Cone head andirons	$16.00
I-250	Heart-shaped andirons	18.00
I-251	Goose head andirons	18.00
I-252	Octagon ball andirons	16.00
I-253	Spit hook attachment	2.00
I-254	Spit rod, pierced arrow point	4.00
I-255	Scroll head andirons	16.00
I-256	Small shoe base andirons	13.00
I-257	Brass tip andirons	20.00
I-258	Simple crane	5.00
I-259	Scrolled small crane	7.00
I-260	Scrolled large crane	10.00
I-261	Crane eyes	1.00
I-264	Pot hooks, large simple	.50
I-265	Pot hooks, twisted	1.00
I-266	Long shovels, simple	5.00
I-267	Wrought scrolled poker	2.50
I-277	Trivet, simple, small	4.00
I-278	Trivet, simple, large	7.00
I-279	Trivet, scrolled	10.00
I-280	Trivet, elaborate	16.00
I-281	Skewer holder, simple	4.00
I-282	Skewer holder, scrolled	6.00
I-283	Skewer holder, heart motive	7.00
I-284	Skewers, each	.35
I-448	Jamb hooks, twisted	4.00
I-449	Jamb hooks	4.50

BOLTS, ETC.

I-270	Heavy door bolts, top, each	$10.00
I-271	Heavy door bolts, bottom, each	6.00
I-272	Square bolts, 4" plain	3.00
I-273	Square bolts, 4" scrolled	4.00
I-274	Square bolts, 8" plain	4.50

Number		Price
I-275	Square bolts, 8" scrolled	$5.50
I-450	Wrought nails, small, 100	2.50
I-451	Wrought nails, large, 100	3.00
I-452	Rag nails, 3", each	.10

FURNITURE BRASSES

Mostly made for us, by hand

Sizes measured from center to center of post holes.

B-1	Oval pulls "Eagle," 3 x 2⅝", each	$0.75
B-6	Oval pulls, oak branch, 4 x 2"	.65
B-N7	Oval escutcheons	.25
B-8	Oval pulls, scrolled, 3¼ x 2⅛"	.75
B-9	Pulls, 2½"	1.20
	Escutcheon to match	.90
B-23	Pulls, 2½"	.85
	Escutcheons to match	.55
B-25	Pulls, 2¾"	1.25
	Escutcheons to match	.95
	Pulls, 3½"	1.55
	Escutcheons to match	1.25
	Pulls, 3¾"	1.70
	Escutcheons to match	1.40
B-35	Plain round or oval Sheraton pulls, 3¼"	.95
	Plain round or Sheraton pulls, 3½"	1.05
B-50	Pulls, 2¼"	1.65
	Escutcheons to match	1.35
B-51	Pulls, 2½"	1.80
	Escutcheons to match	1.55
B-N52	Pulls with 1¾" drop	1.20
B-53	Escutcheons, 2¼"	1.35
B-54	Pulls, 2"	1.85
	Escutcheons to match	1.65
B-70	Escutcheons 4" long	.75
B-N80	Tear drop pulls, 1¾"	.90
B-N81	Escutcheons to match	.25
B-N82	Small pull, ½", $0.18; ¾"	.22
B-N83	Large pulls, 1", $0.25; 1¼"	.30
B-N84	Knobs, ¼"	.15
B-N85	" ½"	.18
B-N86	" ⅝"	.20
B-N87	" ¾"	.25
B-88	Ring pulls	1.20
B-N89	Small knobs	1.00
B-N90	Bed post cover	.45
B-N91	Bed post cover	.40
B-N92	Small ring pull, 2"	.40
B-N93	Escutcheons to match	.32
B-N94	Large knobs	1.05

[7]

Partial Wallace Nutting Ironwork Price List (1926)

Ironwork of the Pilgrim Century Made in 1918
A STATEMENT BY EDWARD GUY, MAKER OF HAND WROUGHT IRON

To Whom It May Concern: -

A copy of the book written by Wallace Nutting showing furniture and ironwork of the Pilgrim century was sent to me, and I thought it was strange business when I saw pictures of ironwork made by me a few years ago, now known as antique ironwork, for students and collectors to study.

I thought it was strange again when the last lines of the author are: "Finally the author begs a kindly judgment on his work, trusting it will be understood all has been guided by fidelity in dealing with the faithful artificers of the Pilgrim century."

For five years I made wrought iron for Wallace Nutting, Inc. Mr. Nutting wrote about my work and praised it. In a booklet given to the public in November, 1917, he wrote: "In Mr. Edward Guy, the mastersmith, he (Mr. Nutting) has secured a man who is a descendant of a line of forgemen of five generations. His ancestors were trained in the Lancashire region of England, famous for its cunning and beautiful wrought ironwork. The workmanship challenges comparison with anything of the sort produced in modern times. The daintiness of the work, together with it's feeling of taste, will certainly commend itself to all discriminating persons."

On page 559 of the Nutting book are two iron candleholders. Both were made by me in 1918. I have the original sketch used by me to make them, which was copied from a book called "Village Homes of England", page 157. They are from Sussex. We changed the candle sockets.

On page 553 of the Nutting book there is shown a pair of pipe tongs or brand tongs. They came out of the same book of English work. They are four years old. They are numbered 184. I also made 181 and 183, but they are copies of the old American tongs. I still have the shop drawings used to make the pair captured at some fort according to Nutting.

On page 573 there are nine door-knockers shown. I made every one of them, and seven out of the nine are my original designs. I have witnesses who saw me make them, and they will say so any time, anywhere.

All the illustrations in the Nutting book, with numbers on the pictures of ironwork, were taken from the catalogue of ironwork sold by Wallace Nutting, Inc. Why show catalogue numbers in a $15 book?

I have counted over 150 pieces shown in both the catalogue and the book. Old and new are mixed together. I make this statement in self defense, because I made much of the ironwork to be sold as modern in the old style, and I still make it.

Honest ironwork is my living. I want to keep the record straight.

Very truly yours,
Saugus Center, Mass., April 1, 1922   *(Signed) EDWARD GUY*

Text of Edward Guy Letter, dated April 1, 1922

The text of Edward Guy's 1922 letter

The reason Nutting would have tried to pass off his reproduction ironwork as original is unclear, having never seen his response to the charges. I have a hard time believing that he would ever intentionally put himself into such an awkward position. Putting both his sometimes overzealous personality and his religious background aside, it's hard to believe that such a nationally renowned expert would put his reputation into question in order to earn what would literally amount to only a few dollars selling his door knockers.

One Nutting researcher speculated that perhaps "Nutting simply thought there should have been seventeenth century American door knockers — Of the style designed and produced under his supervision." Or, perhaps several photographs were inadvertently switched and never caught until after the book's publication. After all, *Furniture of the Pilgrim Century* contained over 1,000 photographs and the possibility exists that an honest mistake was made.

It is also unclear what caused Edward Guy to publicly humiliate Wallace Nutting. Whether there was bad blood after Guy left Nutting's employment in 1921, or whether Nutting himself simply refused to publicly acknowledge the mistake is unclear.

In any event, it would appear that Nutting's ironwork business never flourished the way he had hoped. Although it closed upon the sale of the Saugus Iron Works, he continued to offer his reproduction iron in the 1926, 1927 – 1928, and 1930 furniture catalogs.

The biggest problem facing collectors today is that very little of Nutting's ironwork was marked. Unlike his hand-colored pictures all of which carried the famous Wallace Nutting signature, or the reproduction furniture most of which contained either a paper label or branded signature, his iron was nearly impossible to mark. We suspect that most ironwork was initially marked with a card stock tag attached by a thin wire which, when removed, left the piece unidentifiable. In over 30 years I have only seen two signed pieces of Wallace Nutting ironwork.

And because Nutting so rarely marked his ironwork, positive identification is extremely difficult today. Iron oxidizes and rusts so quickly, and now that his iron has had more than 70 years to age, separating Nutting's iron from the original is nearly impossible. In the absence of any written documentation (e.g., sales

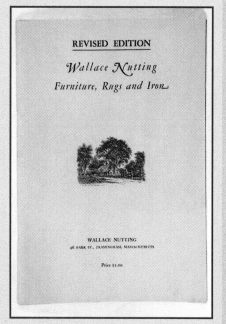

1927 Wallace Nutting Furniture, Rugs, and Ironwork Catalog

receipts), pretty much the only way to positively identify an unmarked piece of Wallace Nutting iron is through a visual match with the item pictured in one of Nutting's sales catalogs.

Without a doubt nearly all Wallace Nutting reproduction ironwork is being sold as original today. Since it is almost always unmarked, it looks like original, and is sold as such at original iron prices. And since it is always unmarked, you will most likely have a difficult time convincing a dealer that his "original" iron is actually a piece of unmarked Nutting iron. Therefore, expect to pay top dollar for it.

No production records are known to have been kept so there is no way of knowing exactly how much Wallace Nutting iron was sold but in our opinion extremely little Wallace Nutting ironwork was sold, despite his advertising it over a 20+ year period.

Wallace Nutting Brass: Although Wallace Nutting devoted 2½ pages in his 1930 furniture catalog to brass, Nutting never attempted to reproduce brass himself. Rather, all handmade and filed brasses which were found on many of his pieces of furniture, and although customers were able to purchase various brass drawer pulls, bolt covers, hinges, casters, ornaments and brass door knockers directly from his company, Wallace Nutting's sales catalog states that "…these brasses are made for us…" by another company.

Summary of Key Points

• Wallace Nutting reproduced early American ironwork between 1919 and 1937.

• He began reproducing iron at the Saugus Iron Works which was located adjacent to Broadhearth, one of his colonial chain of houses located in Saugus, Massachusetts.

• His reproductions included fireplace furniture, candlestands, wall sconces, table lights, movable candlesticks, chandeliers, door knockers, door latches, hinges, and even weather vanes.

• Wallace Nutting ironwork is rarely marked and can be extremely difficult to authenticate.

• Because of its rapid oxidation Wallace Nutting ironwork is difficult to distinguish from original period ironwork.

• Although Wallace Nutting sold reproduction brasses, these were produced for him by another company and his company never reproduced brasses on their own.

#1 – 456 Wallace Nutting wrought iron potato cooker, was the second piece of Wallace Nutting ironwork sold at our auction. It sold for $2,145.00 at our November '01 auction.

A rare "Wallace Nutting" impressed marking upon the potato cooker's handle.

#301 Windsor brace back side chair, script brand, with pieced seat. $400.00 – 625.00

Nutting sold only Windsor chairs and Windsor-style pieces for the first several years. Beginning with only a few different Windsor forms in 1917, he expanded his product line so quickly that by 1918 his Windsor chair catalog included nearly 150 different variations of chairs, beds, stools, cradles, cribs, bassinets, love seats, and settees, all using the Windsor design.

By 1920, with his research into other furniture forms complete and with the *Furniture of the Pilgrim Century* nearly ready for publication, Nutting began to study and copy other forms of antique furniture: chests, tables, desks, and cabinet pieces. Although his production of non-Windsor chair pieces at this time wasn't very large, he did find himself having some initial success in his new endeavors.

Business was growing so well that Nutting decided to consolidate both the picture and furniture business in Ashland, Massachusetts. In 1920 he purchased an old canning factory which was especially attractive because it had its own railway spur enabling Nutting to receive raw materials and ship finished goods by rail. Apparently Nutting borrowed a considerable sum of money to complete this move because he later stated that he owed more than $100,000.00 due to his enlarged studio and facility.

The business still continued to use paper labels for identification at Ashland, although modified somewhat from earlier labels.

But at the same time, Nutting found himself beginning to think of retirement again. His first retirement was short-lived. As a matter of fact, it was almost no retirement at all. In 1904 he seemed to jump from the ministry directly into his first picture studio in New York City, then directly into his new Southbury studio in 1905, where business interests began to consume his life.

His seemingly immediate career change from the ministry into a successful, profit-making business caused some people to accuse him, albeit under their breath, of leaving the cloth in order to make money. Although he continued to deny it to his dying day, some people just never understood how he could leave the ministry because of its hectic pace, only to enter a profession that kept him even busier.

Between 1910 and 1920 while his picture business was growing exponentially:

- Wallace Nutting had moved his home and entire business from Southbury, Connecticut, to Framingham, Massachusetts (1912).

- …he released *Up at the Vilas Farm* (1912).

- …he released *Old New England Pictures* (1913).

- …he opened, restored, then closed his chain of five colonial houses (1914 – 1920).

- …World War I, The War to End All Wars, began and ended (1914 – 1918).

- …he extensively researched, and then published, the most definitive book ever written on Windsor chairs (1917).

- …he started a furniture reproduction business, which involved researching antique furniture, designing and creating 150+ furniture models, creating thousands of manufacturing templates, and then producing a starting inventory that had to approach nearly 1,000 pieces (1917).

- …he created and released his initial reproduction Windsor chair catalog (1918).

- …he completed most of the research needed to publish his *Furniture of the Pilgrim Century* book in 1921.

- …all while managing a business with between 100 – 200 employees which just happened to sell more hand-colored photographs than anyone else in the history of the world.

Regardless of the circumstances surrounding his first retirement, after more than fifteen years in the picture business Nutting once again began to consider retirement. With his picture business booming, with his furniture business growing, with several books already successfully published, and with a name that was nationally known and respected, Wallace Nutting decided to divest himself of all business interests. This time, he intended to enjoy his retirement and pursue a less-exhausting career — collecting and studying early American antiques.

So somewhere between 1921 and 1922, eighteen years after his first retirement, Wallace Nutting decided to retire again.

From a historical perspective this is where things get somewhat tricky. For practically 30 years, since the Wallace Nutting Collectors Club was founded in 1973, it has been a generally accepted fact that Wallace Nutting sold his business, along with the right to continue to use the "Wallace Nutting" name, for a considerable sum of money to another business concern who then took over Wallace Nutting Inc. in Ashland, Massachusetts. Published club research and other published articles referred to Wallace Nutting selling his business. According to a former Wallace Nutting colorist, he sold the business to a chair company in Fitchburg. Nutting supposedly then used that money to accumulate an exceptional collection of original early American antiques. Several years later, disgruntled with the way in which his name was being used, and disgruntled with the way the business that still carried his name was being run, he then supposedly sold his collection of original early American antiques to J.P. Morgan and then used the proceeds from that sale to re-purchase his business in 1924.

However, in the 2003 release of his *Wallace Nutting and the Invention of Old America* book, Tom Denenberg suggests that rather than selling his business outright, perhaps Nutting simply brought in new partners to run the business. As head curator at the Wadsworth Atheneum, Tom has had access to records, documents, research, and contacts available to basically no one else. Tom stated that throughout all of his research he never found any solid evidence, any signed documents or contracts, or any regulatory evidence, that Wallace Nutting Inc. had actually changed hands during this period. Tom suggests that rather than selling his business outright, perhaps Wallace Nutting brought in new partners or investors who took over the business while Wallace Nutting moved into the background.

Nutting's Ashland, Massachusetts furniture facility.
Photo courtesy of the Pedro Cacciola collection.

But something clearly did happen during this 1922 – 1924 period.

The Transition (or Script) Years, 1922 – 1924

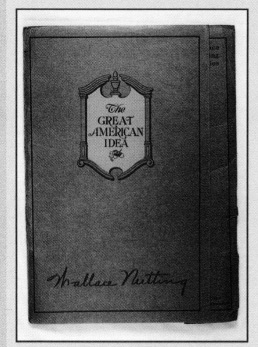

Wallace Nutting: The Great American Idea
script furniture catalog, circa 1922

- Wallace Nutting's 150+ piece 1918 Windsor chair catalog was replace by the *Wallace Nutting: A Great American Idea* catalog (dated January 1, 1922) which contained only 42 different production designs including only 19 Windsor forms. Why the drastic decrease in furniture designs at a time when Nutting was seemingly expanding into new areas almost daily?
- The introduction of the *Wallace Nutting: A Great American Idea* catalog mentioned Mr. Nutting six times on the first page almost making it sound that Mr. Nutting was gone and no longer around. Conversely the 1918 Windsor chair catalog almost sounds like Wallace Nutting himself was talking directly to his customers through the wording and text used throughout that catalog. Why the change in tone?
- The old-school production methods originally used between 1918 and 1921 seemed to be almost immediately replaced in 1922 by newer methods designed to speed up production and cut corners and expenses. This was something totally at odds with the way Nutting described his production techniques several years earlier in his 1918 Windsor chair catalog. Why?
- The light maple finish was all but totally replaced by the darker mahogany finish. Why?
- And if Nutting had indeed brought in new partners and investors, along with new investment capital, logic suggests that any new funding would have gone into the business, not into Wallace Nutting's pockets to enable him to invest in more early American antiques.

So yes, something undoubtedly did happen circa 1921. Whether Wallace Nutting sold his business (as has traditionally been assumed), or simply brought in some new partners (as Tom Dennenberg suggests), it certainly appears that Wallace Nutting left all business interests and retired for a second time.

So around 1921 Wallace Nutting gave up control of his entire picture business and his furniture business, along with the right to use the Wallace Nutting name. It has been thought that he received somewhere around $100,000.00 at this time which he used to pay off creditors for debts arising from his Ashland expansion and to begin what we have already described as Phase II of his antique collecting career.

Nutting began his second retirement enjoyably enough, studying antiques wherever he could locate them. He attended auctions, traveled to near and distant antique shops, toured museums, and visited dealers and friends, buying new pieces when he could, studying, recording, and photographing when he could not buy. Within the next year his keen eye, high energy level, and new-found bankroll enabled him to begin to accumulate what was soon to become one of the finest antique collections ever assembled, all within one year of his second retirement.

But by 1923, things began to trouble him. Undoubtedly retirement didn't suit him. He didn't sit still very long after his first retirement so there was no reason to believe he would relax after his second retirement either. But what apparently disturbed him the most was what he observed happening to the business still bearing his name. Although whatever contractual agreements had been reached between Nutting and the new management are unclear, there's no doubt that Nutting expected them to continue with the same high level of quality that had been associated with the Wallace Nutting name over the past eighteen years.

The Wallace Nutting script brand

They did not.

Records are not clear as to who took over control of Wallace Nutting's business. According to a former colorist, it was a "chair company in Fitchburg." Regardless of the new management's name, Nutting was outraged at the poor quality of the products being produced and sold by this company, still using the Wallace Nutting name. How dare they cheapen the good name that he had worked so long and hard to achieve!

The quality of Wallace Nutting furniture deteriorated at this time. Although they were following Wallace Nutting's patterns and models, corners were cut in order to reduce costs, something that Nutting would never have approved of. The quality of the Wallace Nutting hand-colored pictures deteriorated significantly as well at this time. Although they were still using Nutting's original model pictures and negatives, the coloring was awful. Colors were not nearly as bright or cheerful as before, and the detail began to look muddy and murky, more like a bad water color than a hand-tinted platinotype picture. One colorist complained that the new management was more interested in quantity than quality.

This newer Wallace Nutting furniture, marked by a distinctive script branded signature, were no longer exact copies of the earlier reproductions. At first glance, these newer reproductions looked good, and were probably better than most other reproductions of the period. But upon a closer look, the quality just wasn't the same as when Nutting himself controlled the process.

The Transition (or Script) Years, 1922 – 1924

Script branded chairs were typically constructed of five glued pieces of wood.

The differences between this script branded furniture and Nutting's earlier paper label furniture were obvious. For example, paper label Windsor seats were all carved from one solid 2" plank; the script seats were carved from a piece of wood consisting of five smaller pieces of wood glued together. With script furniture, height specifications were not always followed, the shapes of seats were not nearly as detailed or pronounced, and carvings on the ears were not always as sharp and crisp as before.

On tables, narrower boards were used; on dressers and case pieces, drawers were frequently constructed without dovetailing; and on desks and cabinet pieces, the carvings were either omitted or greatly simplified.

Less expensive woods were frequently used. For example, Welsh cupboards were made from cheaper maple instead of the more expensive oak. More often than not, the standard finish became the darker mahogany style, regardless of whether the original specifications called for it. And fewer coats of finish were applied. We have even seen pieces from this period which carried an atrocious green wash color.

These deviations from the old Wallace Nutting way of doing things may not have been visible to most people, but they were certainly noticeable to him. By 1923, he decided to end his second retirement and get his company back. He did have one major problem however — money. He had used the proceeds he had originally obtained in 1921 to payoff his creditors and to purchase antiques. But he did have one ready source of funds — his own personal antique collection.

Although Nutting may not have been a rich individual, neither was he poor. His national reputation as author, businessman, and authority on antiques had put him in touch with many wealthy collectors — Ford, DuPont, Garvan, Sack, Erving, and J.P. Morgan (the same J. P. Morgan whose grandfather formerly lived in the Cutler-Bartlet House, one of the homes in Nutting's colonial chain).

Anyway, Nutting negotiated the sale of his personal antique collection to J.P. Morgan for approximately $100,000.00 who in turn, donated it to the Wadsworth Atheneum in Hartford, Connecticut.

Nutting immediately used that money to repurchase his picture and furniture business and set out to restore his good name.

Is Script Branded Furniture Actually Wallace Nutting Furniture?

The question arises whether furniture with the script branded signature is indeed Wallace Nutting furniture. I've always maintained that although the quality of the script furniture is not as good as the paper label or block branded pieces, it's still better than most other twentieth century reproductions. It was made from the original Nutting patterns and designs, it followed Nutting's original numbering identification system, was sold under the Wallace Nutting name, and therefore should be considered Wallace Nutting furniture. However, because of its somewhat lower quality, value should be adjusted downward.

How much furniture with the script signature was produced? No one knows because no production records from the transition years are known to exist. But there does seem to have been quite a bit produced. Based on the large quantity of Nutting furniture I have seen, I would estimate that perhaps 10 – 15% of Nutting furniture has a script signature. Let's put this into perspective. Nutting was producing furniture for approximately 20 years, with the greatest volume in the mid-1920s. The 1922 – 1924 production period translates roughly into 8% of total production (two years out of 23). Yet, I have estimated that 10 – 15% of the furniture has the script signature.

How could a company just starting in the business have produced such a large amount of furniture in such a short time? The most logical answer is that since they had access to Nutting's furniture designs, patterns, models, and equipment, their start-up time was minimal. And, because they cut so many corners, they were able to produce more furniture per day than when Nutting himself ran the company.

Who Initiated the Script Brand?

Another area where things get tricky is the question about whether Nutting himself ever produced furniture with the script branded signature? There has indeed been some speculation that Nutting may have initiated the script signature himself just prior to selling his business in 1922 in order to thwart those individuals who removed his paper labels. However I have been unable to find any confirming evidence to support this. Although I have seen a few Wallace Nutting furniture advertisements with the Ashland address that contained a script signature in the advertising copy, I haven't been able to confirm through any other source whether Nutting did indeed use the script branded signature himself.

In the absence of any confirming evidence that Nutting had used the script branded signature, you will probably be safe using the following rule of thumb: Furniture with the script branded signature was produced circa 1922 – 1924 when Wallace Nutting himself was not in control of Wallace Nutting Inc.

Even if he did not reproduce script branded signature furniture, did Nutting himself ever sell furniture with the detested script signature? Somewhat surprisingly, the answer is "yes." Years ago I purchased an entire dining room set, including a gate-leg table and four Windsor chairs, all with the script signature. Accompanying the furniture was a letter indicating that the owner had purchased the set directly from Wallace Nutting himself while in Framingham, in 1936. My speculation is that when Nutting resumed control of the business in 1924, he must have also purchased any existing inventory bearing the script branded signature. Rather than destroy it, he most likely stockpiled it and sold it at reduced prices, especially when business softened during the 1930s.

Anyway, you should be aware that Wallace Nutting furniture bearing the script signature was manufactured during 1922 – 1924, and was of an inferior quality when compared to the paper pabel and block branded furniture produced when Nutting himself controlled the company. Furniture bearing the script brand may be worth anywhere from 25% to 50% less than an identical piece bearing the paper label or block brand.

With things firmly back in his control in 1924, after his second unsuccessful retirement, Nutting was now ready to begin some of his grandest accomplishments of all.

Summary of Key Points

• Wallace Nutting gave up control of his furniture business circa 1922 – 1924 when he retired for a second time.

• Wallace Nutting also gave up control of the Wallace Nutting name during this period.

• A new, smaller *Wallace Nutting: A Great American Idea* catalog featuring only script branded furniture was introduced January 1, 1922.

• Script branded furniture was produced circa 1922 – 1924.

• Script branded furniture is generally inferior in quality to paper label and block branded furniture.

• Only 42 different designs were produced during this 1922 – 1924 script period versus 150+ different designs during the 1918 – 1921 period.

• Wallace Nutting sold his collection of early American antiques to J.P. Morgan in order to acquire the funds necessary to regain control of his business.

• J.P. Morgan donated the Wallace Nutting collection to the Wadsworth Atheneum in Hartford, Connecticut, where it still resides today.

By the time Nutting had regained control of his business in 1924, he had already accomplished more than most individuals could hope to accomplish in a lifetime. The 1921 release of *Furniture of the Pilgrim Century* only seemed to whet his appetite for new challenges. Just as he learned how to reproduce Windsor chairs after his extensive study of the Windsor form, Nutting now found himself desiring to reproduce other forms of early furniture as well. So upon resuming control of his furniture business, Nutting began to expand his furniture reproduction operation beyond Windsor chairs.

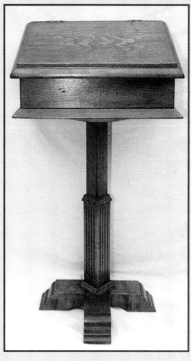

One of the first things that Wallace Nutting did upon regaining control of his business was to renounce the detested script branded signature. Some advertising claimed: "My name in plain capitals thus WALLACE NUTTING is burned into every piece I endorse. I will not be responsible for a script letter formerly used as a mark." Other advertising and catalogs claimed that his new block branded signature "...must appear on all my furniture."

Pilgrim Century oak lift top lectern

#910 Sudbury Court cupboard, now owned by the Society for the Preservation of New England Antiquities (SPNEA)

One of his earliest catalogs issued upon his resuming control is only 32 pages, picturing approximately 70 of the nearly 250 designs he was reproducing at that time. In addition to his wide selection of eighteenth century Windsor chair designs, Nutting was producing seventeenth century oak and maple cabinet and turned pieces, along with a select few eighteenth century pine and maple cupboards, chairs, chests, cables, and desks. Only a few pieces were available in walnut. The light maple finish magically re-appeared at this time. This 1926 furniture catalog represented a stark contrast to the 1922 script catalog which featured only 42 total pieces, all in the darker mahogany finish.

Nutting's new block branded signature.

Wallace Nutting furniture studio, circa 1937. Photo courtesy of the Pedro Cacciola collection.

Beyond the Windsor Form: Other Wallace Nutting Furniture

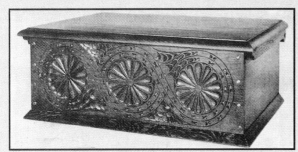

#900 Bible box. From the 1930 furniture catalog.

Wallace Nutting furniture shop employees, circa 1937.
Photo courtesy of the Pedro Cacciola collection.

At this point Nutting had little interest in the later Queen Anne, Chippendale, Hepplewhite, and Sheraton styles. His primary interests were in the late seventeenth and early eighteenth century furniture that he had photographed for *Furniture of the Pilgrim Century*. His catalog stated that he was capable of copying any article of furniture known to have been used before 1720, and he carried his pine and maple reproductions up through 1780. He used very little mahogany and stopped just short of the cabriole leg.

Some of his earlier reproduction pieces included court cupboards; paneled and sunflower chests; oak chest of drawers; butterfly, gateleg, refractory, trestle, folding gate and tavern tables; framed desks; ladderback chairs; joined and rushed stools; pilgrim and carver chairs; and even a day bed and Bible box.

At his peak, Nutting employed a group of approximately 25 craftsmen whom he described in one of his furniture catalogs as "fine American mechanics, men of character, whom it is a privilege to know. Many live on their own little farms. They are trained experts in their lines — turners, chair, and cabinet makers. My greatest asset is these men sought out from every direction, men who love their work, and who are cooperating with me to produce the finest forms of furniture."

In reality, many of the furniture makers he employed were foreign born. Nutting seem to feel that foreign-born craftsmen possessed finer skills and were better disciplined than their American counterparts.

By the mid-1920s, furniture sales were increasing. The country's economy was fairly stable, and America had a renewed interest in early American furniture. Although furniture sales were not yet profitable, they were encouraging. And with his picture business thriving, Nutting expected that the picture business would be able to carry the furniture business until it began to generate a profit. But the sad reality was that although Wallace Nutting truly loved his Pilgrim Century designs, most of America did not. Which forced him to face up to the economic realities of the early twentieth century furniture business.

Moving Beyond the Windsor Form

By 1927 – 1928, the economic reality of Nutting's furniture business began to set in. Sales had not picked up to where he would have liked and expenses were running higher than anticipated. Whereas his earlier furniture catalog stated that he stopped short of the cabriole leg and pieces made of mahogany, by 1927 he found it necessary to copy some of those later Queen Anne, Chippendale, Hepplewhite, and Sheraton styles that he had condemned only a few years earlier. Perhaps he didn't like these higher styles as much as the earlier seventeenth century oak and maple styles, but the public did. If he wished to remain in business, he would have to adapt to the public's taste.

Expanding beyond Windsor chairs and the Pilgrim and William & Mary styles, this catalog included Savery highboys and lowboys; Queen Anne, Chippendale, and Hepplewhite arm and side chairs; carved walnut sideboards; a Goddard chest-on-chest; pine and Welsh dressers; and a carved corner cupboard. In all, Nutting was offering 80 different types of chairs, 30 beds, 60 tables, 20 chests and chest of drawers, 20 cupboards, and 20 desks and secretaries.

#628 mahogany one-drawer Pembroke table. Block brand. $1,825.00 – 2,500.00

#697 Queen Anne card table. Block brand. Sold at our June 2003 auction for $6,600.00

Mahogany three-drawer slant front desk. Block brand. $4,000.00 – 6,000.00

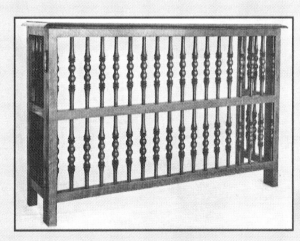

#15 oak radiator mask. From the 1930 furniture catalog $500.00 – 750.00

Beyond the Windsor Form: Other Wallace Nutting Furniture

#746 bank check desk. From the 1930 furniture catalog.
$2,250.00 – 3,250.00

#912 bank table. From the 1930 furniture catalog.
$4,675.00 – 5,675.00

#397 stenographer's leather swivel chair (l)
$925.00 – 1,225.00:
#497 stenographer's short arm swivel chair (r)
$1,000.00 – 1,300.00. From the 1930 furniture catalog.

Commercial Adaptations

Also by 1927 – 1928, not only had Nutting yielded to the later styles of furniture, he began commercially adapting his antique designs to items which had no true antique precedent. His stated purpose in his 1930 furniture catalog for these adaptations was strictly to satisfy a legitimate market demand: "The public are hereby notified that the above object (#735C oak desk) and all following furniture in this (1930 furniture catalog) until (the ironwork section) are adaptations of the antique and are not correct copies. The reason for this is that there is a legitimate demand for a flat top desk, one of which has already been shown, but no others, practical, are known to Mr. Nutting."

But, in reality, this was nothing more than an attempt to bolster sagging furniture sales. He created a commercial line which adapted his furniture to a business setting: bank check writing desks, typewriter desks, executive desks, stenographer's chairs, and even an oak radiator cover. We have rarely seen any of these become available and doubt that many were sold.

Beyond the Windsor Form: Other Wallace Nutting Furniture

It is also interesting to note that by this time, Nutting had expanded the scope of his business operations considerably to include such diverse services as:

- Furniture reproduction
- Hook rugs
- Hardware consisting of hinges, latches, window fastenings, fireplace utensils, sconces, and lighting fixtures
- Panels, mantels, and door heads
- Simple and elaborate carvings
- Hand-colored pictures of all types
- Small calendars
- Illustrations of estates, the interweaving of illustrations, enlargements, and coloring on order (e.g., *Up at the Vilas Farm*)
- Consultation with home owners and architects regarding the architectural aspects of homes
- Interior decorating consultation for homes
- Interior decorating consultation for banks, clubs, hospitals, and offices
- Antique repair and restoration
- A series of lectures on furniture, Colonial interiors, and architecture, offering nearly 3000 photographs and hand-colored glass slides.

Here was a man who only a few short years ago had retired for the second time. Now, by 1927, he had expanded the scope of his business operations to include an even wider variety of services than ever before.

Colonial Williamsburg

One of his customers eventually became Colonial Williamsburg. After unsuccessfully searching for authentic period furniture to use in one of their restored buildings, they commissioned Nutting to produce a set of 12 Flemish arm chairs in 1932. In a move that was characteristically Nutting, he produced the entire set of 12 chairs the way he felt they should have been made prior to receiving approval from the Williamsburg trustees on the initial model.

#747 oak chest executive's desk, adaptable for a typewriter. From the 1930 furniture catalog. $3,500.00 – 4,250.00

#735 seven-drawer executive's desk, adaptable for a typewriter. Available in walnut, oak, mahogany, or maple. From the 1930 furniture catalog. $6,500.00 – 9,175.00

#476 Flemish arm chair, with carved crest and foot rails. $1,075.00 – 1,325.00

Beyond the Windsor Form: Other Wallace Nutting Furniture

Quite unexpectedly, the entire set was rejected as unacceptable. Whether the error was the result of Nutting's personal interpretation of the chairs, whether his craftsmen were unable to read his cryptic style of writing, or whether Williamsburg simply failed to provide clear enough direction really doesn't matter. After considerable debate regarding the merits of his chairs, Nutting produced 12 chairs that were acceptable to Williamsburg and was paid $112.50 each. He then resold the twelve incorrect chairs privately.

Regardless of the unusual circumstances surrounding these 12 chairs, the fact that such a prestigious foundation as Colonial Williamsburg selected Nutting above all other furniture makers in the country exemplifies the high degree of acceptance and respect there was for Wallace Nutting's furniture. These chairs are still on display today in the Colonial Williamsburg Council Chambers.

Construction Techniques

The construction methods and techniques outlined in the chapter on Windsor chairs were similar in scope to the techniques followed on his other furniture. Nutting would first identify the piece of furniture he wished to copy. He would then study and analyze it, create scaled drawings, make whatever "improvements" he felt were necessary, produce the model components, and then begin production.

EXAMPLE OF GOOD AND BAD CONSTRUCTION. WE USE ONLY LEFT HAND

"We use only good construction techniques."
From the 1937 furniture catalog.

The sources for Nutting's reproductions came from many places. Some were antiques that Nutting had privately purchased, generally with the intention of copying. Or sometimes he would borrow the original from a friend or acquaintance. And sometimes he would base his reproduction upon an original antique found in a museum, frequently either the Metropolitan Museum in New York City or the Wadsworth Atheneum in Hartford, Connecticut, which housed his former collection.

You should understand that Nutting was not a craftsman himself. He never lifted a tool, nor did he have any mechanical ability. His major asset was his keen eye for beauty. Nutting knew better than most how to identify a beautiful piece of furniture, but he relied upon his craftsmen to actually reproduce it for him.

It should also be understood that Nutting didn't accomplish everything at once. Each step in his career was a growing process, and each success led to new confidence in his next undertaking. His successful reproduction of his first Windsor chair led to his copying of more than 100 different Windsor designs. His success with Windsor chairs led to his copying non-Windsor chairs; his success with non-Windsor chairs led to copying tables; tables led to chests; and chests led to larger cabinet pieces.

The #733 Goddard Blockfront Nine-Shell Secretary Desk

Nutting claimed his biggest challenge was his reproduction of a Goddard blockfront secretary with nine shell carvings. This was one of his earliest attempts at copying a mahogany piece and he knew that if he could successfully copy this secretary, he could reproduce anything. He took six of his workmen to Providence, Rhode Island, to analyze the piece. They studied it, took measurements, made sketches, and photographed it. When final work was completed, Nutting was pleased with what he considered to be his finest reproduction ever. Only seven were produced, with a 1932 retail price of $1,800.00, and the last one sold at auction in 2002 for $36,750.00, the current auction record for a piece of Wallace Nutting furniture.

#733 Goddard blockfront secretary. Photo courtesy of Sharon & Kenny Lacasse.

Shell carving from the #733 Goddard block front secretary. Photo courtesy of Sharon & Kenny Lacasse.

Note the carvings: Ball & claw feet, highly carved knees, seat rail carving, back splat carvings, and reed post carvings. No wonder this chair cost nearly $300.00 in 1932.

As with his Windsor chairs, his non-Windsor furniture was manufactured in the best manner possible, using the finest woods available. His furniture designs weren't good, they were excellent. The carvings on his furniture weren't average, they were the best.

Each worker was obligated to follow the original model exactly. To insure adherence to his high level of quality, Nutting posted his "10 Furniture Construction Commandments" above each craftsmen's work bench.

Knee carving from a mahogany Chippendale side chair

Beyond the Windsor Form: Other Wallace Nutting Furniture

Wallace Nutting Furniture Construction
Ten Construction Commandments

1. All work to be of the best quality.
2. If the old method is the best, use it.
3. If the work can be done better by hand,
   do it that way.
4. Use long and large mortises, and large
   square white oak pins.
5. Make all joined work fit together perfectly, using draw bore where it is better.
6. Match the color where two pieces come together.
7. Follow the sample strictly. Take no liberties.
8. The hand and the mouth do not work effectively at the same time.
9. Keep busy, do your best, and no fault will be found.
10. Let nothing leave your hands until you are proud of the work.

To Insure Individuality and Make Men While Making Furniture.

At his peak, Wallace Nutting had reproduced an incredibly wide variety of furniture styles and designs:

- Periods ranged from early Pilgrim and William & Mary through, and including, Queen Anne, Chippendale, Hepplewhite, and Sheraton.

- Dates ranged from 1620 to 1830.

- Specific designs included arm chairs, beds, chests, clocks, corner cupboards, court cupboards, desks, dressers, highboys, lowboys, mirrors, settees, settles, side chairs, sofas, tables, treenware, and more than 100 variations of the Windsor chair.

Wallace Nutting had copied more than 500 different forms of early American antiques, more than anyone else before him or since. His reproductions were among the twentieth century's best. The quality was excellent and the designs were diverse enough to furnish any style of home. But there was one important ingredient missing from Wallace Nutting's furniture business.

He was never able to turn a profit.

Summary of Key Points

• Nutting renounced the script brand and replaced it with the block brand immediately upon regaining control of his business in 1925.

• His 1926 furniture catalog was the first to introduce some of his higher furniture designs such as Hepplewhite, Chippendale, Queen Anne, and Sheraton.

• The economic reality of sluggish sales forced Nutting to move even beyond his introduction of higher furniture styles to the introduction of commercial adaptations which had no true antique precedent.

• Only a few years out of his second retirement Wallace Nutting significantly expanded the scope of his business operation to include a diverse line of services.

• Wallace Nutting was so highly regarded as a furniture maker that a diverse assortment of corporations, businesses, and even Colonial Williamsburg commissioned Wallace Nutting to produce special pieces for them.

• Wallace Nutting himself was not a craftsman or tradesman and couldn't even swing a hammer. Rather he was a visionary with a keen eye for beauty and the ability to differentiate between good, better, and best.

• Despite all of this, Wallace Nutting was never able to generate a profit in his furniture business.

Even with the release of his 1927 – 1928 furniture catalog, and despite his ever expanding line of reproduction styles, Nutting was still operating the furniture business at a loss. Lower-than-anticipated sales obviously contributed to this lack of profit.

Unexpectedly high production costs also contributed to business losses. The high expenses certainly didn't come from high salaries as Nutting was not known to have been overly generous with his employees. Rather, the high expenses came from the inordinate amount of time spent producing each piece. As explained earlier, and as dictated in his "10 Commandments," Nutting stubbornly clung to his desire to do things by the old method wherever possible. Few corners were cut, regardless of cost, in order to produce a piece of furniture worthy of the Wallace Nutting name. Wood workers were shaping only three Windsor seats per day, while refinishers could often only turn out three chairs on a good day.

Wallace Nutting (1861 – 1941)

Wallace Nutting, circa 1937 (rear row, second from right, in hat). Photo courtesy of Pedro Cacciola collection

And to further complicate matters, Nutting would frequently change his mind about furniture designs and specifications. Nutting would all too frequently approve a model and then, after actual production began, would make several changes. These changes wouldn't significantly alter the appearance of a piece, but would necessitate significant additional work. Sometimes he would add ¾" to a leg, other times he would slightly change the height of a chest. But his constant meddling would require creating new scaled drawings, cutting new patterns, and preparing new models, thereby adding to overall production costs significantly. But what was even worse, these changes would take several key employees away from the actual production of furniture, which is what really paid the bills.

It didn't really matter whether Nutting was right or not, he didn't care. It was his furniture, it carried his name, and he wanted it to be perfect. He wanted things done his way, regardless of cost.

He always believed that despite his early losses, eventually the furniture business would turn a profit. And even if it was having minor losses, the profits from the picture business would be able to carry it along. But something quite unexpected occurred in 1929 — the stock market crashed and the country fell into the Great Depression. The resulting economic chaos severely impacted both Nutting's picture and furniture businesses.

One important factor you must understand is that Wallace Nutting's picture market was entirely different from his furniture market. The purchasers of Wallace Nutting pictures were generally middle and lower-middle class households. Nutting's hand-colored pictures were quite inexpensive, and as a result, were widely purchased by those individuals who could not afford finer forms of art.

It was also these same middle and lower-middle class households that were the most severely impacted by the crash. With national unemployment over 20%, those families who lost their jobs obviously stopped buying Wallace Nutting

The Decline of the Wallace Nutting Furniture Company

pictures. Unfortunately for Nutting, those who still retained their jobs stopped buying his pictures as well. With the economy so uncertain, very few households were willing to spend their precious cash on something so unnecessary as a Wallace Nutting picture.

On the other hand, the purchasers of Nutting's furniture were generally not the same middle and lower-middle class households who purchased his pictures. The primary market for Wallace Nutting furniture was upper middle and upper class households. These individuals had a much greater overall appreciation for fine antiques, and consequently, for Nutting's furniture. They were generally less severely impacted by the economic uncertainties of the Depression, and as a group had more disposable income. Because although 20% of America was unemployed, 80% of America still had jobs, and many of those people had good jobs with good salaries.

The _Wallace Nutting General Catalog, **Supreme Edition**_, contains a price list for Nutting's reproductions dated February 1, 1932, in the heart of the Depression. Here is a sampling of some prices:

Wallace Nutting staff, circa 1937, down significantly from nearly 200 employees at it peak circa 1915 – 1925. Photo courtesy of the Pedro Cacciola collection.

- A set of four #343 Chippendale side chairs…$1,200.00
- A #579 Sheraton settee…$495.00
- A #682b carved Sheraton sideboard…$650.00
- A #992 carved Savory highboy…$1,230.00
- And the same #773 Goddard block front secretary with nine shell carvings that cost $1,450.00 in 1927, now cost $1,800.00 in 1932.

This was when admission to a movie was only a nickel. And you could purchase many houses for $1,000.00 or less.

The point is that Wallace Nutting furniture was not inexpensive. At a time when many families were worrying where their next meal was coming from, Wallace Nutting was trying to market furniture at a price that many households could not afford to purchase even today.

Not surprisingly, the furniture business continued to lose money during the 1930s. His high prices, resulting from his stubborn refusal to lower his quality standards, basically pre-determined that he would continue to operate at a loss.

But, with the decline in sales, the once-profitable picture business was no longer capable of subsidizing the never-profitable furniture business. By the early 1930s, the fate of Wallace Nutting's furniture business was pretty much inevitable. If he was unable to make a profit selling his furniture when the economy was stable, it was quite unlikely that he would be able to turn things around in the midst of a major economic depression.

By the mid 1930s, sales were off in all areas of the business. In 1936 Nutting had estimated that the furniture business had already lost more than $100,000.00. Although he always felt that "providence" would provide, it never did, and he was forced to begin laying off some of his employees. At one point cash flow was so tight that he tried paying off his employees with unsold furniture. Some accepted the furniture in lieu of their weekly pay. Those who could not accept furniture received personal cash advances from Nutting's bookkeeper, Ernest John Donnelly. (Nutting eventually repaid Donnelly for these loans.)

The Decline of the Wallace Nutting Furniture Company

Nutting's 1937 final edition furniture catalog only introduced six new designs, including such items as a #932 closed Pennsylvania cupboard, #946 open scroll Pennsylvania dresser, #904 six-light cupboard, among others. And prices were greatly reduced into an attempt to attract new business, such as #733 Goddard secretary desk (1932 – $1,800.00; 1937 – $1,000.00); #490 ladderback arm chair (1932 – $66.00; 1937 – $45.00); #921 maple chest-on-chest (1932 – $288.00; 1937 – $100.00); just to name a few.

Things reached the point where the furniture inventory was growing rather than shrinking. Rather than laying off his last few remaining trained craftsmen, Nutting kept them employed for as long as possible. He would sell one chair from inventory and then make five more to replace it. Even price reductions couldn't rejuvenate sales.

The Framingham studio, as it appeared circa 1985.

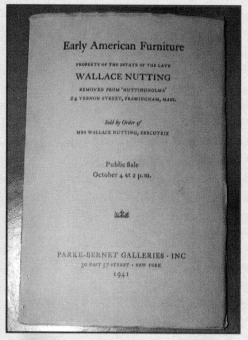

Parke-Bernet Gallery auction catalog for the auction of the Wallace Nutting estate, circa 1941.

Nutting stayed active in the business right to his dying days. However, by the spring of 1941, his visits to the Framingham studio became less frequent and of shorter duration. Most of the day-to-day business activities were carried on by the shop foreman and Ernest Donnelly.

Wallace Nutting died on July 19, 1941, of chronic cardiac degeneration. He was laid to rest in the Mt. Pleasant Cemetary in Augusta, Maine.

Mrs. Nutting inherited the entire Wallace Nutting estate, including the picture and furniture businesses, Wallace Nutting's remaining collection of antiques, and more than $100,000.00 of debt. Apparently Mrs. Nutting was unaware of their mounting bills and the fact that the furniture business had always been a losing venture. In order to raise needed capital, Mrs. Nutting was forced to sell Nutting's remaining collection of authentic American antiques at auction. The sale was conducted by Parke-Bernet Galleries (now Sotheby's) on October 4, 1941, at their New York galleries. The 200 lots sold for slightly more than $20,000.00, which was considerably less than expected. Apparently the market was fairly soft at the time and several experts later indicated that had Mrs. Nutting been able to wait several more years before selling, she probably would have done much better.

With the continued assistance of long-term employees Ernest John Donnelly and Esther Svenson, Mrs. Nutting carried on all aspects of the business until her death in August 1944 at the age of 90.

The picture business was left to Ernest Donnelly and Esther Svenson. They jointly continued selling pictures until 1946 when Ernest Donnelly sold his share of the business to Miss Svenson. Donnelly eventually moved to Philadelphia where he worked as an antiques dealer until moving back to Ireland in 1970, where he died in 1973. Esther Svenson continued the picture business on a very limited basis into the 1950s, working out of her home. She died in 1972, leaving many Wallace Nutting mementos to the Framingham Public Library. The remaining items were left to her sister, Hilda Cushing, who shared many items with Wallace Nutting collectors over the years.

Nutting's will also left a cash bequest of $1,000.00 to his chauffer and gardener, John Kelly. Other gifts ranging from $500.00 – 1,000.00 were left to several nieces and nephews. But having never had any children, and with no close relatives still living, Mrs. Nutting willed the remainder of her estate to Berea College, a long-term favorite charity of the Nuttings.

Berea College

Apparently Nutting's connection with the religiously oriented college began in the late 1890s when he first visited Kentucky. Nutting was impressed with the beauty surrounding Berea and was fascinated with the concept of a liberal arts school for Appalachian area students who could not afford college. In exchange for college tuition, students worked reproducing furniture which would be resold to help pay college expenses.

In 1900 Nutting delivered the commencement address at Berea. He continued to visit the college periodically in later years and formed a close friendship with several of the college's presidents.

By the time he had started his furniture business, his association with Berea became even closer. On various occasions Nutting took several of his workmen to Berea to learn their secrets of making colonial furniture, and Nutting trained several Berea instructors at his furniture factory in Framingham. Through their many years of association with the college, both Mr. and Mrs. Nutting had agreed that most of the furniture business should be left to Berea. Upon her death, Mrs. Nutting basically left everything in the estate to the college. Nuttingholme was sold by Berea to the First Parish Unitarian Universalist Church, which later demolished the home and turned the property into the church's parking lot.

The Log House, Berea College, circa 1985.

All remaining, unsold Wallace Nutting reproduction furniture was transported to Berea for display and use around the college. In 1945, three shipments totaling 196 pieces of furniture arrived via B&A Railroad. Much of this Wallace Nutting furniture was on display when the Wallace Nutting Collectors' Club held its annual convention there in the mid-1980s, occupying three rooms upstairs at The Log House, the retail outlet for the college's crafts industries.

Summary of Key Points

- Wallace Nutting's constant changes and stubborn desire to do things the old way created an environment where it was difficult to turn a profit.

- Wallace Nutting's furniture market was primarily upper class households whereas his primary picture market was middle class and lower middle class households.

- The high cost of Wallace Nutting furniture at a time when the country was in an economic depression greatly contributed to Nutting's financial woes.

- A lack of sales caused Wallace Nutting's business to shrink from a high of 100 – 200 employees circa 1920 – 1925 to only a handful by the mid-1930s.

- Wallace Nutting died in 1941, leaving his wife, Mariet Nutting, with the business and a considerable amount of debt.

- Mrs. Nutting sold many of Wallace Nutting's remaining antiques at the Parke-Bernet Auction Galleries in 1944 to help to pay off a portion of the remaining debt.

- Mrs. Nutting died in 1944 leaving the picture business to long-time employees Esther Svenson and Ernest John Donnelly, and leaving the furniture business and its contents to Berea College.

After all patterns and blueprints were copied for use by Berea College, Berea sold the remaining portion of the Wallace Nutting Furniture Company to the Drexel Furniture Company in Drexel, North Carolina, in the early 1950s. Drexel purchased the right to produce furniture with the Wallace Nutting name as part of Wallace Nutting Furniture, Inc., a Delaware Corporation, with its principal place of business in Framingham, Massachusetts.

Around 1954 Drexel Furniture introduced what it called its Wallace Nutting Cherry Highlands Collection. Its introductory 12-page sales catalog featured more than 60 bed, bench, chest, dresser, vanity, night table, mirror, dining room table, end table, lamp table, buffet, corner cabinet, china cupboard, and breakfront designs. Some of its introductory sales copy read as follows:

The Wallace Nutting Cherry Highlands Collection was one of several other furniture collections contained in Drexel's 1954 furniture catalog.

Two Honored Furniture Names Combine to Give You This Delightful Style

For nearly 50 years, Drexel has been famous for distinguished, high quality furniture at sensible prices. And now Drexel joins with Wallace Nutting to offer you authentic designs carefully selected from his authoritative work "Furniture Treasury"…As you will see, many items in the Cherry Highlands Collection closely resemble priceless originals in the "Treasury." Others, inspired by the originals, fit them to your needs today…Cherry wood, from which the entire collection is made, has unique beauty and warmth of its own, in perfect keeping with the pleasant nature of the design. The United States Bureau of Standards has found that not even mahogany exceeds cherry in quality and performance as a cabinet wood."

The Wallace Nutting Cherry Highlands Collection had little resemblance to Wallace Nutting's original reproduction furniture.

But although the Wallace Nutting name was used liberally throughout the Cherry Highlands Collection sales literature, frankly this furniture had nothing to do with Wallace Nutting's 1918 – 1941 reproduction furniture. Rather, Drexel tried to lend greater credibility to its Cherry Highlands Collection by attempting to tie in the Wallace Nutting name and the *Furniture Treasury* book.

For example, the following represent several of what I would call Drexel myths found in their 1954 Wallace Nutting Cherry Highlands Collection sales literature.

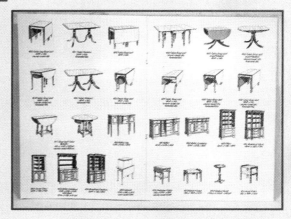

A few of the 60+ pieces included in the Cherry Highlands Collection.

Drexel Furniture

- *Drexel Myth*: "…now Drexel joins with Wallace Nutting to offer you authentic designs…."
  Reality: Wallace Nutting had been dead for 13 years when this collection was introduced.

- *Drexel Myth*: "…many items in the Cherry Highlands Collections closely resemble priceless originals in the 'Treasury'…."
  Reality: Nothing Drexel produced "closely resembled" anything in the *Furniture Treasury*.

- *Drexel Myth*: "…Cherry wood, from which the entire collection is made, has unique beauty and warmth of its own, in perfect keeping with the pleasant nature of the design…."
  Reality: I can't think of a single piece of furniture that Nutting ever reproduced using cherry wood.

- *Drexel Myth*: "…Drexel has selected the outstanding examples in this *(Furniture Treasury)* treasure trove, adapted them to today's scale and style of living, crafted them in mellow, friendly cherry wood on selected cabinet woods, and offers them to you now, at delightfully moderate prices…."
  Reality: These pieces look nothing like Wallace Nutting's reproductions, which were never "delightfully moderately priced." And Wallace Nutting never dreamed that his reproduction furniture could be used to house televisions or other 1950s gadgets.

- *Drexel Myth*: "…The graceful simplicity of the corner china is typical of the best colonial styles from Nutting's early photography…."
  Reality: The corner china looked nothing like anything Wallace Nutting ever produced or pictured in his colonial interior scenes.

- *Drexel Myth*: "…A Drexel #801 breakfront china cabinet…repeats a theme from the Plummer Collection which Nutting gathered for Yale University…."
  Reality: Although Drexel also tried to tie in the prestige of Yale University to their Wallace Nutting Cherry Highlands Collection, Nutting never produced anything closely resembling a breakfront china cabinet.

- *Drexel Myth*: "…A butterfly dropleaf table bears a dramatically close resemblance to the one shown in Plate 912, Volume I, of the Furniture Treasury. Wallace Nutting himself once owned the priceless original…."
  Reality: "Dramatically close resemblance" in fact bears little resemblance to Nutting's reproduction butterfly dropleaf table.

Apparently, relatively little of the Drexel furniture was ever produced. Despite the fact that it was sold through literally hundreds of furniture stores around the county I have only seen a few pieces and the quality does not come close to resembling the earlier Nutting reproductions. Rather, the pieces I have seen look more like "used" 1950s furniture rather than 1920s bench made reproduction furniture.

Drexel's Wallace Nutting New Cherry Highlands Collection was introduced in 1954 and discontinued in 1957. Similar Drexel Wallace Nutting Collections included "C" Nutting Maple (January 1954 – 1957); "F" Framingham Genuine Mahogany (January 1954 – 1957); 607 – 657 – 687 American Treasury (October 1960 – 1964); and 141 – 142 – 144 – 146 Wallace Nutting (October 1960 – 1968).

A Wallace Nutting Drexel sideboard

Drexel pieces seem to be branded with the name "Wallace Nutting, by Drexel." This Nutting/Drexel furniture is not, and should not, be considered true Wallace Nutting furniture. Value should be determined by what it really is — 1950s second-hand furniture, not legitimate Wallace Nutting reproductions. In my opinion, the name "Wallace Nutting" adds nothing to the value of a piece of Drexel furniture.

And with the discontinuance of the last of the Drexel collections, so ends the story of Wallace Nutting reproduction furniture.

The Drexel brand inside a drawer.

Summary of Key Points

• Berea College, who inherited the Wallace Nutting furniture business upon Mrs. Nutting's death in 1944, sold the remaining portion of the Wallace Nutting Inc. furniture business to the Drexel Furniture Company of Drexel, North Carolina, after all of Wallace Nutting's patterns and blueprints were copied by Berea.

• Drexel introduced a series of Wallace Nutting furniture lines between 1954 and 1968 which in reality had nothing to do with Wallace Nutting.

• Drexel's Wallace Nutting furniture carried a small "Wallace Nutting by Drexel" brand.

• Drexel's Wallace Nutting lines of furniture are in reality nothing more than "used furniture" and are of extremely little interest to true Wallace Nutting collectors.

Wallace Nutting (1861 – 1941)

The following narrative was written by William L. Bowers many years ago concerning his association with Wallace Nutting in the late 1930s. Bill Bowers, a furniture maker, worked for Wallace Nutting first hand circa 1939 – 1940. This article was originally published in 1974 by *The Antique Trader* (Dubuque, Iowa) who was kind enough to give us permission to reprint the article in its entirety.

Although some of the smallest details are not 100% accurate, most information is generally correct and I think you will agree that it provides a fascinating insight into the inner workings of the Wallace Nutting Furniture Studio, and into the unique personality of Wallace Nutting.

"I had been corresponding with Wallace Nutting perhaps a year or two, before meeting him at Washington and Jefferson College where he received an honorary degree, Doctor of Humanities in 1935.

"I plied him regularly with about a letter a week with so many questions about his work. He never ever failed to answer me promptly. I suppose I was his number one fan and first true admirer to receive such consideration.

"It all finally culminated in the form of a telegram in the fall 1939, offering me a year's work, at thirty dollars a week. This certainly needed no thought. In less than a week I was off to Framingham to start my new adventure. About a month later I found a place to rent and moved my wife and two small daughters to Massachusetts to join me.

"My arrival in Framingham was rather dismal. Fall was well advanced this far north, and everything looked bleak. I had to see the WN (Wallace Nutting) Studio before anything else. It was back of the Congregation Church on Park Street, in the center of town, and very easy to locate. It was not an object of beauty. A great, gaunt, unpainted, three story, frame building that was at one time a straw hat factory. No trees or shrubbery adorned the outside, not even grass. And this was the place that housed all that beauty? Everything was closed up tightly so I retired to my hotel room for the night. No visions of sugar plums danced through my head!

"I was there in the morning to present myself. Apparently WN had done this hiring quietly and on his own, for no one knew who I was or why I was there. The foreman of the cabinet-makers was an understanding man and put a few tools in my hand and said, start in, you may as well — no one else knows what he is doing. From that moment I realized all would be played by ear, plus what you could see. This was right, for at no time were there any hard and fast rules about anything, except starting and quitting work. Everything was run according to how WN felt about the affairs of the day. He did not operate an efficient workshop and would not listen to practical advice, that is, from his foreman and older workers. He was the boss and if it was wrong, he would take the blame.

"I could see how things were going and in about six months the big order that brought me up there was filled and then it was all downhill. Several men were laid off, picture business was slow, and furniture sales off the floor were few and far between. The place carried a huge inventory and he kept adding to it, to try and keep his men. At this time there were only six of us working on furniture, two wood finishers upstairs, two or three girls coloring pictures, one photo finisher, and three in the office.

"The cabinet shop was on the ground floor, or basement. The worst shop I ever worked in for conditions, poorly lighted and heated, and sanitary conditions, deplorable. No doubt WN had visited shops in foreign countries that were worse and got the idea this somehow made good furniture. He was always quoting how he liked beauty about him, but he never spent much time down there with us. He did not employ a janitor — waste of money, everyone sort of helped, but no one ever cleaned the plumbing fixtures so they were slowly turning green, algae was slowly covering the lavatory. WN said he hated cheap plumbing fixtures so upstairs he had his own private toilet of marble fixtures, taken from an old hotel in Boston, marble floor and the door was locked, of course I and nobody ever got in there.

"The office was in front on the first floor, a great hall leading to the front door separating it from the rest of the floor given over to the picture business. WN had his great flat top desk in the center of the room and used a writing arm Windsor to work on. The desk was piled high with his books and brochures, and catalogues. When the northeasters blew and rattled the building, the temperature generally fell to about 55 – 60 degrees. Then WN would wrap a huge muffler about his neck and put his hat on, calmly cutting his nails with a huge pair of tailor shears with which he opened mail. Esther Svensen was always afraid he would injure himself with these, but he never did.

"Ernest Donnelly, his right-hand man and invaluable asset in all ways, kept the whole ship from sinking by his constant watchfulness and guidance. At one time Ernest told me the treasury was almost down to nothing. WN replied 'providence will provide'. Well, long about March or April, providence didn't show up and everybody was laid off except me. I had a written contract and took a job as night watchman there. Things didn't get any better to speak of, times were still tight, so about the end of June, 1940, I gave up and returned to Chambersburg, Pennsylvania. I felt I had accomplished what I went for, in that WN let me copy most of his patterns and furniture pictures. So in reality, I brought the WN furniture business back to Chambersburg, on paper that is.

"We still corresponded until his death in July 1941. WN always said he was going to leave the business to his employees, as neither he nor Mrs. Nutting had any close relatives left. He left everything to his wife and her discretion. She gave the picture business to Ernest Donnelly and Esther Svenson, the two oldest and most trusted employees. They didn't have the capital to find new quarters, etc , so sold it to a Mr. Currier in Boston, one of their retailers of pictures there. I suppose he got the negatives also, but never heard what he did with them nor did I ever see anymore pictures made, or for sale. The rights to make WN furniture were sold to Drexel Furniture Company who planned a line of WN pieces. They abandoned it as too costly and I never heard anything more. *The Furniture Treasury* was sold to the present publishers. WN's antique collection, what was left of it, sold at Parke Bernet Galleries in New York in 1942, things bringing only a fraction of their present worth. At Mrs. Nutting's death in September, 1944 all went to her pet charity, Berea College, in Kentucky for distressed mountain folk.

"Mrs. Nutting was a kindly, generous woman, very small and bird-like, really gracious. It was she that gave the employees Christmas gifts, for she had a kind heart. WN scoffed at this gesture as he deemed this 'both humiliating to giver and receiver.' She loved gardening and had a beautiful place up at Framingham Center, where they lived and which they called 'Nuttingholme.' A Mr. Kelly worked for her full time and did the driving. WN never had anything nice to say about Mr. Kelly. Mrs. Nutting was the one that designed, and had made the rugs that were sold by the mountain people she was interested in, down in Kentucky. She had a loom there at the house and gave it what time she could, but her interests were so varied, especially in the summer with the garden. WN took many pictures in her garden. Nuttingholme was also a surprise when I first saw it. A great old Victorian mansion with everything about out of taste according to WN's precepts of beauty. I judged that this was Mrs. Nutting's home and if Wallace didn't like it, he could stay at the studio; he was there most of his time anyhow. Never the less, it was a quiet, dignified place and at their time of life they didn't want anymore projects. After all, WN had bought and furnished some six or eight places for his furniture and pictures so no doubt felt he had done about everything.

Recollections

"Wallace Nutting was not well liked by the townspeople. Of course they didn't understand him and his search for beauty. And furthermore he said it was too late in the day to change them. He had an aloof attitude toward the employees, those that didn't understand him didn't stay long. One had to see things his way or there was no room. Of course, I was top of the class, being so devoted, along with Ernest Donnelly and Miss Svenson. It was odd how the other employees treated me, nothing malicious, but very watchful and secretive as if WN and I were partners. I can understand their distrust in a way, as many a time he would take me from the shop on a picture taking trip, or to Boston antiquing. I got to meet the best dealers in Boston and see a lot of fine things. I remember one old time dealer up on Beacon Hill who had a shop and remarked to me on the side one day 'I knew him, way back when he wasn't so holy.' There may be something to this as WN liked to tell of a picture circulated of him in his ministerial days, showing him seated with a strumpet (i.e., prostitute) on his lap. Of course, said he, someone superimposed his head on someone else's shoulders in making the picture. Occasionally he filled a pulpit as a guest and took me along on Sunday. He spoke well and very commandingly, never at a loss for words or ideas.

"It is good things turned out as they did for as my wife said at one time — 'this is all too much Wallace Nutting and no time for me.' And I couldn't afford a gardener like Mr. Kelly.

"I also remember going along several times on trips to take pictures. I was impressed in that he worked quickly and with confidence that the results would be exactly what he wanted. Always sure of himself.

"Wallace Nutting was quite deaf, but considered this an asset. It certainly served as an excuse to ignore people and unpleasant situations. He had a hearing-aid, but most of the time I doubt it was turned on, because generally he spoke in a booming manner. Many of his personal affairs were conducted behind a screen in the office, a small narrow room with thin partitions and lined with filing cabinets. One day his physician called and they retired back of the screen. It seems WN had a problem, as he told the doctor, he was bothered with youthfulness and needed some advice. As the doctor spoke rather low, no one ever learned the remedy. WN at one time told Ernest Donnelly he wished his people would come to him for advice with their problems. Little did he know how quickly and thoroughly he was watched, and that his problems were theirs, really. Even his waste basket was gone through well, before being burned. Everybody in the whole building was just plain nosey, or rather their own life was so drab they rode on his coat tails for the interest he generated. None of them ever thought of doing anything on their own, without being told how. He knew this and remarked they would all be paupers if it weren't for him.

"No one ever really knew Wallace Nutting as he presented a formidable figure of politeness and reserve. However, he had a humorous side and could enjoy a joke or situation. He tried to present a father image to his employees, but it didn't work out. They knew his promises were made on sunny days and not dependable. He relied heavily on his bad memory, old age, and being tired. One old employee, George Sturgen, the Windsor chair maker was WN's pet workman. He was a workhorse, spent hours over his regular time, was dependable, and everything you would want. He was the first to be laid off. I heard WN say that he would go hungry before laying off George, but he loved to say things like that and always gave a little smile.

"We had a wood turner that did the legs and spindles on the furniture, and George bent the hoops in a steam chest, shaped the seats by hand, bored the holes properly for the parts, and then assembled the piece. The finishers took care of it from there.

"George usually put up two dozen at a time, of course depending on orders, but at this time the stock was heavy. They would sell one chair, and make five more. The back arm bows with the knuckle termination were made ahead so the wood carver could do these before being assembled.

"The best cabinet maker was a Swede, Ernest Gerstan, a small, wiry man that moved fast. He was the best joiner I ever knew; his work was perfect. I learned a great deal from him. On the other side of me was Joe Babrunos, from Riga, Latvia. He was a heavy, ponderous man that moved slowly, but precisely; a fine workman, but slow and from the old school. He told me he served his time in Moscow and often spoke of the Cossacks in a hushed voice as a most dreaded and feared group. That was under the old Czar and a way of life he knew as a young man in Russia before the Revolution. He came to America before the first World War with that big flood of immigration. Wallace Nutting mentioned there were more foreign born people in Boston than what remained of the Old New England stock.

"Mr. Johnson, the wood carver, had a small shop in Cambridge and called for and delivered his work as needed. He was from Sweden, a very fine workman the best WN ever had. He could carve almost as fast as a machine, improvising with his feelings as he went along. He was not a mechanical carver, as most are, that just repeats a thing monotonously.

"Wallace Nelson was a good mechanic and was shop foreman. He was WN's right hand man there and WN relied on his judgement to produce what he wanted. Nelson was from Canada, French I think, a small man that spent a lot of time not working. He was capable all right, but Wallace Nutting did make his life difficult, especially when things didn't go well. There were several other men that were good workmen, but nothing remarkable about them.

"The finishing room was on the third floor. Two men were there most of the time, nothing but shellac was used, each piece taking between six and nine applications and then was hand rubbed. If it was to be stained, this step was first. The amount of time on the finish was approximately a third or half of the building time. At the time I was there, fine cabinet woods like Cuban mahogany were still available and used exclusively. It seemed a shame to cover up such quality with a lot of finish, but that was the taste of the time.

"Wallace Nutting did not make any money on his furniture, perhaps at the best of times he did, but over all, it was the picture business that carried it all along. Mr. Donnelly told me that between 1926 – 1929 they sold about a thousand dollars worth of photos a day and also turned out a lot of furniture, having about thirty employees then. It all came to sudden stop with the stock market crash in 1929. WN had a very large collection of antiques then, most of it from the furnishings of his houses. This was sold to John Wannamaker in New York who put out a catalogue and merchandised it in the arts magazine. For the next ten or twelve years it was mighty rough going to keep things up to Wallace Nutting standards and ideals. Too bad he died then, for in another two years he would have seen better conditions and a great demand for his furniture. The picture business, however, never regained its popularity, color photography and cheap color prints taking over by this time.

"As far as I know Drexel never did anything more with the Wallace Nutting furniture line, nor did anymore pictures appear. Mr. Donnelly moved into Boston and tried a line of miniature paintings and silhouettes with his old picture customers, but it didn't turn out very well so he moved to Philadelphia to work for David Stockwell in the antique business. Donnelly left him in 1970 to retire to Ireland where he died of a heart attack in the fall of 1973.

"Esther Svenson never did anything more when she retired from WN's in 1944. I know she had a great deal of information and mementos as she was there the longest of all, but I do not know what happened to these.

"One might say WN contributed more for the preservation of our past heritage of American arts and culture than anyone else. We had greater names in the arts, but they reached selected few. Wallace Nutting was for everybody and everyone appreciated him. He put everything he had, both finances and all his time, to explain how and why our ancestors lived and felt.

"Our great museums, and names like Henry DuPont at Winterthur, are unquestionably the epitome of quality and taste — but these are the results of many millions of dollars and the employment of well-trained personnel.

Recollections

"Our best institutions are the sum total of many people working at it full time and having unlimited amounts of money. Wallace Nutting did all this first, and single-handedly. It took a lot of judgement, foresight and study to determine what was the best, before there were any guidelines in books or pictures. We had a few good names about this time that WN thought a lot of and consulted such as Henry Wood Erving, J. Stodgell Stokes, and of course, the best dealers at that time. He knew them all well.

"When H. F. DuPont was first forming his great collection Wallace Nutting was invited down to view his things. Nutting must have made severe criticism as he was never asked again, or consulted, or ever quoted in their writings or publications.

"I spent a lot of time with Mr. Donnelly as we were about the closest to WN and really the most interested in him. There were always new antidotes for me about WN, even things that had happened long ago, like the time WN lost control of his car, mounted the sidewalk, and struck a storefront in Sudbury. Neither of them was seriously hurt , but quite shaken up. Another time WN bought a court cupboard from a woman and she sued him to return it, claiming he underpaid her. They took it to court and WN won the case by proving he paid her more than anyone else on record at that time for a similar item. It was all in the papers and some say it wasn't good for his reputation. WN never ever listened to advice — he did the deciding. As he once said, 'I'll even pay to be wrong.' I suppose he found a lot of satisfaction doing just what he wanted. This is what upset the management of the business. They would have things going well, and WN would upset all for no reason at all, perhaps some foolish whim to which no thought was given.

"When things were going wrong or there was some sort of crisis at the shop, WN disappeared for a few days till it blew over, Mr. Donnelly taking charge. One time there was no money to meet the payroll, so WN left instructions to give each employee a piece of furniture. A few took it, but most others had to have money and Mr. Donnelly paid them from his funds. Later WN reimbursed him.

"Quoting the last letter I received from WN, in the spring of 1941 , he says 'It is really old age that compels me to quit. I am so tired and no longer able to cope with the increasing problems of business.' The fun and challenge had gone from his work, as the times demanded stricter attention to business, as government controls and interference made it impossible to do things the old way.

"I suppose he died a satisfied but saddened man, as the world was changing and he was too tired to start over. However, he did not give up, but was at the studio everyday, even if it was only for a few hours. He was only ill a few days at home before his death.

"A word about the actual making of his furniture. One or two men did the mill work on the lumber, processing it to correct size and put it at the workman's bench. Here, the hand-work started such as dovetailing parts together, and assembling the whole according to the patterns. The completed piece was finished by hand-scraping, very little sandpaper being used. Nothing was glued up to make a thick piece. Only solid planks of full thickness were used, such as on the block front pieces which required a plank three inches thick to saw out the required shape.

"The cabinetmaker carried out the entire job or piece, so it was the product of one man, with the exception of the finish and applying the hardware. The hardware was supplied by William Ball, Sr. of West Chester, Pennsylvania, according to WN's specifications. The fine Cuban mahogany was bought in Boston from Palmer and Parker, imported lumber dealers. They are the ones that supplied WN with a French walnut plant 6" thick, 30" wide and 16 feet long for the library table legs on the Andover Academy job. Nutting made four of these tables for the school, in the seventeenth century style. In the early 1920s, *Furniture of the Pilgrim Century* was much in demand. That is, oak court cupboards, Hadley chests, Brewster chairs and early William and Mary looking glasses. Also, gate leg tables and slat back chairs were much in demand. The public taste began to change about 1928 to walnut and mahogany pieces of the better type. The earlier style never revived and is still a slow seller today. Even the antique pieces don't bring near the old prices of the 1920s.

"Mr. Nutting had a blacksmith working over at Saugus. He was an Italian and a superb workman, fashioning the most delicate items on his anvil. WN complained that he always smelled of wine. The demand for iron objects ceased with no new building and he gave up supporting the venture.

"Volume three of the *Furniture Treasury* is a monumental work of Ernest Donnelly in that the drawings are all his free-hand sketching, requiring countless hours to complete. They were all copied from photographs of original pieces. It was quite a task to ascertain correct proportions, not to mention perspective, which was most important. Donnelly also worked up a line of silhouettes that emphasized furniture details. These did not sell too well.

"I feel that everyone that worked with WN never regretted a minute of it. Everyone came in each day with the expectation of WN confounding them with some new project or idea."

Block banded signature

One question I am frequently asked is "How do I know if I have a piece of Wallace Nutting furniture?" In most instances, the answer is quite obvious. Nutting intended to clearly mark all of his furniture, in a manner that no one could miss, for two reasons.

First, Wallace Nutting was proud of his furniture reproductions. His company produced the finest furniture of the twentieth century and he wanted everyone to know it. Placing his name on each piece served as an excellent form of advertising.

But just as important as the advertising function, Nutting was fearful that unscrupulous people might try to re-sell his reproductions as original, period antiques, something that eventually did happen, on more than several occasions.

So Nutting went out of his way to clearly identify each piece of his furniture and signed Wallace Nutting furniture will almost always be more valuable than unsigned Wallace Nutting furniture. The type of Wallace Nutting furniture marking is extremely important in determining its value. Certain collectors prefer certain markings and will pay more for their preferred marking. In this chapter we'll discuss the various ways that Wallace Nutting marked his furniture, we'll explain how to date Wallace Nutting furniture, and we'll introduce you to the Wallace Nutting furniture numbering system.

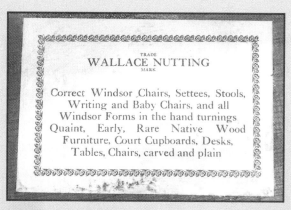

Paper label, circa 1920

Paper Labels

The earliest method Nutting used to identify his reproduction furniture was to glue a paper label to some inconspicuous location. On Windsor chairs, it was generally on the underside of the seat; on tables it was usually on the underside of the table top or in the drawer; on chests and case pieces it was on the backside or inside the drawer.

The earliest paper label, measured approximately 6"x 8", was marked "Wallace Nutting Inc, Saugus, Mass" and contained several paragraphs of sales copy within a value-border design. Over the next few years Nutting used several different paper labels, but each had the same purpose: to advertise the piece of furniture as Wallace Nutting and to differentiate his reproductions from authentic antiques.

Occasionally Nutting also used a paper tag which was affixed to the furniture by means of a thin wire. This was usually done on chairs having rushed seats or those pieces where a paper label could not be inconspicuously placed. One such tag is shown at the top right of page 69.

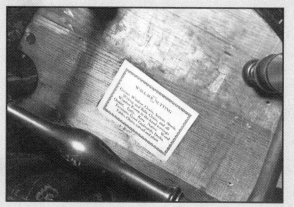

Paper label, on the underside of a chair

One way to determine the approximate date of a piece of Wallace Nutting furniture with a paper label is through the address on the label:

- Saugus, Massachusetts: 1917 – 1920
- Ashland, Massachusetts: 1920 – 1922
- Framingham, Massachusetts: 1923 – 1926

Many collectors prefer paper label furniture because they feel that this was the period when Nutting worked harder at producing his furniture, and a time when he paid more attention to his production process, and before the years when he streamlined his furniture production process.

The biggest problem with paper labels was their durability. Sometimes the paper label disappeared due to age or environmental factors (heat, humidity, etc). And sometimes it was removed intentionally. Either for innocent reasons, such as people removing tags from bedding or clothing today. Or for more disingenuous reasons such as someone trying to artificially age a Nutting piece and then pass it off as an original period antique.

One story has it that an unscrupulous antiques dealer in the early 1920s was buying Wallace Nutting child's chairs, removing the paper labels, and then "loaning" the chairs to a certain household filled with children. The dealer would then recover the chairs several years later, when they looked significantly "older" than when they had left Nutting's shop. This story supposedly contributed to Nutting's switching his furniture marking from paper label to the branded marking.

Anyway, when you see a piece of Wallace Nutting furniture with only a paper label, you can assume that is was produced circa 1918 – 1921.

> Wallace Nutting
> Furniture
>
> **STYLE AND STRENGTH**
> All Hand Turned
> All Maple
> Amber Finish
> Mortised and Pinned
> Square Pegs
> In Round Holes.
> Supremacy
> In Reproductions
> A Good Name Is Better
> Than Great Riches
> Name Burned In

Partial paper label, with most of the label missing

Script Branded Signature

In 1904 Wallace Nutting had originally retired from the ministry and then quickly opened up his first photography studio in New York City. By the time 1921 – 1922 rolled around Nutting had already been selling hand-colored photographs for nearly 20 years, he had written several books, and he had opened and closed his colonial chain of homes. Apparently he became tired of what he was doing and in 1921 decided to retire from both the picture and furniture businesses, as we discussed earlier.

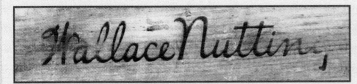

Script branded signature, circa 1922 – 1924

Script brand, under the rear chair stretcher, circa 1922 – 1924

Identifying and Dating Furniture and the Numbering System

Paper label and script branded signature, with pieced construction seat. Circa 1921 – 1922.

But it was right around this time that the Wallace Nutting script branded signature was introduced. Just to clarify what we mean by the script branded signature, instead of using the paper label, the "Wallace Nutting" name was literally branded into to wood, with a fire-heated branding iron, using large script letters, approximately 1" high x 12" wide x ¼" deep. You couldn't miss it. And it couldn't easily be removed without noticeably altering the piece.

There has been considerable speculation about whether the new management of Wallace Nutting, Inc., or Wallace Nutting himself, introduced the script branded signature. For years it was a generally accepted fact that the new management had introduced the script brand in order to differentiate themselves from Wallace Nutting, and that Nutting was never associated with the script brand.

There is also a school of thought that Wallace Nutting himself introduced the script branded signature, just prior to selling the furniture business in 1921. It is known that Wallace Nutting was frustrated that unscrupulous individuals were removing his paper labels in order to perpetuate a fraud, and it has always been assumed that he introduced the branded mark to stop the frauds from occurring.

Did Nutting himself, or the new owners, introduce the script branded signature? No one seems to know for certain. But we do know the following:

- Nutting used a paper label from 1918 to 1921.

- Nutting wanted to frustrate potential frauds by introducing a branded signature.

- Most furniture pieces with the script brand are lower quality construction, and almost all script branded pieces are limited with only a few exceptions to the 42 different furniture models that were contained in the 1922 *Wallace Nutting: The Great American Idea* catalog. Since Nutting's 1918 Windsor catalog had 150+ furniture designs, it is more likely that the new management started their fledgling Wallace Nutting Inc. business by introducing only a very limited number of Wallace Nutting's many furniture designs.

- We have seen an extremely limited number of pieces with both the paper label and script brand, almost always with pieced construction. This would suggest that upon re-purchasing his business in 1924, Nutting "inherited" all remaining script branded inventory. Perhaps rather than trash the inferior merchandise he simply added an old paper label prior to the introduction of the next generation of Wallace Nutting marking: the block branded signature.

As we've already mentioned, Nutting gave up control of his business in 1921, along with the right to use the "Wallace Nutting" name. It would appear that most furniture made by the new management was marked with a distinctive script branded signature. However, the possibility does exist that the new owners may have used paper labels for a very short period of time before changing to the script brand. In all my years of collecting, aside from the one piece mentioned above, all transition pieces I have seen were marked with the distinctive script brand.

There has also been some speculation that Nutting himself may have initiated the script brand just prior to selling the business in 1921. After all, his script signature was the trademark of his picture business and, for the sake of consistency, a script marking on his furniture would have made a great deal of sense. The possibility does exist that because of his extreme displeasure with the quality of the transition pieces bearing the script branded signature, Nutting may have been willing to renounce a few of his own "script" pieces in order to clear his name of all other script branded pieces.

But this is nothing more than a theory put forth by certain collectors. Neither research compiled by the Wallace Nutting Collector's Club, nor all of my 30+ years research, nor any information put forward by Tom Denenberg or anyone else to date, has solidly confirmed that Wallace Nutting himself used the script branded signature. And, in the absence of any confirming information that Nutting himself ever used the script brand, I still feel comfortable making the following statement:

Furniture marked with the script branded signature was produced between 1922 and 1924 and was made when Nutting did not control the company.

Script branded furniture, although still quite collectible, is generally regarded as the least collectible of all three major Wallace furniture markings.

Block Branded Signatures

One of the first things Nutting did upon resuming control of his company circa 1924 was to renounce the script branded furniture of his predecessors. Beginning in his 1924 furniture catalog, and in future catalogs, Nutting made the following claim:

My name in plain capitals thus
WALLACE NUTTING
is burned into every piece I endorse. I will not be responsible for a script letter formerly used as a mark.

Statement from the Wallace Nutting furniture catalog

Thus, furniture produced after Nutting re-purchased his company circa 1924 is clearly marked with the block branded signature. This brand was approximately 1" high, nearly 12" long, and about ¼" deep. The only way to remove it would be to chisel it out of the wood, leaving an unrepairable gouge that would alert any potential buyer of an "original" piece.

Sometimes the first and last names "WALLACE NUTTING" would be on one line; other times the "WALLACE" would be on a separate line above the "NUTTING."

One-line block branded signature

Two-line block branded signature

Identifying and Dating Furniture and the Numbering System

Block brand and paper label

Many people prefer Nutting's block branded furniture because they feel that this represents the period most typical of high quality Wallace Nutting furniture, and because he had already worked out many of the production problems that he faced during his start-up paper label period.

You will find more block branded furniture than either script branded or paper label furniture. This is because the script brand was only used for three years (1922 – 1924), and the paper label was only used for four years (1918 – 1921), whereas the block brand was used during Nutting's most productive furniture years (1924 – 1941).

Based upon the number of pieces I have seen with both a paper label and a block branded signature, there was probably a period of several years where both markings were used, probably up through 1925 or 1926.

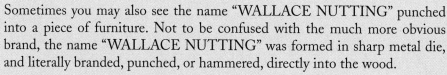

Punched Wallace Nutting Name

Punched marking

Sometimes you may also see the name "WALLACE NUTTING" punched into a piece of furniture. Not to be confused with the much more obvious brand, the name "WALLACE NUTTING" was formed in sharp metal die, and literally branded, punched, or hammered, directly into the wood.

This marking is much smaller than either type of brand, and was generally used where the brand was either inappropriate or would not fit, for example, on the bottom of a small article. However, I have even seen this marking used on chairs, tables, and even an item as large as a corner cupboard.

Although this punched marking is more unusual than either the paper label and script or block branded signatures, value is not impacted either positively or negatively. Although most collectors would prefer a paper label or block branded signature, the quality and condition of the piece is much more important in determining value than the type of marking used, and the punched brand always appears on a high quality piece.

Punched marking on Wallace Nutting treenware

Punched Furniture Design Numbers

Over a period of 20 years, Nutting produced nearly 1,000 different furniture designs. Obviously he needed a method of identifying each of these different designs, both within his studio and workshop, and in his sales literature. To accomplish this he developed his furniture design numbering series. Wallace Nutting introduced his current numbering system in the 1918 Windsor catalog, but he did make some changes in later years (i.e. cribs moved from very low numbers to the 800 series).

Probably the largest collection of furniture design numbers can be found in the back of the 1932 *Wallace Nutting General Catalog, Supreme Edition*. Here you will see design numbers ranging from 1 – 1000, with each number representing a specific furniture design.

These furniture design numbers were further broken down into specific subcategories:

1 – 36	Small articles including treenware and assorted smalls
34 – 58c and 76 – 98	Finials
59 – 70	Clocks
101 – 292	Stools
301 – 399c	Side chairs
401 – 499c	Arm chairs
513 – 599b	Settles, sofas, and settees
601 – 699	Tables and stands
700 – 749	Desks
750 – 777b	Mirrors
801 – 850b	Beds
900 – 1000	Chests, dressers, case and cabinet pieces

Punched number

It was not uncommon for the furniture design number to be literally punched, or stamped, into the piece. Generally when the furniture design number was included, it was near the paper label or the brand.

How can you use this to your advantage as a collector? Well, we've already talked about paper labels being intentionally removed for unscrupulous purposes. But it was also fairly common for the paper label to simply fall off over the years. Or sometimes they were intentionally removed by the owner, not unlike removing a label from a pillow or mattress. After all, whoever would have thought (besides Nutting himself) that Wallace Nutting furniture would ever become so collectible.

Anyway, how can this information help you? Once you learn to identify Wallace Nutting furniture by its excellent form, and once you understand the furniture design numbering system, you're armed with valuable information unknown by most other collectors.

For example, on more than several occasions I have been at an auction where I saw a piece of Wallace Nutting furniture with the punched furniture design number, but without the paper label. Without a paper label or brand, few people in the country are experienced enough to realize its true identity.

So, if you're at an auction where a very nice Pennsylvania comb back Windsor arm chair is being sold, a chair that is obviously not period, but a piece that is probably an early twentieth century reproduction, the appearance of a punched "412" on the bottom should tip you off to the chair's true identity.

You should be aware that the punched furniture design numbers have been found on both script and block branded pieces so the appearance of a punched furniture design number should not be taken as an absolute sign of quality.

Which Marking Is The Best?

One question that frequently arises concerns which marking, paper label or block brand, is best. There are really two schools of thought here.

One group believes that all paper label furniture is better. They believe that this furniture was the earliest made, and was made with more attention to detail than later furniture. They believe that more time went into each piece, and that paper label furniture was less prone to the problems associated with larger scale production.

The other group believes that block branded furniture is better. They believe that although paper label furniture is good, there were more production difficulties with paper label furniture (e.g., cracking bows) because it was the earliest furniture produced and was somewhat experimental in nature. Many early paper label designs were later discontinued due to production difficulties or for quality reasons. These production difficulties were later resolved by the time the block branded furniture was produced and this group believes that furniture with the block brand is of better quality.

Which theory is correct? The truth probably lies somewhere in the middle. The quality of both were very good. I am aware of collectors who prefer each specific marking if they can get it, but if they are unable to locate the marking of their choice, the other is more than acceptable.

Wallace Nutting Furniture Dateline

You can generally date Wallace Nutting furniture by its markings as follows:

- Paper label only   1918 – 1921
- Script branded signature   1922 – 1924
- Script brand and paper label 1924 – 1925
- Block brand and paper label 1924 – 1926
- Block brand only   1926 – 1941

Summary of Key Points

• Wallace Nutting almost always clearly marked his furniture in one of five styles.

• Signed Wallace Nutting furniture will almost always be more valuable than unsigned Wallace Nutting furniture.

• The type of Wallace Nutting furniture marking is extremely important in determining its value. Certain collectors prefer certain markings and will pay more for their preferred marking.

• Paper label furniture is generally the earliest and normally dates circa 1918 – 1921. Many people prefer paper label furniture because they feel that this was the period when Nutting worked harder at producing his furniture, and a time when he paid more attention to his production process.

• Script branded furniture is the middle period and dates circa 1922 – 1924. Although still quite collectible, is generally regarded as the least collectible of all three major Wallace Nutting furniture markings.

• Block branded furniture is the latest marking and normally dates circa 1926 – 1941. Most people prefer Nutting's block branded furniture because they feel that this represents the period most typical of high quality Wallace Nutting furniture, and because he had already worked out many of the production problems that he faced during his start-up paper label period.

• Occasionally you will find a paper label and a script brand or block brand.

• You will find more block branded furniture than either script branded or paper label furniture. This is because the script brand was only used for three years (1922 – 1924), and the paper label was only used for four years (1918 – 1921), whereas the block brand was used during Nutting's most productive furniture years, 1924 – 1941.

• Occasionally you may also see Wallace Nutting furniture with punched numbers or a punched Wallace Nutting name. These are also desirable Wallace Nutting furniture markings.

In determining the value of any antique or collectible, condition is universally recognized as the primary determinant. Wallace Nutting furniture is no exception. Condition is everything. The rarest piece of Wallace Nutting furniture, in poor or damaged condition, is of little value to anyone but the furniture refinishers or bottom feeders. The most common piece of Nutting furniture, in beautiful and excellent condition, is desirable to nearly everyone.

Let me introduce you to my furniture numerical grading system which I use when evaluating the condition of Wallace Nutting furniture. I should remind you that this furniture numerical grading system is nothing more than my personal system for grading Wallace Nutting furniture as it comes through my auctions. It is not perfect and it is very subjective. Yet I feel comfortable with it and I believe that most other Wallace Nutting furniture experts will agree with my gradings most of the time. In the absence of a better system you are welcome to use this system. And if you have any ideas on improving it, I would like to hear from you.

So, here is the five-point furniture numerical grading system that I use when evaluating Wallace Nutting furniture.

5.0 — Excellent Condition

In order to be graded a 5.0 the furniture must be in absolutely excellent condition. There can be no flaws whatsoever and it must look as if it just came out of the Nutting showroom while still having 60 – 85 years of wonderful patina. Perhaps less than 5% of Wallace Nutting furniture will be in this condition.

- There can be no repairs or restoration.
- The finish must be completely original and in excellent condition without blemish.
- The construction must be absolutely solid with no sign of weakness.
- All parts (pulls, brasses, hinges, etc.) must be original.
- If rush is involved, the rush must be original and completely intact with no breaks.
- If there is a paper label it must be complete and intact.

A 5.0 grading means that the piece is in excellent condition with absolutely no visible flaws.

4.0 — Very Good Condition

In order to be graded a 4.0 the furniture must be in very good, but not excellent condition. It must look like a great piece of furniture showing no sign of damage and less than the normal amount of wear that you would expect to see on a piece of 60 – 85 year old furniture. Perhaps 20 – 30% of Wallace Nutting furniture will be in this condition.

- There can be no repairs or restoration.
- The finish must be completely original and in very good, but not quite excellent condition. A few minor dings, and less than normal wear, is acceptable for this grade.
- The construction must be absolutely solid with no sign of weakness.
- Any parts replacement must be transparent and invisible to the normal person's eye.

A 4.0 grading means that the piece is very good, but not excellent.

- If rush is involved, the rush can have only very minimal damage, or if the rush has been professionally restored, the new rush must be in excellent con dition.
- If there is a paper label it must be mostly (85 – 95%) intact.

3.0 — *Good Condition*

In order to be graded a 3.0 the furniture must be in good, but not very good or excellent condition. It must look like a good piece of furniture showing only nominal damage, or showing the normal amount of wear that you would expect to see on a piece of 60 – 85 year old furniture. Perhap 35 – 50% of Wallace Nut-ting furniture will be in this condition.

- Professional repairs or restoration are acceptable.
- The finish must be either original in less-than very good condition or it may have been professionally refinished. Dings, minor blemishes, and a normal amount of wear are acceptable in this category.
- The construction should be solid.
- If rush is involved, the rush can have only a minor amount of damage, or the rush must have been professionally restored.
- If there is a paper label it must be mostly (50 – 60%) intact.

This desk would be a 3.0 because it was refinished.

This chair would be a 3.0 because it has been poorly re-rushed.

This chair would be a 3.0 because it has a normal, yet noticeable, amount of wear.

This stool would be a 3.0 because of the dings and normal wear.

This table would be a 3.0 because of the top finish blemish.

Evaluating Condition

The chair on the left would be a 4.0 grading because the rush damage is so minimal. The chair on the right would be a 2.0 grading because the rush damage is so great that you could not sit upon the chair.

2.0 — *Poor Condition*

In order to be graded a 2.0 the furniture must be showing some form of repairable damage, and must be capable of moving up to a 3.0 grading if the repairs are professionally made. It must look like a good piece of furniture showing noticeable damage or showing much more than the normal amount of wear that you would expect to see on a piece of 60 – 85 year old furniture. Perhaps 10 – 20% of Wallace Nutting furniture will be in this condition.

- Repair or restoration must be visibly required, or must have been poorly made.
- The finish must be either very rough (yet capable of being re-finished) or must have been poorly re-finished. Major dings, larger stains or blemishes, a greater than normal amount of wear are all signs of this category.
- The construction is probably weak, damaged, or in need of re-gluing.
- If rush is involved, the rush will have a major amount of damage or no rush whatsoever.
- If there is a paper label it will be damaged or nearly entirely gone.

This chair would be a 2.0 because of the rough finish and because of the major rush damage. It could be upgraded to a 3.0 if the rush were replaced and if it was refinished.

These two pieces would be graded a 2.0 because each has been painted over the original finish. They could be upgraded to a 3.0 if stripped and refinished.

1.0 — *Extremely Poor Condition*

In order to be graded a 1.0 the furniture must be basically non-repairable or, even with good repair the best-possible condition could be a 2.0. It must look like a good piece of furniture showing noticeable damage and a piece of furniture that should probably have been discarded years ago. Broken chair legs, cracked chair seats, severely damaged drawers or physical structure, parts may be missing, or other major damage will be apparent. Perhaps the piece is only good for parts. Only 0 – 5% of Wallace Nutting furniture will be in this condition because by the time that it reaches this stage, it has usually been discarded or trashed.

• Repair or restoration must be nearly impossible.
• The finish might be beyond repair.
• The construction is extremely weak, parts are missing, or the damage is absolutely major.

You should note that there can also be slight variations between the grade levels. For example, a large stain on a table top might be a 3.0 grading, while a much smaller dime-sized stain might be a 3.5 – 3.75 grading.

How severely does condition impact value? Probably more than you think. Let's take a piece of Wallace Nutting furniture that, for arguments sake, is valued at $1,000.00 if in excellent condition or having a grading of 5.0.

This chair is an example of a 1.0 and is basically only good for parts.

Grading	Impact on Value	Estimated Value in This Condition
5.0	n/a	$1,000
4.0	less 20 – 30%	$700 – $800
3.0	less 40 – 60%	$400 – $600
2.0	less 70 – 80%	$200 – $300
1.0	less 90 – 95%	$50 – $100

Let me share a story with you about condition. Several years ago I had a potential consignor bring me a #415 fan back Windsor chair for possible consignment. The chair had a major crack in the seat, it was missing one of the knuckles on the arm, it had two broken spindles, and the chair had been painted blue many years ago. When I told him that the chair would be fortunate to bring $50.00 – 100.00 at auction, he was dumfounded. "But it's a Wallace Nutting chair. I paid much more for it than that," he said. I lost the consignment and he took the chair away, presumably to another auctioneer who most likely told him what he wanted to hear.

My message to you is fairly simple: Don't overpay for damaged Wallace Nutting furniture. And don't expect to receive 5.0 pricing for damaged goods. Value is not predicated solely upon the fact that a piece carries the Wallace Nutting name. Rather value is predicated upon the fact that a piece carries the Wallace Nutting name *and* it is in very good to excellent condition.

And just to further clarify, I'm not telling you not to buy Wallace Nutting furniture in the 1.0 – 2.0 – 3.0 categories. Rather, I'm suggesting that you should not pay 4.0 – 5.0 prices for 1.0 – 3.0 furniture. Because as in all other areas of collecting, the best merchandise rises in value at a much faster rate than damaged merchandise.

Summary of Key Points

• Condition and rarity will be the primary determinants of value.

• I use a 5-point furniture numerical grading system when evaluating the condition of Wallace Nutting furniture.

• Very few pieces of Wallace Nutting furniture will be graded a 5.0.

• Very few pieces of Wallace Nutting furniture will be graded a 1.0 because by the time they reach that point they have usually been discarded.

• Pieces graded 4.0 will normally be the best that you can locate and is what you should strive to collect.

• There can be ¼ point and ½ point degrees of difference between the major grade levels to reflect major and minor damage.

• Patina, identification markings, color and condition of finish, amount of wear, solidness of construction, repairs and restoration, and overall look will all factor into the grading of a piece of Wallace Nutting furniture.

• You should not pay top dollar for damaged merchandise.

• You can reasonably expect the value of a clean and undamaged piece of furniture to rise faster than a blemished or damaged piece of furniture.

Several years ago we were offered a "Wallace Nutting" table by an antique dealer from Ohio. The dealer's letter included a poor-quality photograph of a drop leaf table and, although the details of the table were not totally clear, the table appeared to be of good quality and consistent with Wallace Nutting's style. Throughout two telephone discussions, the dealer assured us that the table had a block branded signature.

After traveling several hours, we met the dealer in Adamstown, Pennsylvania, and had our first opportunity to personally inspect the table. The table was a cherry six-leg double gate leg drop leaf table with rope-turned legs. It was old, it was attractive, and it was a well-constructed table. But after a few minutes of close inspection, we determined that the table was a Wallace Nutting fake.

Someone apparently had taken an original antique table, probably circa 1860 – 1870, and worth approximately $250.00 – 350.00 at the time and literally branded the Wallace Nutting name into the bottom of the table, thereby creating a table worth between $1,200.00 – 1,750.00. The original perpetrator of the fraud obviously had created a Wallace Nutting branding iron which probably cost less than $50.00 and which was capable of branding an unlimited number of pieces of furniture.

A corner cupboard with a fake Wallace Nutting block brand

There were several tell-tale signs that led me to conclude that the table was a Wallace Nutting fake.

1) The brand was approximately ¼" taller, and approximately 2" longer, than most other
   Wallace Nutting block brands I had previously seen.
2) There was a dark finish over the block branded signature which almost looked like black
   paint, which was intended to make the brand appear older than it was.
3) The table looked older than a piece of authentic Wallace Nutting furniture should have appeared
   (circa 1860 – 1870 vs. 1925 – 1940).
4) The exact table did not appear in any Wallace Nutting furniture catalog.
5) The construction of the table was inconsistent with Wallace Nutting furniture.
   a) The leg turnings were not as bold or attractive as Nutting would have created.
   b) There were no wooden pegs whatsoever used in the construction of the table.
   c) There were too many screws used throughout the table.

The dealer reported that he had purchased this table at an "as is" auction in Ohio, where it was sold along with several other pieces of Wallace Nutting furniture. It was subsequently reported that other fake Wallace Nutting furniture was also sold at the same auction house using the same branding iron.

It was my opinion that the individuals who attempted to sell me the table were honest dealers who were quite embarrassed by the incident. They had little experience dealing in Wallace Nutting furniture and had no way of knowing that they were selling a fake. They bought it with the best of intentions and got burned by their Wallace Nutting inexperience.

Another Wallace Nutting fake story involved Bill Hamann, president of the Wallace Nutting Collector's Club and one of the Wallace Nutting furniture experts whom I collaborated with for this book. Several years ago Bill had learned about a Wallace Nutting block branded corner cupboard that was being sold at an Indiana auction. Bill was unable to attend the actual sale but after several reassuring conversations with the auctioneer, he placed a telephone bid. Bill won the corner cupboard, immediately sent payment to the auctioneer to settle accounts, and made arrangements to pick up the piece later.

Wallace Nutting Fakes

Fake corner cupboard. Courtesy of Bill & Gretchen Hamann.

Only upon arriving to pick up the piece did Bill determine that the cupboard wasn't right. Although is was block branded, the brand was a fake, probably done with the same branding iron that branded the table that I had seen several years prior. Anyway, Bill explained to the auctioneer that the cupboard was a fake and requested a refund (his check had already cleared). The auctioneer refused the refund request and Bill had no choice but to take the corner cupboard home with him.

Again, the modus operandi was comparable to my experience.
1) A larger than actual block branding iron was used.
2) The piece wasn't pictured in any of Wallace Nutting's furniture catalogs.
3) It was dumped through an "as is" auction.

The only difference between Bill's experience and mine was that I was fortunate enough to personally see the piece prior to paying for it.

Bill estimates that perhaps as many as 10 – 12 fakes have been reported in his area, normally being sold through auctions in Ohio or Indiana.

The lesson here should be quite clear:
• Know what you are buying.
• Know whom you are buying from.
• And make certain that whatever you buy is returnable if it is not as represented.

Caveat Emptor.

Summary of Key Points

• There are indeed fake pieces of Wallace Nutting furniture in circulation.

• Anyone can make a branding iron and any piece of furniture can be fraudulently branded with the Wallace Nutting name.

• Know what you are buying.

• Know whom you are buying from.

• Make certain that whatever you are buying is returnable if not as represented.

• Caveat Emptor.

Fake block brand found in Bill Hamann's corner cupboard. Courtesy of Bill & Gretchen Hamann.

Although not as precise as some of the previously mentioned methods, another way to identify a piece of Wallace Nutting furniture is visual identification through Wallace Nutting's furniture catalogs.

It's a fact that pieces of unmarked, unidentified Wallace Nutting furniture are in circulation. Some of these pieces have lost their paper label, some have no identifiable furniture design number, and time and age has removed any evidence of the former paper label on other pieces. As mentioned earlier, Wallace Nutting occasionally sold his furniture in the white (unfinished), and whenever Nutting sold a piece of furniture in the white, it was sold unmarked. And some early pieces having inadequate space for a paper label (e.g., chairs with rushed seats) were sold with a card stock tag that has long ago been removed.

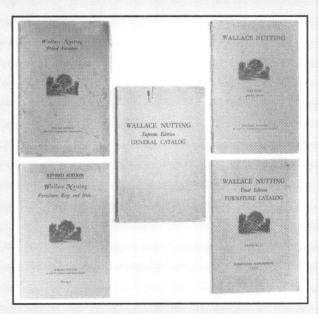

Original Wallace Nutting furniture catalogs

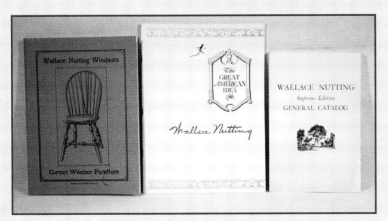

Three re-printed furniture catalogs

So the net effect is that there are indeed pieces of unsigned and unmarked Wallace Nutting furniture still in circulation. Some of these are probably being passed over as someone else's twentieth century reproductions, and some of them are still being bought or sold as authentic antiques.

How do you identify such pieces? As a last resort, in the absence of any distinguishing markings — paper label, script brand, block brand, punched name, or punched number — you may be able to refer to one of Wallace Nutting's furniture catalogs. To the best of my knowledge Wallace Nutting released only the following eight furniture catalogs:

Wallace Nutting Furniture Catalogs

1918:	*Wallace Nutting Windsors: Correct Windsor Furniture*
1922:	*Wallace Nutting: A Great American Idea*
1926:	*Wallace Nutting Period Furniture*
1927:	*Wallace Nutting Furniture, Rugs, and Iron*
1927 – 1928:	*Wallace Nutting 7th Edition Catalog*
1930:	*Wallace Nutting General Catalog, Supreme Edition*
1932:	*Wallace Nutting General Catalog, Supreme Edition*
1937:	*Wallace Nutting Furniture Catalog, Final Edition*

Visual Reference Tools

The good news is that each of these catalogs can be used to visually identify and authenticate a piece of unmarked Wallace Nutting furniture. The bad news is that no single catalog includes all of the various pieces that Nutting produced over a 20+ year period. For example, the 1918 *Wallace Nutting Windsors: Correct Windsor Furniture* catalog includes many Windsor pieces that were later discontinued due to production problems or poor sales. The only place to find any script branded furniture is through the 1922 *Wallace Nutting: A Great American Idea* catalog. And new designs were still being introduced as late as the 1937 *Final Edition Catalog* which means that they will not appear in any earlier catalog.

Is It Real...or Is It Wallace Nutting?

We frequently hear from people who confuse original period antiques, or even Centennial pieces (those items made around the 1876 American Centennial period) with Wallace Nutting reproductions. One thing you should keep in mind is that early, authentic furniture was handmade, not machine produced. As a result each piece was slightly different from the next. Wallace Nutting furniture, on the other hand, was intended to be copied from a pre-designed production model. Each piece was intended to look exactly like the production model, it should have almost exactly the same measurements as the production model (allowing for a minimal amount of age shrinkage), and Nutting's craftsmen would be terminated if they deviated too far from the production model.

So if the piece of furniture you are viewing looks exactly like the comparable piece in any catalog, if the turnings, carvings, and design appears exactly the same, if the measurements from the book correspond to what you are previewing, there is a real good chance the piece you are looking at is a Wallace Nutting reproduction.

Where Do You Find These Catalogs?

Original Wallace Nutting furniture catalogs are available through many of the more traditional sources: eBay, other Internet book resources, antiques dealers, flea markets, and of course, auctions. We usually have one or more Wallace Nutting furniture catalogs consigned to each of our auctions. By doing a little legwork you can usually locate an original furniture catalog, often in the $50.00 – 175.00 + range.

Or, you can purchase a re-printed copy of several of these furniture catalogs through Michael Ivankovich Antiques. For example, we offer three re-printed furniture catalogs, including:

1918: *Wallace Nutting Windsors: Correct Windsor Furniture*, 48 pages, listing 150+ Windsor designs, 100+ photographs, the most complete Wallace Nutting paper label Windsor furniture visual reference book in print, $12.95

1922: *Wallace Nutting: A Great American Idea*, 40 pages, listing 42 script brand designs, with photographs of each, the most complete Wallace Nutting script branded furniture visual reference book in print, $12.95

1932: *Wallace Nutting General Catalog, Supreme Edition*, 160 pages, listing nearly 1,000 designs, 330+ photographs, the most complete Wallace Nutting furniture block brand visual reference book in print, $15.95

If you are going to obtain just one furniture catalog, we would recommend the 1932 *Wallace Nutting General Catalog, Supreme Edition*. This was his most complete furniture catalog and is well worth the money.

Orders can be placed through our website: www.michaelivankovich.com. Or you can mail a check to Michael Ivankovich Antiques, PO Box 1536, Doylestown, PA 18901. Add $4.95 P&H for first book ordered, $2.25 for each additional book.

Summary of Key Points

• Wallace Nutting issued eight different furniture catalogs between 1918 and 1937 and each can help to visually identify unmarked Wallace Nutting furniture.

• Each specific furniture design number should have the exact same measurements and dimensions as all other pieces produced under that same furniture design number.

• The 1918 *Wallace Nutting Windsors: Correct Windsor Furniture* catalog is the best and most complete visual reference of Wallace Nutting's paper label Windsor furniture. It offers 100+ visual reference pictures (more than in any other catalog), including sizing specifications, of nearly all Nutting Windsor furniture produced between 1918 and 1921. This catalog also includes many Windsor forms that were sold, and then later discontinued and not found in later catalogs.

• The 1922 *Wallace Nutting: A Great American Idea* is the best and most complete visual reference of Wallace Nutting script furniture. It offers 42 visual reference pictures, along with sizing specifications, of nearly all script branded furniture that was produced between 1922 and 1924.

• The 1932 *Wallace Nutting General Catalog, Supreme Edition,* is the best and most complete visual reference of Wallace Nutting block branded furniture. It contains 330+ visual reference pictures and the most complete listing of furniture numbers found in any other catalogs.

• Original and re-printed copies of these furniture catalogs are available.

BEAUTY CONSTRUCTION STYLE

Above is a Sudbury Cupboard

If you can find an old Court Cupboard like this you can probably obtain $25,000 for it. If you want a new one, as this is, at a modest price, it is something that you can get.

Shown at my Studio 46 Park Street (close to Station) Framingham, Massachusetts

WALLACE NUTTING

Antiques, full page ad, #910 Sudbury court cupboard, circa 1925

Wallace Nutting sales brochure

One of the keys to Wallace Nutting's success was his ability to market his products. There were other photographers selling hand-colored pictures throughout New England, but none marketed them as effectively as Wallace Nutting.

Other individuals published furniture books, but none sold more than Wallace Nutting.

And others were reproducing furniture in the early twentieth century, but none were more aggressive marketers than Wallace Nutting.

Tom Denenberg revealed in his 2003 book, *Wallace Nutting and the Invention of Old America*, that Wallace Nutting had hired the George Batten Company of New York City to create many of his advertisements in the early 1920s. (George Batten Co. later became part of BBD&O, one of the country's leading advertising agencies.) Old advertising proof sheets examined by Tom provide evidence that Wallace Nutting's advertising agency created certain Nutting ads for *Ladies Home Journal*, *Vogue*, and several other publications.

But in the early 1920s when the furniture business was just beginning, and later in the financially-depressed 1930s, Wallace Nutting and his staff more than likely were responsible for the bulk of his advertising creation. My guess is that Nutting seems to have written much of his own advertising copy. His flowery prose and inability to sound humble were truly Nutting trademarks. He sincerely believed that he produced the finest furniture anywhere, and he had no reservations about telling the world about it.

But part of the beauty of Wallace Nutting, Inc. advertising was that each business segment helped to cross-market the other segments. The hand-colored pictures helped to sell the books, the books helped to sell the furniture, and the furniture rounded out the national exposure of the Wallace Nutting name. I've isolated nine distinct areas which I consider to be advertising centers for Wallace Nutting Inc. and all of its inter-related products and services.

1) Wallace Nutting's Hand-Colored Interior Scenes — Wallace Nutting's hand-colored pictures not only financially carried the furniture business for most years, they also helped to promote the beauty of authentic early American furniture. Quite often these interior scenes featured Wallace Nutting's reproductions rather than period antiques. His pictures helped to sell his furniture. His furniture helped to sell his pictures.

2) Sales Brochures — Wallace Nutting produced at least three different sales brochures over the years. Each was designed to promote Wallace Nutting Inc., the hand-colored photographs, the books, the reproduction furniture, and all of the other services available through Wallace Nutting, Inc. Each product line helped to cross-sell the other product lines.

3) Furniture Books — Wallace Nutting's six furniture books released between 1917 and 1933 helped to promote Wallace Nutting Inc. They helped to make Americans better aware of the furniture used by their ancestors, and they taught readers the difference between the good-better-best of early American antiques. And if one was unable to acquire the real thing, a Wallace Nutting reproduction was almost as good as having the original. The furniture books also helped to foster the image of Wallace Nutting as one of America's leading experts in early American antiques.

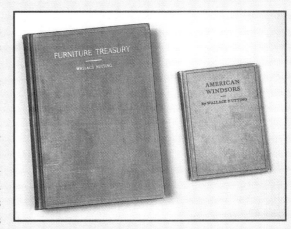

Wallace Nutting furniture books

4) Furniture Catalogs — Wallace Nutting's eight furniture catalogs released between 1918 and 1937 spread the word of his high quality reproductions through both the private and retail markets. Select department stores sold Wallace Nutting furniture directly to their customers. Or customers could visit Wallace Nutting Inc. in Framingham, Massachusetts, and see his furniture first-hand. The high expense of these catalogs often times necessitated Wallace Nutting to sell his catalogs in order to eliminate browsers and non-serious buyers: "Illustrated Catalog $1.00, Refunded on first purchase."

5) Wallace Nutting Inc. Show Room Displays — According to the 1937 *Wallace Nutting Final Edition Furniture Catalog*, Wallace Nutting's Framingham Studio offered "…about fifty rooms with something like one thousand pieces on exhibition, about nine-tenths of which are new." This meant that if Wallace Nutting could get his potential customers to visit his Framingham Studio his 1000+ piece furniture display could probably sell them on the beauty and merits of Wallace Nutting furniture. And while they were there, they could purchase a few Wallace Nutting pictures and books as well.

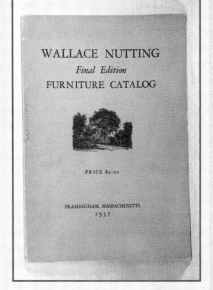

1937 Wallace Nutting Final Edition Furniture Catalog

6) Department Store Displays — Many stores that carried Wallace Nutting's pictures and furniture actually had entire Wallace Nutting departments. His hand-colored pictures were displayed alongside his reproduction furniture. If you bought a picture, you might as well buy a piece of furniture. If you bought a piece of furniture, you might as well buy a picture. And if you didn't see what you wanted on the show room floor, you could order a piece directly from the store's Wallace Nutting furniture catalog, or you could order a piece specially-built to your own personal specifications.

7) Published Magazine Articles — Wallace Nutting helped to hone his personal image as an antiques expert by publishing a series of articles in prestigious national magazines. For example, between 1922 and 1930 he published articles on the following subjects in

One of Wallace Nutting's 50 showroom displays

Advertising

Antiques, full page ad, circa 1925

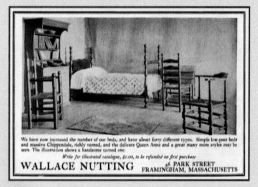

Antiques, half page ad, circa 1925

WALLACE NUTTING

Will talk on Old Furniture in the Lecture Room

at the

PHILADELPHIA ANTIQUES EXPOSITION

Illustrated by colored screen pictures in great number and variety

EVERY AFTERNOON AT HALF PAST TWO

Beginning Tuesday, May Third

And will exhibit many of his exquisite Colonial reproductions. The addresses, however, will make no reference to them.

Dummy and prospectus of the new work on furniture details and designs will also be shown and subscriptions taken. A thousand sketches.

These features were a notable element of interest at the New York Antiques Exposition.

Antiques, ad for lecture in Philadelphia, Pennsylvania, circa 1925

WALLACE NUTTING

whose pictures are in all homes

AUTHOR

of Six Books on Early Furniture and

Fourteen Other Volumes on

OLD AMERICA - In and Out of Doors

WILL LECTURE HERE

Showing 180 Colored Lantern Slides

AT

Advertising poster for furniture lecture, circa 1930

Antiques Magazine: Windsor Chairs (no surprise here); The Prence-Howes Court Cupboard (the cupboard he was sued for); Turnings on American Furniture: Parts I and II; Carved Spoon Racks; Notable Furniture of the Pilgrim Century (again, no surprise); and A Sidelight on John Goddard. Each of these articles helped to solidify the image of Wallace Nutting as a national expert in early American antiques, which helped to cross-sell his other product lines.

8) Trade Paper Advertising — Although Wallace Nutting advertised in a variety of national magazines, without doubt he carried a larger advertising presence in the magazine *Antiques* than in any other national publication. *Antiques* was the first major national scholarly magazine devoted to quality early American antiques and Wallace Nutting absolutely needed a presence there if he was going to sell his reproduction furniture nationwide. From 1922 through the 1930s most issues carried one to three Wallace Nutting ads. When revenues were strong Nutting sometimes carried a full page ad for his furniture. In other months he utilized only a quarter or half page ad. Smaller ads were often devoted to his furniture books, and most months his business was listed under the Antique Shops Directory as well. Once again, he used a traditional *Antiques* magazine venue to help sell his reproduction furniture and to help to craft his national image as an antiques expert.

9) Lecture Series — Wallace Nutting had created approximately 3000 hand-colored glass magic lantern slides which he used in his various lecture series. According to his 1930 furniture catalog, Nutting offered "six lectures covering the entire period of American Homes and Furnishings." What is especially interesting about these lectures is that Nutting not only made his presentations to men's clubs, but also to women's groups, including "Women's Colleges or Classes in Decoration." Nutting was astute enough to recognize that the woman of the house often made the household's furniture purchasing decisions and, if she was going to purchase furniture, it may as well be Wallace Nutting furniture.

The following advertisements will give you a better indication of the type of products Wallace Nutting advertised and the image he presented, in *Antiques* magazine.

Magic lantern and Wallace Nutting glass slides

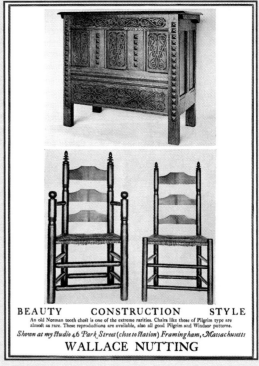

BEAUTY　　　CONSTRUCTION　　　STYLE

An old Norman tooth chest is one of the extreme rarities. Chairs like these of Pilgrim type are almost as rare. These reproductions are available, also all good Pilgrim and Windsor patterns.

Shown at my Studio 46 Park Street (close to Station) Framingham, Massachusetts

WALLACE NUTTING

Antiques, #933 oak Norman tooth chest (rare) & #493 and #393 Pilgrim chairs ad, circa 1925

BEAUTY　　　CONSTRUCTION　　　STYLE

THE reproduction of the Connecticut Sunflower and Tulip Court Cupboard is the only reproduction, known by me, to be made. It is of quartered oak, and is a very careful copy of the best original that has come to my attention. Every measurement is worked out to the thirty-second of an inch. I also make the Connecticut two-drawer Sunflower Chest.

Shown at my Studio 46 Park Street (close to Station) Framingham, Massachusetts

WALLACE NUTTING

Antiques, #911 Connecticut sunflower & tulip court cupboard ad (rare), circa 1925

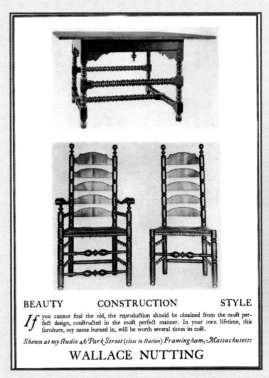

BEAUTY　　　CONSTRUCTION　　　STYLE

If you cannot find the old, the reproduction should be obtained from the most perfect design, constructed in the most perfect manner. In your own lifetime, this furniture, my name burned in, will be worth several times its cost.

Shown at my Studio 46 Park Street (close to Station) Framingham, Massachusetts

WALLACE NUTTING

Antiques, #613 ball-turned tavern table and #490 and #390 New England five-back ladderback chair ad, circa 1925

Advertising

BEAUTY   CONSTRUCTION   STYLE

The above is a very perfect and important reproduction of the Connecticut Sunflower and Tulip two-drawer chest. The stools are examples of our minor pieces.
It is a beautiful drive to Framingham. You will find there 120 different patterns of reproductions. Also there is on the floor one of the finest old court cupboards of American origin.
Interested persons may, by sending a postal, be waited on with pictures at their homes.

Shown at my Studio, Framingham, 46 Park Street (close to Station)
21 miles to Boston

WALLACE NUTTING

Antiques, #931 oak sunflower chest and #165 and #166 joined stool ad, circa 1925

BEAUTY   CONSTRUCTION   STYLE

THE "lowboy" table here shown is beautiful, small and fashionable. It is made in solid walnut or in maple. I make also 200 other reproductions, including everything that could possibly be required in an American dwelling before 1720, and all maple and pine after that date.

Shown at my Studio, Framingham, 46 Park Street (close to Station)
21 miles to Boston

WALLACE NUTTING

Antiques, #727 trumpet turned lowboy table ad, circa 1925

LARGE OFFICE DESK AND SOME CHARITY REPRODUCTIONS OF FINE OLD PIECES, PERHAPS MORE DOMESTIC IN TYPE
Illustrated Catalogue $1.00. Refunded on first purchase
WALLACE NUTTING 46 PARK STREET FRAMINGHAM, MASSACHUSETTS

Antiques, room setting offering both "correct reproductions" alongside "office adaptation" desk and office chair, circa 1930

Summary of Key Points

• Wallace Nutting used a variety of advertising techniques to cross-market his products.

• Although he at times did use the services of a professional advertising agency, more often he coordinated his own advertising.

• Low sales usually meant low advertising expenditures which forced Wallace Nutting to coordinate much of his advertising himself.

• *Antiques* magazine was probably Wallace Nutting's #1 print advertising vehicle.

Perhaps the greatest misconception surrounding Wallace Nutting furniture is that many people outside of the Wallace Nutting collecting niche confuse authentic, original antiques found in the *Furniture Treasury* or other Wallace Nutting furniture books with Nutting's reproductions. "I have a chair that looks almost like Plate xxx in the *Furniture Treasury*. Could mine be a Wallace Nutting?"

Hopefully after reading this book you now understand the difference between an original antique found in a Wallace Nutting book and a Wallace Nutting reproduction.

If someone were to ask me whether they should purchase authentic American antiques or Wallace Nutting reproductions of comparable form and condition, I would without hesitation recommend the authentic antiques, *if they could afford them*. The authentic antique in excellent condition undoubtedly represents a true piece of Americana and will most likely prove to be an excellent long-term investment.

Original Windsor braced back side chair, circa 1750, once owned by Wallace Nutting. **Furniture Treasury, Volume II,** *Plate #2560.*

Wallace Nutting #301 Windsor braced back side chair, circa 1920

Unfortunately, most people cannot afford the finest authentic antiques, especially at today's high prices. When the most desirable paintings start bringing more than $50,000,000.00 with increasing regularity, when the finest forms of early American furniture break the $12,000,000.00 barrier, when the finest pieces in nearly all areas of antiques and collectibles seem to reach record levels on a regular basis, the other remaining great pieces also travel upwards in price, beyond the means of all but the wealthiest collectors.

And if Wallace Nutting couldn't locate the best-of-the-best circa 1920, what are your chances of finding it at an affordable price today. This leaves most collectors with two choices:

a) You can collect authentic antiques having less than excellent form and design, or antiques that have been repaired or restored over the years. Or…

b) You can collect top quality twentieth century reproductions which make up for their lack of age with fine lines and correct proportions.

Summary – What Does the Future Hold?

If someone were to ask me whether I would prefer to own a Wallace Nutting reproduction, an authentic antique that has been repaired and restored, or an authentic antique with less than desirable form and design, I would select the Wallace Nutting reproduction for several reasons:

1) Wallace Nutting reproductions offer the finest in form and design. Most of the originals he copied can only be found in museums or private collections today.

2) The high quality that Wallace Nutting achieved in his reproductions would be extremely difficult to duplicate today. He worked with the finest woods, he employed the same techniques used by seventeenth and eighteent century furniture makers, and he didn't cut corners.

3) There is only a finite amount of Wallace Nutting furniture, and no more will ever be produced, making what little remains even more valuable as time passes.

4) Wallace Nutting furniture will stand up to daily wear and usage. You can still use it without fear of damaging your investment as with eighteenth and nineteenth century antiques.

5) This furniture has the added-value of its association with the most famous name in American antiques — *Wallace Nutting*. The name is there for everyone to see, paper label or branded signature, a name that is associated with quality, antiques, and Americana.

Will Prices Continue To Rise?

Not only will Wallace Nutting furniture not get any cheaper, I am supremely confident that prices will continue to rise, and probably at a much more dramatic rate, than in previous years. Here are 10 good reasons why I'm sure about this:

1) Both the winning bidder and underbidder for the $36,750.00 record-setting #733 Goddard block front secretary desk in 2002 were members of the Wallace Nutting Collector's Club. Which tells me that the real money — the Oprah Winfrey's, the Bill Gates, the Hollywood crowd, the New York auction crowd, and America's fabulously "unknown" wealthy, have yet to learn about the Wallace Nutting furniture market. Trust me, it's only a matter of time before the very big money learns about Wallace Nutting furniture. Because what other undiscovered high quality collectible areas are still out there and available to collect. Once the really big money learns about Wallace Nutting furniture, watch the prices soar.

2) For nearly 30 years Michael Ivankovich and members of the Wallace Nutting Collector's Club have been praising the merits of Wallace Nutting, and relatively few people have listened. With the Wallace Nutting Collector's Club boasting approximately 250 households nationally, most of whom only collect the pictures, this is not a huge collectible field, especially when compared to other groups which boast memberships in the thousands. This is about to change as several recent developments are suggesting.

3) Tom Denenberg, head curator at the Wadsworth Atheneum in Hartford, Connecticut, one of America's most prestigious museums, released a new book in 2003 titled *Wallace Nutting and the Invention of Old America*. Tom's position at the Wadsworth Atheneum opened countless new documents and doors for research into Wallace Nutting and Tom's book is already gaining national attention which is already serving to put the national spotlight on Wallace Nutting.

4) In conjunction with the release of Tom Denenberg's book, the Wadsworth Atheneum has opened a wonderful exhibition in 2003 also called Wallace Nutting and the Invention of Old America which featured the pictures, books, furniture, and memorabilia of Wallace Nutting. This exhibition introduced Wallace Nutting to many new potential collectors as well as to those who previously shunned Nutting's work as kitsch, but who are now beginning to hold his work in much higher regard. The Wallace Nutting Collection of Original Period Antiques, which is on permanent display at the Wadsworth Atheneum, will also continue to position Wallace Nutting as one of the twentieth century's antiquarians, which will continue to draw attention to his works.

5) SPNEA, or the Society for the Preservation of New England Antiquities, has recently acquired a major piece of Wallace Nutting Furniture — a #910 oak Sudbury court cupboard — which they plan on using as a focal point in an upcoming colonial revival exhibition. That piece came from the Michael and Susan Ivankovich collection. We were sad to see it leave our collection because we will probably never have the opportunity to pur chase another comparable piece of Wallace Nutting furniture. Yet we were happy to see it go to SPNEA because when SPNEA decides to focus upon Wallace Nutting, you know that Wallace Nutting has arrived.

6) Other institutions are also beginning to focus upon Wallace Nutting as well. The Museum of Early Trades & Crafts (New Jersey), the Indiana University Art Museum (Indiana), and the Allentown Art Museum (Pennsylvania) are just a few of the organizations now starting to host exhibitions focusing upon Wallace Nutting. We expect this number to increase in the future.

7) Most antiques and collectibles trade papers have been extremely generous with us in helping to promote Wallace Nutting in the past. But when the *New York Times* published two articles on Wallace Nutting within the same week, when articles on Wallace Nutting begin appearing in the *Philadelphia Inquirer*, *Boston Globe*, *Hartford Courant*, *Cleveland Plain Dealer*, and most other major newspapers throughout the country, it's another sign that Wallace Nutting is up and coming.

8) As new buyers continue to enter the Wallace Nutting furniture market, you now have more buyers than sellers, which almost assures an upward pricing spiral. Because when you have more people chasing after fewer goods, prices always rise over the long run.

9) Since 1988, our Michael Ivankovich auctions have provided collectors with a national buying and selling forum. For 15 years Wallace Nutting buyers have had a place where they can bid with confidence in an auction environment where they receive strong auction guarantees. And Wallace Nutting sellers can consign their merchandise knowing that their consignment will receive national exposure when placed in a competitive bidding situation in front of the country's leading collectors.

I will get to reason #10 shortly.

No one in the history of American antiques has ever accomplished the types of things done by Wallace Nutting.

- He sold nearly 10,000,000 pictures, all bearing his name.
- He published nearly 20 books, all bearing his name.
- He gathered one of the most extensive collections of important antique furniture ever assembled, still on display in a major institution, still bearing his name.
- He reproduced thousands of the finest pieces of furniture ever made, all bearing his name.

I think Bill Bowers said it best in Recollections. "One might say that Wallace Nutting contributed more for the preser-vation of our past heritage of American Arts and Culture than anyone else. We had greater names in the arts, but they

Summary – What Does the Future Hold?

reached relatively few. Wallace Nutting was for everybody and everyone appreciated him. He put everything he had, both finances and all his time, to explain how and why our ancestors lived and felt. Our great museums and names like Henry DuPont at Winterthur, are unquestionably the epitome of quality and taste…but these are the results of many millions of dollars and the employment of well-trained personnel. Our best institutions are the sum total of many people working at it full time and having unlimited amounts of money. Wallace Nutting did it first…and single-handedly."

Which takes us to reason #10 on why I feel that Wallace Nutting furniture will continue to increase in price.

There is a word in the English language called *synergy*. Quite simply defined, synergy means that the total effect of an action is greater than the sum of its individual parts or components. This is what differentiates Wallace Nutting from nearly every other market today.

• Wallace Nutting pictures have become a major market.
• Nearly 20 different books authored by Wallace Nutting are being widely collected today.
• Wallace Nutting furniture is now sought after at a higher rate than ever before.

These separate and independent markets, pictures, books, furniture, each have one thing in common — the Wallace Nutting name. This is what separates Wallace Nutting from all of his competitors. His name stands out above all of the other early twentieth century photographers, all of the other early twentieth century furniture authors, and all of the early twentieth century furniture makers. His competitors specialized in one area. Wallace Nutting's name transcended these three areas, setting him far above his competitors.

Wallace Nutting.
• It's the synergy of the name.
• It's the inter-relationship of the picture, book, and furniture markets.
• It's the effect of his cross-marketing.
• It's the diverse combination of high and low end collectors.

As always, the spotlight will eventually shift to another area. It always has, it always will. But, a strong Wallace Nutting market will remain. Because the name Wallace Nutting means quality, it means style, it means Americana.

Americana is here to stay. And so is Wallace Nutting.

– Chapter 17: An Introduction to Values –

The first part of the book provided you with the general background and history of Wallace Nutting furniture. In it we talked about:

- Wallace Nutting, the man
- His furniture reproduction business
- His furniture styles and construction techniques
- Various Wallace Nutting furniture markings
- The Wallace Nutting furniture numbering system
- The Wallace Nutting furniture grading system
- How to date Wallace Nutting furniture
- Visual reference tools
- The potential for fakes
- Our thoughts on the future direction of Wallace Nutting furniture

But the book from here on will focus on the price guide to Wallace Nutting furniture, which is probably why you purchased this book. Value is what it is all about. If you are reading this book right now, you are probably attempting to determine one of two questions:

1) What's your piece of Wallace Nutting furniture worth?
2) How much should you expect to pay in order to acquire a particular piece of Wallace Nutting furniture?

The second part of this book will attempt to answer both of these questions by providing you with three possible approaches to valuing Wallace Nutting furniture:

1) Actual Auction Prices of Wallace Nutting furniture sold through our Michael Ivankovich Auction Co. auctions between 1998 and 2003.

2) Two General Rules of Thumb which are designed to help you easily gauge the rarity and current market value of most Wallace Nutting furniture pieces.

3) Current Market Value Estimates provided by a team of five Wallace Nutting furniture experts which are designed to provide consensus current market value estimates on nearly each piece of Wallace Nutting furniture sold between 1918 and 1941.

Chapter 26: Listing of Recent Auction Prices is the starting point for valuing Wallace Nutting furniture.

Chapter 26: Listing of Recent Auction Prices at the end of this book provides actual auction prices for several hundred pieces of Wallace Nutting furniture that sold through Michael Ivankovich Auction Company auctions since 1998. These prices represent actual auction prices, and they represent fair market value transactions that occurred when Wallace Nutting furniture was sold in a competitive bidding situation in a well-advertised, nationally-attended auction. These prices should help to point you in the right direction in determining the appropriate value for many pieces of Wallace Nutting furniture.

The number one problem with trying to place an estimated value on certain pieces of Wallace Nutting furniture is that because some of it is so rare, there is no known public pricing history. When we (Wallace Nutting furniture collectors, as a group) first starting collecting and researching Wallace Nutting furniture in the 1970s, no one had any idea how much was out there or what was available to collect. No production records ever survived so we had no idea what quan-

An Introduction to Values

tities remained in circulation. We simply looked at the furniture catalogs, saw what Wallace Nutting was selling, and assumed that it would eventually turn up for sale somewhere. Now 30 years later, many examples of Wallace Nutting furniture have still not surfaced.

In the 1970s – early 1980s there were relatively few people actively collecting Wallace Nutting furniture which, in hindsight, made it appear more plentiful than it actually was. As new collectors and dealers began entering the hunt for Wallace Nutting furniture in the 1990s, the market became saturated with more buyers than sellers, making it harder than ever before to acquire a quality piece at a reasonable price.

I've been at this for more than 30 years, buying, selling, auctioning, writing appraisals, and answering letters and e-mails from people who actually have Wallace Nutting furniture. Yet despite all of this exposure to Wallace Nutting furniture, I have seen barely 40% of the items pictured in the 1932 furniture catalog. If I haven't seen it, and if you haven't seen it, where is it?

Some Wallace Nutting collectors have speculated that perhaps Wallace Nutting never produced more than the initial production model for certain designs. If no orders were ever received for a particular style or design number, no additional copies of that design would have been produced. Considering the harsh economic climate during the depression years of 1930 – 1940, and considering Nutting's high asking prices, Wallace Nutting probably never received one single order on many items in his catalog.

How much Wallace Nutting furniture produced between 1918 and 1941 still remains in circulation today? We suspect that most is still around somewhere. Wallace Nutting pictures were held in considerably lower regard by the public 75 years ago than they are today and, quite often, after their useful life was over they were simply discarded or trashed. Even his books were often discarded after becoming old or outdated.

But rarely would anyone throw away a piece of Wallace Nutting furniture. Perhaps certain commercial items such as radiator covers or office furniture might have been discarded by larger corporations or businesses after its useful life had passed, but I can't imagine much other furniture being thrown into the trash bin. The quality was simply too good. Unless it became inadvertently broken or damaged, or perhaps destroyed in a fire or accident, you can pretty much rest assured that the vast majority of all Wallace Nutting furniture produced between 1918 and 1941 is still sitting in someone's house today.

So, if most of the Wallace Nutting furniture that was ever produced still survives today, where is it?

And, if we have never seen it, and if no known sales record exists, how does one put a value on the rarest Wallace Nutting Furniture?

The Rarity and 20 Times Rules of Thumb

First let me share with you two very basic rules of thumb that I follow when beginning to place a value on Wallace Nutting furniture. And then I will share with you how we actually arrived at the values that we list in this section of the book.

Rule of Thumb #1...The Rarity Rule: The original selling price of a piece of Wallace Nutting furniture usually correlates to its rarity and value today. That is, the more expensive it was when originally produced, the fewer units were ever produced, and the rarer it is today, the greater its potential current market value.

What this means is that as you review the values provided in this section, first take a look at the 1932 list price. The higher the 1932 list price, the rarer that piece most likely will be today, and the higher its potential current market value.

> ***Rule of Thumb #2…The 20 Times Rule:*** The 20 times rule states that today's starting point for valuing a piece of Wallace Nutting furniture should be no less than the 1932 list price multiplied by 20.

What this means is that as you review the values provided in this section, take a look at the 1932 list price and multiply it by 20. This will provide you with a very general starting point for placing a value on a piece of Wallace Nutting furniture. It isn't always 100% accurate but more often than not it will get you reasonably close to today's current market value.

For example a #31 treenware candlestick with a 1932 list price of $1.80 times 20 suggests a current market value of $36.00, which is not even close to the current market value suggested in the 0 – 99 Series section section. Because of treenware's low 1932 list price, and it's high demand today, the 20 times rule does not seem to apply to treenware.

However, let's take a #165 low joined stool with a 1932 list price of $22.50 times 20 suggests a current market value of $450.00. A little lower than our price guide suggests in the 100 – 200 Series section, but not all that far off. In this case a 25 times or 30 times rule might be more appropriate, but the 20 times rule is not out of line.

Consider a #415 Windsor comb back arm chair with a 1932 list price of $59.00 times 20 suggests a current market value of $1,180.00. This falls within the $1,000.00 – 1,500.00 value range suggested in the 300 – 400 Series section.

How about a #628 mahogany Pembroke table with a 1932 list price of $96.00 times 20 suggests a current market value of $1,920.00. This again falls within the value range suggested in the 500 series section.

Or a #589 wainscot settle with a 1932 list price of $186.00 times 20 suggests a current market value of $2,720.00. Once again, very close to the value range suggested in the 600 Series section.

As one last example, take a #733 Goddard block front secretary desk with a 1932 list price of $1,800.00 times 20 suggests a current market value of $36,000.00. Not too far off the current auction record price of $36,750.00 paid for the last one to sell at auction in 2002.

So although the 20 times rule is not infallible, it does offer a good starting point for determining the current market value of many, but not all, pieces of Wallace Nutting furniture.

> ***Special note regarding 1932 list price:*** You will note throughout the value guide that certain items do not include a 1932 list price. This means that particular piece is from the 1918 Windsor furniture catalog which did not include a price list and we do not know the actual list price for that piece. ***Also:*** Any piece designated "script" means that the list price is from 1922 and not 1932.

How We Arrived at the Estimated Current Market Values in This Price Guide

When I first started this book, my original thought was that I would place an estimated current market value on each item listed in this section by myself. I could have done it alone, and I would have been right far more often than I would have been wrong, but then I had a better thought.

I thought back to my earlier days as a corporate human resources trainer and remembered that in certain personnel training sessions we would administer tests called the Desert Survival Test and the Moon Survival Test. The basic premise of these tests was that each member of a team was first asked a series of questions relating to how they could best survive if stranded in/on the Desert/Moon. Then the entire group would join together, as a team, and answer the same series of survival questions, as a team. In more than 10 years of administering these tests I never once saw a single individual out-perform the entire team. The group always provided a more accurate response than did any single individual.

That's what I decided to do here. Rather than supply all of the pricing estimates by myself, I invited a group of five teams, 10 people in all, whom I consider to be Wallace Nutting furniture experts to help me arrive at a consensus decision on the current market value of each item listed in this section. The teams I selected have a total of more than 150+ years of combined experience buying, selling, researching, and chasing after Wallace Nutting furniture. No one has less than 15 years experience, the most has nearly 30 years experience. I don't think I could have found a team with more Wallace Nutting furniture experience than I did with this group.

And I believe that this group came up with significantly more accurate current market value pricing estimates than I could have done myself. It was a long and tedious process for all involved. We had to look at nearly 1,000 different items, and consider the low estimate, the high estimate, and the rarity factor — nearly 3,000 opinions (educated guesses) per team, nearly 15,000 opinions (educated guesses) for the five teams combined. It took several months to accomplish but we did it and, in my opinion, the results are a realistic estimate of today's Wallace Nutting furniture market.

First, let me introduce you to this group, listed alphabetically after our biography, and then I will share the criteria on how we arrived at our pricing estimates. And let me be the first to extend our many thanks to each of these collectors and friends who, through this labor of love, have provided invaluable information to all Wallace Nutting furniture collectors.

Meet Our Team of Wallace Nutting Furniture Experts

Michael & Susan Ivankovich
Doylestown, Pennsylvania

Michael and Susan Ivankovich have been collecting Wallace Nutting furniture for nearly 30 years. They have bought and sold more than 100 pieces of Wallace Nutting furniture over the years but, more importantly, they have been selling Wallace Nutting furniture through their auctions, in a competitive bidding situation, since 1988. As a result they handle more Wallace Nutting furniture than anyone else in the country, and they are closer to the national pulse of Wallace Nutting furniture values than anyone else in the country.

Michael & Susan Ivankovich

Just as importantly, they have a 20+ year history of corresponding with other collectors around the country. Mike is often the first source people contact about their Wallace Nutting furniture. "What's my piece worth?" and "What can you tell me about it?" are the two most frequently asked questions. These 20+ years of answering questions have enabled Mike and Sue to learn what pieces other people have. If Mike and Sue have never seen or even heard about the existence of a particular piece, you can pretty much be assured that very few were ever produced.

Sue served as secretary of the Wallace Nutting Collector's Club for four years. They live and work in Doylestown, Pennsylvania. Their www.michaelivankovich.com website is actually seven different websites but, most importantly, you may want to visit their Wallace Nutting furniture gallery (www.wallacenuttingfurnituregallery.com) or their Wallace Nutting furniture image library (www.ivankovichimagelibrary.com) which features nearly 150 digital images of Wallace Nutting furniture. You can either e-mail them at: ivankovich@wnutting.com or you can write them at: PO Box 1536, Doylestown, PA 18901.

Jim & Sharon Eckert
Colfax, Illinois

Jim and Sharon Eckert are natives of central Illinois. Since 1979 they have lived in Colfax, Illinois, a small farm community about 120 miles south of Chicago. They have been collecting, buying, and selling Wallace Nutting pictures and furniture for nearly twenty years. They have made dozens of trips east and hundreds of trips in the Midwest, stopping at thousands of shops, antique malls, shows, flea markets, and auctions in search of items for their collections. For more then ten years they were active dealers at Midwest shows and flea markets.

Jim has been employed in commercial banking since 1968 and since 1979 has been president, C.E.O., and trust officer of Anchor State Bank in Anchor, Illinois. Sharon, now a part-time

Jim & Sharon Eckert

An Introduction to Values

bank officer and full-time homemaker, worked in the insurance industry for many years prior to the birth of their son, James Jr., who recently married his college sweetheart, Eriko at a ceremony in Hawaii. In addition to their Wallace Nutting collecting and activities with the Wallace Nutting Collector's Club (where Jim has served as treasurer for more than five years), the Eckerts also collect Bessie Pease Gutmann pictures, cast iron doorstops, glass baskets, stoneware, and figurines. In her spare time Sharon is an avid gardener and enjoys old movies. Jim (an acknowledged workaholic) is an avid (although not good) golfer and enjoys reading (particularly history and politics).

Jim and Sharon enjoy helping other collectors (whether beginners or advanced) and can be contacted by mail at: P. O. Box 62, Anchor, IL 61720 – 0062 or by e-mail at anchorsb@mtco.com.

Bob & Pam Franscella

Bob & Pam Franscella
Sparta, New Jersey

Bob and Pam Franscella have been collecting Wallace Nutting pictures and furniture for the past two decades. As active members of the Wallace Nutting Collector's Club, they are always on the lookout for unknown items and facts regarding Wallace Nutting. Their collection consists of over 1,300 hand-colored photographs and 30+ pieces of Wallace Nutting furniture.

Pam's antique business Depression Classics features depression-era glassware, pottery, china, and of course Wallace Nutting pictures. Bob and Pam can be seen at many of the major shows in the northeast, either setting up or just buying. Throughout the last few years they have loaned numerous items to museum exhibits, and provided lectures for antique shops, museums, and private groups.

The Franscellas reside in the northwest corner of New Jersey with their two golden retrievers, Rosa and Aretha.

Bill & Gretchen Hamann
Shaker Heights, Ohio

Bill and Gretchen Hamann have been collecting Wallace Nutting pictures, books, and furniture for 30 years. Their primary focus became Wallace Nutting furniture after collecting Wallace Nutting pictures for approximately 15 years.

They have one of the larger privately owned collections of Wallace Nutting furniture in the country. Their collection has been recognized by the *New York Times*, the *Cleveland Plain Dealer,* and the Wallace Nutting Collector's Club. Selected pieces, both photos and furniture, were loaned to the Wadsworth Atheneum in Hartford, Connecticut for the Wallace Nutting and the Invention of Old America exhibit. They loaned photos to the Indiana University Art Museum in Bloomington, Indiana, for an exhibition on behalf of the center for the Study of Religion and American Culture at the Indiana University campus in Indianapolis in 1994. This unique interdisciplinary exhibition, Religion in the American Visual Arts: Regional Variation on National Themes focused on photography as a reflection of religious expression in American culture.

Bill and Gretchen have been members of the Wallace Nutting Collector's Club for 17 years and Bill has been serving as president of the Wallace Nutting Collector's Club since 1997. They reside in Shaker Heights, Ohio, and are still actively collecting.

Bill & Gretchen Hamann

Sharon & Kenny Lacasse

Sharon & Kenny Lacasse
West Barnstable, Massachusetts

Sharon and Kenny Lacasse have been Wallace Nutting collectors and dealers for the past 15 years. Like most Wallace Nutting collectors they began collecting Nutting's photos before they began to appreciate the fine craftsmanship of Wallace Nutting furniture.

Sharon once said, "It's too expensive," but Kenny said, "The pictures are nice but the furniture is a work of art!" They were once advised by an antique dealer friend to "buy the best" and they then set out to do just that. Their first purchase was a #301 Windsor bow back side chair. Over the past 15 years they have collected and sold hundreds of pieces of Wallace Nutting furniture and currently have over 50 pieces in their private collection including the #733 Goddard-Townsend mahogany nine-shell secretary which they purchased at auction in 2002 for a record setting price.

Sharon has written numerous articles for major trade papers and Kenny has done consulting work for auction houses. They have been active members of the Wallace Nutting Collector's Club for the past 10 years. They are considered one of the leading authorities on Wallace Nutting furniture on the East Coast. You may contact them at: Sharon Lacasse Antiques, PO Box 170, West Barnstable MA, 02668, (508) 428 – 0562, or via e-mail: slacasse@capecod.net.

An Introduction to Values

How We Arrived at These Wallace Nutting Furniture Values

We arrived at the consensus current market values as follows:

1) Each team — Ivankovich – Eckert – Franscella – Hamann – Lacasse — were given a master list containing approximately 1,000 items, which included each piece of Wallace Nutting furniture that appears in the three main Wallace Nutting furniture catalogs:

   - *Wallace Nutting Windsors: Correct Windsor Furniture* (1918)
   - *Wallace Nutting: The Great American Idea* (1922)
   - *Wallace Nutting General Catalog, Supreme Edition* (1930)

These three catalogs were selected because they represent the most comprehensive paper label, script brand, and block brand catalogs that Nutting issued between 1918 and 1930. Each item in these three catalogs were sorted and listed by furniture design number to allow for easier cross-referencing to pictures found within each catalog. There were approximately 1,000 different furniture design numbers to consider, as well as cross-referencing these numbers with the corresponding pictures in each catalog.

2) Each team was given the following instructions:

For Value — Please provide your opinion as to the estimated retail or auction value of each piece of Wallace Nutting furniture in the accompanying inventory listing. You should assume that each item is in very good condition without damage or blemish.

   a) If you are aware of a realistic actual retail/auction price, provide a low estimate and high estimate of approximately 10 – 15% on either side of the actual retail price.
   b) If you are unaware of such a piece ever being sold at the retail or auction level, provide a reasonable low estimate and high estimate that you feel the piece would sell for if it appeared at a reputable and well-advertised auction
   c) If you feel uncomfortable providing a price on any specific piece, it is ok to skip it.

For Rarity — each team was asked to make a rarity estimate based upon these criteria:

   1) Fairly common — Probably more than 500+ total pieces were produced between 1918 and 1937
   2) Uncommon — Probably 250 – 500 total pieces were produced between 1918 and 1937
   3) Unusual, but not rare — Probably 50 – 250 total pieces were produced between 1918 and 1937
   4) Rare — Probably 10 – 50 total pieces were produced between 1918 and 1937
   5) Extremely rare — Probably fewer than 10 total pieces were produced between 1918 and 1937

3) Each team's results were complied onto a master spreadsheet.

4) For each furniture design number we then dropped the lowest estimate and the highest estimate provided by the group. If there were matching low and high estimates, we dropped one low and/or one high estimate, and then averaged the remaining estimates to provide us with a consensus low estimate and high estimate of current market value.

5) We then rounded the number to the nearest $25.00, $50.00, or $100.00, depending upon the final level.

Is this system perfect? No. But we felt that it was best, fairest, and most unbiased way to provide reasonable and honest value estimates to many items which literally have no known record of public sale. This approach prevented any one of us from attempting to price our own collection by providing inflated values because the highest estimate was eliminated. And it minimized the overall effect when one of us may have totally "missed the boat" on something because the highest and lowest estimates were thrown out.

The Rarity Factor

The low and high value estimates should be fairly clear. But let me take just one final minute to interpret and help you the better understand the rarity factor included with the value estimates.

First, as with estimated values, the rarity factor is nothing more than an educated guess by a group of knowledgeable collectors about how many copies of each piece might have been produced by Wallace Nutting over a 20+ year period. No Wallace Nutting production records were ever found. No one has any idea how many of each design were ever produced. The only way to even come close to estimating the rarity of any particular design is to make a best-estimate guess. Which is what we did here. And, to the best of my knowledge, this was the first time that this has ever been done. We are happy to share these results with you and you are welcome to use this as you wish.

Rule of Thumb #3: This higher the rarity factor, the rarer the piece. The lower the rarity factor, the more common the piece.

You can interpret the rarity factor as follows:

Rarity Grading	# of Estimated Pieces Produced
5.0	Fewer than 10 total pieces were probably produced
4.5	Perhaps 10 – 25 total pieces were produced
4.0	Perhaps 25 – 50 total pieces were produced
3.5	Perhaps 50 – 125 total pieces were produced
3.0	Perhaps 125 – 250 total pieces were produced
2.5	Perhaps 250 – 375 total pieces were produced
2.0	Perhaps 375 – 500 total pieces were produced
1.5	Perhaps 500+ total pieces were produced
1.0	Perhaps many more than 500+ total pieces were produced

Smalls can sometimes bring large dollars and Wallace Nutting smalls are no exception. This 0 – 99 Series consists of four diverse categories of Wallace Nutting items: treenware, clocks, finials, and several other assorted items.

Treenware frames and salt & pepper shakers, from the Wallace Nutting furniture catalog

Treenware plates, saucers, and salt dishes, from the Wallace Nutting furniture catalog

Treenware goblet, candlestick, cup & saucer, from the Wallace Nutting furniture catalog

#27 and #28 treenware maple salt dishes, punched Wallace Nutting name, $125.00 – 275.00

3" treenware salt shaker, unmarked, $275.00 – 400.00

#30 treenware curly maple plate, punched Wallace Nutting name, $225.00 – 325.00

#31 treenware curly maple candlestick, punched Wallace Nutting name, $200.00 – 375.00

Pair #2 round treenware curly maple frames, each with Wallace Nutting silhouette, Wallace Nutting silhouette labels, $125.00 – 225.00 each

Pair oval treenware curly maple frames, each with Wallace Nutting silhouette, unmarked, $100.00 – 200.00 each

The 0 – 99 Series: Treenware, Clocks, Finials, and Miscellaneous

Treenware: Wallace Nutting treenware consists of small wooden utilitarian items created by Wallace Nutting including such things as plates, saucers, cups and goblets, candlesticks, frames, salt and pepper shakers, ink wells, pin boxes, snuff boxes, handy boxes, pen and desk trays, etc. These were typically made from regular maple, tiger maple, and mahogany. These were relatively inexpensive in 1930 (original list price: $0.45 – 4.50 ea.) and are highly sought after by collectors today. Their small size obviously eliminated any possibility of the larger block brand or paper label so they were either marked with the much smaller punched brand or more often than not, sold unmarked. As a result most treenware is unmarked and therefore usually unidentifiable as Wallace Nutting. Sometimes the marking was covered up by a felt bottom on such items as candlesticks and handy boxes. Wallace Nutting treenware items typically sell for $100.00 – 300.00 and we have even sold a treenware candlestick at auction for $1000.00+.

Treenware and Smalls Price Guide

#	Treenware	Low Est.	High Est.	Rarity	1932 list price
1	Frame, 3⅝", curly maple	$100.00	$200.00	2.00	$1.00
2	Frame, 4¾", curly maple	$125.00	$225.00	2.00	$1.50
3	Frame, 5⅝", curly maple	$125.00	$225.00	2.00	$2.00
3A	Shaving glass, 4½", curly maple	$250.00	$425.00	3.00	$2.75
3B	Shaving glass, 5½", curly maple	$300.00	$475.00	3.00	$3.75
4	Pepper shaker, curly maple	$250.00	$375.00	2.33	$1.00
5	Salt shaker, curly maple	$275.00	$400.00	2.33	$2.75
6	Ink well, curly maple	$175.00	$300.00	2.50	$1.25
7	Snuff box, curly maple	$220.00	$325.00	2.50	$1.75
8	Handy box, 3", curly maple	$250.00	$350.00	2.50	$2.50
9	Handy box, 4", curly maple	$275.00	$375.00	2.50	$3.00
10	Shot well, curly maple	$175.00	$325.00	3.33	$1.00
11	Pen tray, curly maple	$175.00	$300.00	2.50	$2.50
12	Candlestick, 8"	$300.00	$400.00	2.50	$3.50
19	Wafer holder, boxwood	$175.00	$400.00	3.67	$3.00
20	Handy box, 7"	$275.00	$325.00	2.50	$7.50
25	Cup, curly maple	$200.00	$325.00	3.00	$1.20
25B	Goblet, curly maple	$250.00	$400.00	3.00	$1.80
26	Reversible plate, 8"	$225.00	$325.00	2.50	$3.00
27	Salt, 2½", curly maple	$175.00	$275.00	2.33	$0.60
28	Salt, individual	$125.00	$225.00	2.33	$0.45
29	Saucer, curly maple	$150.00	$300.00	3.67	$0.80
30	Plate, 9", curly maple	$225.00	$325.00	3.67	$3.60
30B	Plate, 8", curly maple	$225.00	$325.00	3.00	$3.00
31	Candlestick, low	$200.00	$375.00	2.67	$1.80
31B	Candlestick, small	$200.00	$325.00	2.00	$0.75
41	Toddy stick, large	$100.00	$150.00	3.00	$1.00

The 0 – 99 Series: Treenware, Clocks, Finials, and Miscellaneous

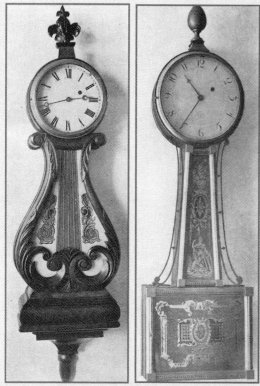

#63 Curtis Lyre clock (l); #61 banjo gold leaf clock (r), both from the Wallace Nutting furniture catalog

#68B Philadelphia clock, with added panel (l); #59B Willard inlaid clock (r), both from the Wallace Nutting furniture catalogs

#65 Goddard hall clock, with block front and shell carvings (l); #60 Goddard hall clock, mahogany, with shell carving, both from the Wallace Nutting furniture catalog

#65 Goddard hall clock, with block front and two shell carvings. Photo courtesy of the Bill & Gretchen Hamann collection.

Close-up #65 Goddard hall clock, with block front and two shell carvings. Photo courtesy of the Bill & Gretchen Hamann collection.

The 0 – 99 Series: Treenware, Clocks, Finials, and Miscellaneous

Clocks: When it comes to Wallace Nutting clocks, we have only personally seen and sold one banjo clock, and are aware of only one unsigned case clock which is even attributed to Wallace Nutting. As a result I don't have many photographs to share with you here. Although Wallace Nutting wrote a book on clocks (*The Clock Book*, 1924), and although he pictured both case clocks and banjo clocks in his furniture catalogs, speculation is that he sold extremely few clocks over the years because long-time collectors as a group report hearing of so few Wallace Nutting clocks. It should also be understood that although Wallace Nutting did make the clock cases, the movements were purchased elsewhere and added to his cases.

Because so few collectors have ever heard of a Wallace Nutting clock, some collectors have speculated that many of the clocks pictured in Nutting's furniture catalogs were old (period) clocks rather than reproductions. In his 1937 *Wallace Nutting Furniture Catalog, Final Edition* Nutting states: "We have specialized for a long time on clocks. We almost always have rare or unusual old clocks on sale. In particular we have the pillar and scroll clock, old, or we would make new ones…. We are also making the banjo clock…." This wording certainly seems to suggest that Wallace Nutting spent more time selling and working on older, period clocks than he did reproducing newer clocks. The possibility exists that Wallace Nutting pictured "old" clocks in his catalogs, implying that he could make a clock that looked just like the one pictured in the catalog.

Either way, you should recognize that Wallace Nutting clocks are extremely rare and will have substantial value associated with them if located and authenticated. Hence, the high estimated value and rarity factors here.

Please note that the clock values suggested in this section are strictly nothing more than educated guesses by knowledgeable Wallace Nutting collectors. None of us are aware of a single case clock ever appearing in the public marketplace.

Clock Price Guide

#	Clocks	Low Est.	High Est.	Rarity	1932 list price
59	Clock, Willard, quarter column	$14,850.00	$18,000.00	5.00	$450.00
59B	Clock, Willard (w\o, quarter column)	$14,675.00	$17,900.00	5.00	$425.00
60	Clock, hall, mahogany, shell	$11,000.00	$22,500.00	5.00	$560.00
61	Clock, banjo, gold leaf	$3,000.00	$4,275.00	4.33	$110.00
62	Clock bracket, gold leaf	$100.00	$150.00	4.50	$20.00
63	Clock, Curtis, lyre	$3,500.00	$4,925.00	4.33	$200.00
64	Clock, Curtis, mahogany & gold	$13,000.00	$17,000.00	4.67	$570.00
65	Clock, Hall, block & shell	$16,675.00	$23,675.00	5.00	$600.00
66	Clock, Hall, block & shell, brass face	$17,825.00	$22,000.00	5.00	$625.00
68	Clock, Philadelphia type	$14,000.00	$17,175.00	5.00	$475.00
68B	Clock, Philadelphia type, w\added panel	$14,500.00	$17,675.00	5.00	$500.00
69	Clock, shelf, mahogany	$3,450.00	$5,500.00	4.50	$250.00
70	Clock, shelf, painted	$3,450.00	$5,500.00	4.50	$250.00

The 0 – 99 Series: Treenware, Clocks, Finials, and Miscellaneous

Assorted finials, from the 1937 furniture catalog.

Wallace Nutting finials advertisement, **Antiques***, July, 1929*

Finials: One Wallace Nutting product line that you will rarely (never) see are finials. Advertised in most of his furniture catalogs, I have never even heard of a confirmed Wallace Nutting finial being available, let alone seen one. And even if I saw one, I don't think that I could confirm it with a 100% degree of certainty. Nutting's furniture catalogs showed more than 60 different finials that he was supposedly creating but none were ever marked and to the best of our knowledge, none are ever identifiable. Therefore, we have not even attempted to place a value on any of Nutting's finials in this book. However, the following is a listing of finials from his furniture catalog.

Finials

#	Finials	1932 list price
34	Finial, big ball, 7½"	$3.00
37	Finial, highboy spiral	$7.00
38	Finial, Chapin open scroll, 11½"	$9.00
42	Finial, Queen Anne, walnut, 7¼"	$1.80
42B	Finial, Queen Anne, spiral, 7"	$5.00
43	Finial, Pennsylvania, clock, 6"	$5.70
43B	Finial, miniature, for glass	$0.60
44	Finial, Goddard clock	$7.50
44B	Finial, Goddard clock (wider)	$9.00
45	Finial, clock or highboy	$6.90
45B	Finial, seventeenth century drop (for table)	$0.60
46	Finial, bookcase, spiral	$6.00
46B	Finial, acorn\banjo, pine, gilded	$4.50
47	Finial, large spiral, 6¾"	$7.50
48	Finial, urn, spiral, 6"	$7.50
48B	Finial, urn, roll edge, 7¼"	$9.00

The 0 – 99 Series: Treenware, Clocks, Finials, and Miscellaneous

#	Finials	1932 list price
49	Finial, slender spiral, 8"	$7.50
49B	Finial, mahogany spiral, 7"	$7.50
50	Finial, Goddard highboy	$13.00
50B	Finial, mirror, pine, gilded, drop	$7.50
51	Finial, Goddard highboy (larger)	$13.00
51B	Finial, secretary or highboy (odd)	$7.50
52	Finial, Philadelphia, 7½"	$9.00
52B	Finial, Chapin, 7"	$1.25
53	Finial, largest Penn. chest on chest	$9.90
53B	Finial, crude maple, 8"	$6.00
54	Finial, bed, 4 ⅞"	$1.00
54B	Finial, bed, 4¾"	$1.00
54C	Finial, small bed, 5"	$1.00
54D	Finial, bed, 1⅜"	$1.00
54E	Finial, bed, 1⅜" (narrower)	$0.75
55	Finial, seventeenth century drop leaf table, 3¼"	$0.75
55B	Finial, seventeenth century drop leaf mirror, 3¼"	$0.60
55C	Finial, Queen Anne drop, 2¾"	$0.60
55D	Finial, Queen Anne table drop, ¾"	$0.60
55E	Finial, Queen Anne drop, miniature	$0.60
56B	Finial, gilded, 3½"	$4.50
57	Finial, large table, 8¼"	$2.00
57B	Finial, larger intersection	$2.00
58	Finial, for X intersection, 4¼"	$2.75
58C	Finial, tambour secretary, 4"	$1.00
76	Finial, largest carved	$22.50
77	Finial, large carved Foliage	$18.00
78	Finial, reeded lid, narrow frame	$9.00
79	Finial, carved, with Festoons	$90.00
80	Finial, Pennsylvania, large carved urn	$30.00
81	Finial, Chapin secretary finial	$4.00
82	Finial, Chapin, small deep cut	$3.00
83	Finial, urn & spike, like brass	$2.00
84	Finial, urn & spike, like clock	$2.00
85	Finial, spiral, like #46	$5.70
86	Finial, shelf clock, center	$3.00
87	Finial, Thomas Harland	$5.70
88	Finial, Thomas Harland, small	$5.25
89	Finial, tall clock, 4¾"	$1.00
90	Finial, Pennsylvania tall clock, large	$9.00
91	Finial, drop for 3-leg stand, 3½"	$6.00
92	Finial, Connecticut chest-on-chest, 6"	$2.00
93	Finial, shelf clock, 3¼"	$0.90
94	Finial, carved, pointed	$7.50
95	Finial, highboy, 8"	$11.50
96	Finial, drop for lowboy, 3½"	$0.60
97	Finial, large hollow urn, 4½"	$6.00
98	Finial, Connecticut highboy	$5.70

The 0 – 99 Series: Treenware, Clocks, Finials, and Miscellaneous

#17 Windsor tripod candlestand,
pine and maple. Block brand.
$425.00 – 575.00

#21 screw (whirling) tripod
candlestand, tiger maple. Block brand.
$825.00 – 1,500.00

#22 cross base candlestand, pine and
maple. Block brand.
$450.00 – 675.00

Other Assorted Items: Wallace Nutting included some additional pieces of furniture within the 0 – 99 Series, most likely because they didn't conveniently fit under any other the other primary categories. Such items included a pedestal tray, radiator mask, Windsor tripod candlestand, fluted stand, screw (whirling) candlestand, dictionary rest, costumer (coat rack); pole screens, and a mahogany knife box.

Other Assorted Items Price Guide

#	Other Assorted Items	Low Est.	High Est.	Rarity	1932 list price
14	Pedestal tray, mahogany	$375.00	$650.00	3.33	$9.00
15	Radiator mask (price per foot)	$550.00	$825.00	3.33	$12.00/ft
16	Tripod hub stand, Pennsylvania turnings	$575.00	$875.00	2.00	
17	Candlestand, NE Windsor tripod (Block)	$425.00	$575.00	1.00	$13.00
17	Candlestand, NE Windsor tripod (paper label)	$425.00	$625.00	1.00	
17	Candlestand, NE Windsor tripod (script)	$375.00	$575.00	1.33	$11.00
18	Fluted stand	$400.00	$625.00	2.50	$30.00
21	Candlestand, screw	$825.00	$1,500.00	2.00	$36.00
22	Candlestand, cross base	$450.00	$675.00	2.00	$18.00
23	Dictionary rest	$425.00	$625.00	2.33	$25.00
24	Costumer	$450.00	$725.00	3.00	$24.00
32	Pole screen, Hepplewhite	$1,400.00	$2,125.00	3.67	$36.00
33	Knife box, mahogany	$525.00	$825.00	3.50	$9.00
35	Pole Screen, mahogany	$1,375.00	$1,625.00	3.50	$34.00
36	Pole Screen, carved	$1,725.00	$2,450.00	3.67	$75.00
40	Hat rack, spinning wheel, maple	$525.00	$825.00	2.00	$12.00

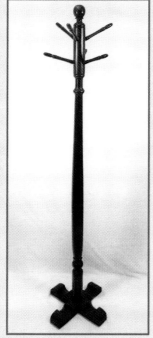

#24 costumer (coat rack), pine and maple.
Block brand. $450.00 – 725.00

#40 spinning wheel hat rack, maple. Block brand.
$525.00 – 825.00

Summary of Key Points

• Wallace Nutting treenware is often unmarked and can command strong prices if marked or properly attributed.

• Wallace Nutting clocks are extremely rare and will be difficult to authenticate if unmarked. If found and authenticated, certain Wallace Nutting case clocks could command $10,000.00 – 20,000.00.

• Wallace Nutting finials were never marked and are almost impossible to authenticate.

• Certain miscellaneous items such as candlestands, pole screens, knife boxes, coat and hat racks may also be found in the 0 – 99 Series.

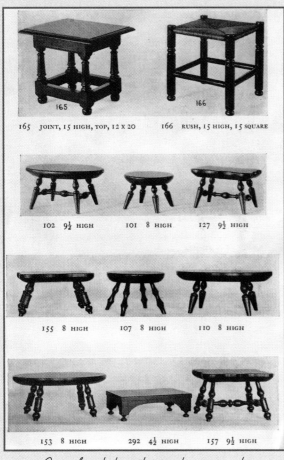

165   JOINT, 15 HIGH, TOP, 12 X 20   166   RUSH, 15 HIGH, 15 SQUARE

102   9½ HIGH   101   8 HIGH   127   9½ HIGH

155   8 HIGH   107   8 HIGH   110   8 HIGH

153   8 HIGH   292   4½ HIGH   157   9½ HIGH

Assorted stools, from the 1930 furniture catalog

#101 round Windsor stool, light maple finish, paper label.
$250.00 – 500.00

#102 oval Windsor stool. Block brand. $275.00 – 525.00

#143 Pennsylvania ogee stool,
dark finish, paper label.
$425.00 – 475.00

#161 joint stool, 18" splayed
legs, light maple finish. Block
brand. $500.00 – 825.00

#153 Pennsylvania oval stool, light mahogany.
Block brand. $375.00 – 625.00

The 100 – 200 Series: Stools, Signs, and Children's Chairs

#161-C joint stool, 24" splayed legs, light maple finish. Block brand.
$500.00 – 850.00

#164 Brewster three-leg stool, original rush, dark finish. Block brand under stretcher.
$400.00 – 700.00

18" rush #167 rushed four-leg stool, replaced rush, light maple finish. Block brand under stretcher. $450.00 – 700.00

#162-B, joint stool, short form with four splayed legs, light maple finish. Block brand. $500.00 – 850.00

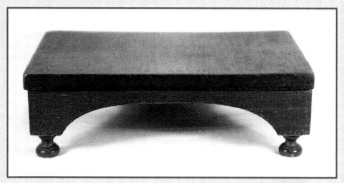

#292 gothic stool, light maple finish, block brand. Can't explain why WN gave this stool a 200 number. $425.00 – 750.00

Stools: Wallace Nutting stools are fairly common, primarily because of the rarity rule. That is, the lower the original cost, the greater the quantity that were most likely sold. Some Wallace Nutting stools were relatively inexpensive when first sold and would be considered fairly common today. Most Nutting stools appear in the Windsor form, with both New England and Pennsylvania turnings, light maple and darker mahogany finishes, and with or without stretchers. But other stool forms are also fairly common including joint stools, Jacobean stools, Brewster stools, three-leg, four-leg, and six-leg stools, among others. Most other stools were made of maple with the light maple finish.

They are petite, can fit basically in any house or apartment environment, and their relatively low price makes stools often the first Wallace Nutting furniture purchase for many newer collectors.

The 100 – 200 Series: Stools, Signs, and Children's Chairs

Stool Price Guide

#	Stools	Low Est.	High Est.	Rarity	1932 List Price
101	Stool, Windsor, round (block)	$250.00	$500.00	1.33	$5.50
101	Stool, round cricket (paper label)	$300.00	$600.00	1.00	
102	Stool, Windsor, oval (block)	$275.00	$525.00	1.67	$9.00
102	Stool, oval cricket (paper label)	$325.00	$625.00	1.33	
103	Stool, milking, with handle (block)	$325.00	$550.00	2.67	$2.00
103	Stool, 3-leg cricket with stretchers (paper label)	$400.00	$625.00	2.33	
104	Stool, boot jack, fish shape	$400.00	$600.00	3.00	$3.00
105	Stool, square ogee cricket	$400.00	$625.00	2.33	
106	Stool, 3-leg cricket	$400.00	$625.00	2.33	
107	Stool, bamboo, round	$325.00	$600.00	2.33	$5.50
110	Stool, New England, oval	$300.00	$525.00	1.67	$7.50
111	Stool, bamboo round cricket	$350.00	$625.00	2.67	
112	Stool, bamboo oval cricket, with stretchers	$375.00	$650.00	2.67	
115	Stool, bamboo square ogee cricket	$375.00	$650.00	2.67	
121	Stool, Pennsylvania, round	$350.00	$625.00	2.33	
122	Stool, Pennsylvania, round with stretcher	$350.00	$625.00	2.33	
124	Stool, Pennsylvania, 3-leg	$350.00	$625.00	2.33	
125	Stool, Pennsylvania, square ogee	$350.00	$625.00	2.33	
127	Stool, New England, ogee (block)	$350.00	$600.00	2.00	$10.00
127	Stool, oblong ogee cricket with stretchers (paper label)	$350.00	$625.00	2.33	
136	Stool, square ogee Rhode Island cricket	$350.00	$625.00	2.33	
143	Stool, Pennsylvania, ogee (block)	$375.00	$600.00	2.33	$15.00
143	Stool, Pennsylvania, ogee (paper label)	$425.00	$725.00	2.00	
144	Stool, Sheraton window seat	$825.00	$1,600.00	4.00	$100.00
145	Stool, Windsor, round	$400.00	$625.00	2.67	$13.50
145	Stool, Northern round	$375.00	$650.00	2.00	
145	Windsor stool (script)	$350.00	$650.00	2.00	$12.00
153	Stool, Pennsylvania, oval (block)	$300.00	$600.00	2.67	$7.50
153	Stool, Pennsylvania round stool, no stretcher (paper label)	$375.00	$625.00	2.33	
155	Stool, Pennsylvania, ogee	$350.00	$650.00	2.67	$7.50
156	Stool, oblong ogee cricket, no stretchers	$375.00	$650.00	2.67	
157	Stool, Pennsylvania oblong ogee	$225.00	$650.00	2.50	
161	Stool, joint, 18", splayed leg	$500.00	$825.00	2.33	$24.00
161A	Stool, joint, 20"	$500.00	$850.00	3.00	$27.00

The 100 – 200 Series: Stools, Signs, and Children's Chairs

#	Stools	Low Est.	High Est.	Rarity	1932 List Price
161B	Stool, joint, 22"	$500.00	$850.00	3.00	$28.00
161C	Stool, joint, 24"	$500.00	$850.00	3.00	$29.00
162	Stool, 4-leg long form	$750.00	$1,150.00	3.00	$54.00
162B	Stool, 4-leg short form	$650.00	$975.00	3.00	$50.00
163	Stool, 6-leg long form	$825.00	$1,325.00	3.00	$70.00
164	Stool, Brewster, 3-leg	$400.00	$700.00	1.33	$17.00
165	Stool, low joint	$475.00	$750.00	2.33	$22.50
166	Stool, 15", rushed seat	$400.00	$675.00	2.33	$13.00
167	Stool, 18", rushed seat	$450.00	$700.00	2.67	$19.50
168	Stool, 22", rushed seat	$500.00	$800.00	2.67	$21.00
169	Stool, 29", rushed seat	$525.00	$825.00	2.67	$24.00
170	Stool, Jacobean, 20" long	$675.00	$1,000.00	3.00	$27.00
171	Stool, Jacobean, 30" long	$825.00	$1,175.00	3.33	$32.00
173	Stool, pine trestle	$775.00	$1,200.00	3.67	$37.50
174	Stool, Dutch walnut	$550.00	$900.00	3.50	$54.00
174B	Stool, Dutch walnut with carved knee	$750.00	$1,700.00	2.67	$59.00
179	Stool, Chippendale	$625.00	$1,000.00	4.00	$66.00
179B	Stool, Chippendale, carved hip	$700.00	$1,200.00	4.00	$88.00
180	Stool, Chippendale	$525.00	$825.00	3.67	$42.00
290	Bench, maple, 6 legs	$1,100.00	$1,600.00	2.00	$42.00
292	Stool, Gothic	$425.00	$750.00	3.00	$6.60

Signs: There isn't a great deal to say about Wallace Nutting signs because I have never seen one and have never even heard of one existing. The 1930 furniture catalog listed tavern signs as well as simple and elaborate signs, with a total of seven signs appearing in that catalog. It is doubtful that they were ever marked and it is even more doubtful that any clearly identifiable and verifiable signs will ever appear.

Sign Price Guide

#	Signs	Low Est.	High Est.	Rarity	1932 List Price
175	Sign, lettered tavern	$500.00	$900.00	4.33	$36.00
175B	Sign, lettered tavern, with stage coach	$576.00	$1,000.00	4.50	$52.00
176	Sign, tavern, large oval	$625.00	$950.00	4.50	$52.00
176B	Sign, tavern, large oval, with stage coach	$750.00	$1,100.00	4.50	$70.00
177	Sign, simple light	$675.00	$1,200.00	4.00	$24.00
178	Sign, large elaborate	$800.00	$1,425.00	4.33	$80.00
178B	Sign, large elaborate, with painted design	$850.00	$1,500.00	4.33	$100.00

#175 lettered sign, from the 1930 Wallace Nutting furniture catalog

The 100 – 200 Series: Stools, Signs, and Children's Chairs

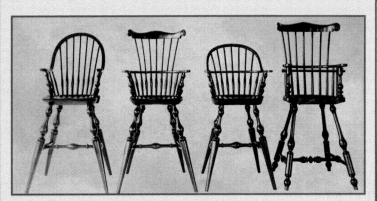

Four child's chairs from the 1937 furniture catalog, left-to-right:
#210, #201, #205, #209

#210 child's Windsor high chair. Block brand.
$1,500.00 – 2,000.00

Unknown, child's Windsor high chair with liftable food tray. Block brand.
$1,500.00 – 2,000.00

#211, child's comb back Windsor arm chair. Block brand. Sold at our March 2003 auction for $2,970.00

Windsor fan back child's chair, with plain ears and no stretchers. Block brand. Photo courtesy of the Sharon & Kenny Lacasse collection.
$1,200.00 – 1,800.00

Three-back New England ladderback child's chair, with rush seat and sausage turned foot rest. Photo courtesy of the Sharon & Kenny Lacasse collection. $1,250.00 – 1,750.00

Child's Chairs: Wallace Nutting child's chairs represent a highly popular and increasingly expensive category of Nutting furniture. Child's chairs come in the form of high chairs and smaller versions of adult-sized chairs. Most child's chairs are Windsors, but at least one style of New England ladderback child's rushed chair was also produced. Their petite size makes them desirable to nearly all collectors today. Few people would readily allow a child to use a Nutting child's chair today, but some are used to display dolls.

It was actually his child's chairs that apparently led Nutting to phase out his paper label which was replaced by the hard-to-delete branded signature. In the 1930 furniture catalog Nutting tells the following story: "A child's high chair made by me, and sold as new for nineteen dollars, was artificially aged and resold for a cool thousand. Nobody but the maker could have discovered the imposition."

Child's Chair Price Guide

#	Child's Chairs	Low Est.	High Est.	Rarity	1932 List Price
201	Child's high chair, comb-back Windsor	$1,300.00	$2,000.00	3.67	
204	Baby's chair, slat back (block)	$900.00	$1,300.00	3.50	$24.00
204	Child's high chair, New England Windsor (paper label)	$1,200.00	$1,725.00	4.00	
205	Child's high chair, bow-back Windsor	$1,200.00	$1,676.00	3.67	
207	Child's arm chair, NE low Windsor	$1,700.00	$2,525.00	3.33	
208	Child's arm chair, low bow-back Windsor	$1,700.00	$2,525.00	3.33	
209	Baby's chair, Pennsylvania high chair (block)	$1,550.00	$2,125.00	3.67	$48.00
209	Child's high chair, Pennsylvania comb back Windsor (paper label)	$1,700.00	$2,300.00	3.50	
210	Baby's chair, Windsor high chair (block)	$1,500.00	$2,000.00	3.67	$42.00
210	Child's arm chair, low Pennsylvania Windsor (paper label)	$1,650.00	$2,250.00	4.00	
211	Baby's chair, Windsor low comb back (block)	$1,500.00	$2,000.00	3.67	$24.00
211	Child's arm chair, low comb-back Windsor (paper label)	$1,800.00	$2,400.00	4.00	

Summary of Key Points

• Wallace Nutting stools are fairly common, came in a variety of forms, are usually marked and reasonably priced, and are often the first piece of Wallace Nutting furniture purchased by new collectors.

• Wallace Nutting signs are extremely rare. They were probably never signed or marked, would be extremely difficult to authenticate, and we have never seen one single sign in 30 years.

• Wallace Nutting child's chairs are quite unusual, very popular with collectors, and command top prices when they appear in the marketplace.

#451 Windsor writing arm chair, with New England turnings, and drawer under seat. Block brand. From the 1930 Wallace Nutting furniture catalog.
$2,500.00 – 3,500.00

#440 Windsor writing arm chair, with Pennsylvania turnings, and drawer under seat. Block brand. From the 1930 Wallace Nutting furniture catalog.
$2,500.00 – 3,500.00

Spanish footed baluster side and arm chairs. #380 side chair (l) and #480 arm chair (r).

People didn't necessarily need fine beds, chests, cupboards, desks, dressers, settees, settles, or case and cabinet pieces. But they did need chairs. Kitchen chairs, dining room chairs, bedroom chairs, hall chairs, and parlor chairs. Everyone needs to sit down at some point throughout the day. Therefore, Wallace Nutting sold more chairs than any other single form of furniture. And considering that many of Nutting's chairs were lower in price and that chairs were typically produced in sets of four, that translates in Wallace Nutting reproducing more side chairs and arm chairs than any other single furniture form.

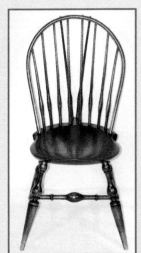

#301 Windsor brace back side chair, New England turnings. Block brand.
$525.00 – 800.00

#326 Windsor brace back, fan back side chair, New England turnings and carved ears. Block brand.
$50.00 – 925.00

#311 Windsor fan back side chair with imposed comb, paper label.
$725.00 – 1,150.00

#349 Windsor slipper side chair, New England turnings and turned ear. Only 15"high to aid in slipper removal. Block brand.
$625.00 – 1,000.00

#349 Windsor slipper side chair, New England turnings and carved ear. Only 15" high to aid in slipper removal. Block brand.
$625.00 – 1,000.00

Side chairs: Windsor chairs are the most common Wallace Nutting chair form that you will find for several reasons. First, the Windsor chair form has probably been the most popular chair form with most Americans throughout the early twentieth century. It was comfortable, dignified, and was most closely identified with early colonial America probably more-so than any other furniture form.

Secondly, Nutting started producing Windsor chairs in 1918. They were the first form that he began reproducing and selling to the general public. Therefore he had 24 years (1918 – 1941) to sell Windsors chairs. This contrasts the only 16 years (1926 – 1941) that he was able to market and sell his later furniture designs which included the financially depressed 1930s.

And finally, in the early years Nutting had nearly 100 different Windsor designs. Some were dropped because of production difficulties or a lack of sales, while a few others were added in the later years. But with nearly 100 different Windsor designs, often sold in sets of four it shouldn't be surprising that you will find more Windsor chairs, both side chairs and arm chairs, than any other type of Wallace Nutting chair or furniture form.

#305 Windsor bent rung side chair, bamboo turnings. Block brand. Although this chair is fairly unusual, the bamboo turning is not as popular as the New England or Pennsylvania turnings with collectors.
$700.00 – 950.00

#329 Windsor swivel side chair. Block brand. Note that this chair actually "swivels" upon a metal rod in the seat, similar to a piano stool, which is what this chair was often used for. $675.00 – 925.00

#374 Maple light three-back ladderback side chair. A very plain chair and Nutting's simplest rushed chair. Block brand.
$500.00 – $700.00

#393 maple pilgrim side chair. Block brand.
$475.00 – 725.00

#392 maple four-back ladderback side chair. Block brand. $625.00 – 825.00 (with minor rush damage)

#390 maple five-back ladderback side chair. Script brand. $575.00 – 775.00 (with minor rush damage).

#365 maple wild rose side chair. Note that "wild rose" refers to the carving on the crest rail. Block brand.
$675.00 – 950.00

#380 Spanish footed baluster side chair. Block brand.
$800.00 – 1,100.00

119

The 300 – 400 Series: Side Chairs and Arm Chairs

#334 Philadelphia Chippendale side chair, with highly carved knees and back. Block brand.
$1,000.00 – 1,500.00

Hepplewhite John Goddard side chair with exquisite egyptian wing-type back. Block brand. Photo courtesy Sharon & Kenny Lacasse collection.
$1,000.00 – 2,000.00

#356 Chippendale mahogany carved side chair. Block brand. Photo courtesy Sharon & Kenny Lacasse collection.
$1,100.00 – 1,725.00

#359 Chippendale mahogany carved four-back side chair. Block brand. Photo courtesy Sharon & Kenny Lacasse collection.
$1,000.00 – 1,500.00

#391 Delaware Valley five-back ladderback side chair. Block brand. Photo courtesy Sharon & Kenny Lacasse collection.
$725.00 – 925.00

#393 Dutch walnut side chair. Block brand. Photo courtesy Bill & Gretchen Hamann collection.
$1,000.00 – 2,000.00

Mahogany upholstered bedroom side chair. Block brand.
$750.00 – 1,500.00

But the Windsor form wasn't the only type of chair that Wallace Nutting produced. Chairs were reproduced in more than 100 different styles ranging from Brewster, Carver, Chippendale, Hepplewhite, Queen Anne, Sheraton, Dutch, Flemish, Cromwellian, and Pilgrim chairs. There were Martha Washington, Connecticut Senate, Goddard, and Philadelphia chairs. Woods included maple, tiger maple, mahogany, and walnut. Plain chairs and highly carved and decorated chairs were offered. Many chairs were rushed, upholstered, or leathered. Some chairs were fairly inexpensive, but the best-of-the-best were not cheap.

Rushed Side Chairs: Wallace Nutting produced approximately ten different rushed side chairs. Some were apparently good sellers because they are fairly common today. The biggest problem with rushed chairs today is damage to the original rush. A collector's biggest dilemma with rushed chairs is this: If you sit, you run the risk of harming the original rush, especially if there is already some damage. Conversely, if you replace the original rush, you can use the chair, but you harm the value. What should you do?

My Advice: Enjoy the chair. If you want to sit in the chair, do it. If the rush breaks, re-rush it. The value of any Wallace Nutting rushed side chairs will not make or break your financial portfolio so my suggestion is that you enjoy it.

Queen Anne, Chippendale, Hepplewhite, and Other High-Styled Side Chairs: These chairs represent the finest and rarest chairs made by Wallace Nutting and extremely few have surfaced. These were usually mahogany, usually hand carved, often upholstered, and are quite rare today. If you already own some, congratulations. If you plan on acquiring some, they will probably cost you dearly.

Side Chair Price Guide

#	Side Chairs	Low Est.	High Est.	Rarity	1932 List Price
301	Side chair, Windsor bow back, with brace (block)	$525.00	$800.00	1.00	$29.00
301	Side chair, Early braced bow-back (paper label)	$500.00	$775.00	1.00	
301	Side chair, early bow-back, braced Windsor (script)	$400.00	$625.00	1.00	$24.00
302	Side chair, Windsor bow back, no brace	$450.00	$775.00	1.00	$25.00
303	Side chair, small braced bow back, Rhode Island leg	$525.00	$800.00	1.00	
305	Side chair, bamboo, bent rung (block)	$700.00	$950.00	3.00	$30.00
305	Side chair, bent rung bamboo Windsor (paper label)	$550.00	$850.00	1.33	
305	Side chair, bent-rung bamboo (script)	$500.00	$675.00	1.33	$28.00
306	Side chair, bamboo Windsor with straight stretcher	$525.00	$875.00	2.00	
309	Side chair, Windsor fan back, no brace (block)	$600.00	$825.00	1.00	$25.00
309	Side chair, Pennsylvania fan back Windsor (paper label)	$600.00	$925.00	1.50	
310	Side chair, Windsor, no brace (block)	$600.00	$825.00	1.33	$25.00
310	Side chair, light fan back Windsor with plain ear (paper label)	$575.00	$775.00	1.00	
310	Side chair, light fan back, plain ear (script)	$450.00	$625.00	1.00	$28.00
311	Side chair, Windsor w/imposed comb (block)	$800.00	$1,050.00	1.67	$36.00
311	Side chair, fan back with imposed comb (paper label)	$725.00	$1,150.00	1.33	
311	Side chair, fan back, imposed comb (script)	$625.00	$1,000.00	1.00	$32.00
312	Side chair, northern early braced fan back Windsor	$675.00	$1,000.00	2.00	

The 300 – 400 Series: Side Chairs and Arm Chairs

#	*Side Chairs*	*Low Est.*	*High Est.*	*Rarity*	*1932 List Price*
313	Side chair, Pennsylvania square seat braced fan back Windsor	$675.00	$1,000.00	2.00	
316	Side chair, small braced bow back, Rhode Island leg, with larger seat	$675.00	$1,000.00	2.00	
319	Side chair, hub & spoke bamboo Windsor	$675.00	$1,050.00	2.00	
323	Side chair, Pennsylvania slipper Windsor	$575.00	$900.00	1.67	
325	Side chair, Chippendale (block)	$1,100.00	$1,500.00	2.33	$150.00
325	Side chair, light plain braced fan back (paper label)	$850.00	$1,175.00	2.50	
325B	Side chair, Queen Anne	$1,150.00	$1,525.00	2.33	$120.00
326	Side chair, Windsor fan back w/ brace (block)	$650.00	$925.00	1.00	$29.00
326	Side chair, braced fan back Windsor (paper label)	$650.00	$925.00	1.00	
326	Side chair, fan-back Windsor chair (script)	$625.00	$800.00	1.50	$32.00
326B	Side chair, Windsor fan back with brace, in curly maple	$825.00	$1,200.00	2.67	$36.00
327	Side chair, standard fan back Windsor	$750.00	$900.00	2.00	
329	Side chair, Windsor swivel	$675.00	$925.00	2.00	$42.00
333	Side chair, Windsor comb back (block)	$800.00	$1,200.00	2.33	$33.00
333	Side chair, braced bow-back Windsor, imposed comb (paper label)	$775.00	$1,275.00	2.00	
333	Side chair, braced bow-back imposed comb (script)	$700.00	$925.00	2.00	$28.00
334	Side chair, Chippendale, carved, fluted	$950.00	$1,500.00	3.33	$180.00
335	Side chair, Sheraton, carved (block)	$850.00	$1,325.00	3.00	$120.00
335	Side chair, high, flat bow back (paper label)	$650.00	$1,000.00	2.50	
336	Side chair, high, flat bow, braced-back	$700.00	$1,050.00	2.00	
337	Side chair, John Goddard Hepplewhite	$925.00	$1,575.00	3.00	$135.00
338	Side chair, Hepplewhite, tied reed back	$825.00	$1,400.00	3.00	$135.00
338B	Side chair, Hepplewhite, no carving	$825.00	$1,300.00	3.00	$90.00
341	Side chair, Hepplewhite, 3-feather	$900.00	$1,450.00	3.00	$147.00
342	Side chair, Hepplewhite, 3-reed back	$825.00	$1,400.00	3.00	$135.00
342B	Side chair, Hepplewhite, not carved	$725.00	$1,050.00	3.00	$100.00
343	Side chair, Chippendale, richest type	$1,200.00	$1,750.00	3.00	$300.00
346	Side chair, round seat Pennsylvania Windsor	$650.00	$950.00	3.33	
349	Side chair, Windsor slipper chair (block)	$575.00	$850.00	1.50	$26.00
349	Side chair, fan back, plain ear slipper chair (paper label)	$625.00	$1,000.00	1.67	

The 300 – 400 Series: Side Chairs and Arm Chairs

#	Side Chairs	Low Est.	High Est.	Rarity	1932 List Price
350	Side chair, Pennsylvania square seat braced slipper chair	$675.00	$1,050.00	2.33	
355	Side chair, Windsor high desk chair	$600.00	$850.00	1.50	$31.00
356	Side chair, Chippendale, mahogany	$1,100.00	$1,725.00	3.33	$150.00
358	Side chair, Chippendale, carved, fluted	$825.00	$1,375.00	3.33	$130.00
359	Side chair, Chippendale, 4-ladder back	$1,000.00	$1,500.00	3.33	$135.00
359	Side chair, Carver (script)	$700.00	$1,100.00	2.67	$40.00
359B	Side chair, Chippendale, carved ladders	$925.00	$1,500.00	3.33	$130.00
360	Side chair, Cromwellian, leather	$600.00	$800.00	3.00	$78.00
360B	Side chair, Cromwellian, grain leather	$550.00	$800.00	3.00	$63.00
361	Side chair, Dutch, turned, rush seat	$525.00	$800.00	3.33	$29.00
362	Side chair, Chippendale, 3-ladder	$825.00	$1,100.00	3.00	$75.00
363	Side chair, Chippendale, ribbon back	$900.00	$1,450.00	3.00	$75.00
363B	Side chair, Chippendale, ribbon back, fully carved	$1,100.00	$1,675.00	3.00	$80.00
364	Side chair, Carver, maple, rush seat	$575.00	$800.00	2.50	$40.00
365	Side chair, wild rose, maple, rush seat	$675.00	$950.00	2.67	$36.00
369	Side chair, Chippendale, French scroll	$900.00	$1,550.00	3.00	$195.00
371	Side chair, Hepplewhite, shield back	$900.00	$1,550.00	3.00	$150.00
375	Side chair, Spanish foot, fiddleback	$675.00	$925.00	2.67	$54.00
375B	Side chair, Spanish foot, fiddleback, Turned foot	$650.00	$900.00	2.67	$51.00
375C	Side chair, Spanish foot, fiddleback, carved back	$1,050.00	$1,000.00	2.67	$57.00
376	Side chair, Flemish, carved	$950.00	$1,450.00	3.00	$240.00
377	Side chair, 3-slat, maple, rush seat	$475.00	$650.00	1.50	$27.00
380	Side chair, Spanish foot, baluster	$800.00	$1,100.00	2.67	$69.00
390	Side chair, New England 5-back, maple, rush seat	$625.00	$850.00	2.00	$45.00
390	Side chair high back, rush seat (script)	$575.00	$775.00	2.00	$40.00
391	Side chair, Pennsylvania 6-back, rush seat	$725.00	$925.00	3.00	$48.00
392	Side chair, light 4-back	$625.00	$825.00	2.33	$36.00
392B	Side chair, light 4-back, curly maple	$700.00	$850.00	3.00	$42.00
394	Side chair, leather, carved	$775.00	$1,075.00	3.00	$81.00
397	Side chair, Stenographer's swivel	$925.00	$1,225.00	4.00	$81.00
398	Side chair, Dutch, walnut	$775.00	$1,100.00	3.00	$99.00
399	Side chair, Queen Anne, scrolled posts	$1,125.00	$1,450.00	3.00	$147.00
399C	Side chair, ball foot, carved knee	$1,300.00	$1,725.00	3.00	$240.00

The 300 – 400 Series: Side Chairs and Arm Chairs

Arm Chairs: There is not much more to say about arm chairs that hasn't already been said about side chairs, except that arm chairs are much rarer than side chairs. Although some sets of chairs were entirely composed of arm chairs, most sets of four, eight, or twelve chairs were more often than not comprised primarily of side chairs with perhaps only one arm chair per four chairs produced.

#402 New England lady's continuous arm chair with comb. Paper label.
$925.00 – 1,550.00

#405 Windsor bent rung arm chair, bamboo turnings. Block brand. Although this chair is fairly unusual, the bamboo turning is not as popular as the New England or Pennsylvania turnings with collectors.
$750.00 – 1,125.00

#410 Windsor light comb back arm chair. Paper label.
$800.00 – 1,325.00

#412 great Pennsylvania Windsor comb back arm chair. Block brand.
$1,000.00 – 1,500.00

#415 Windsor comb back knuckle arm chair. Block brand.
$1,000.00 – 1,500.00

#419 Windsor double comb back arm chair. Script brand.
$825.00 – 1,150.00

#420 Windsor bow back knuckle arm chair. Block brand.
$950.00 – 1,325.00

#422 Windsor comb back tenon arm chair. Block brand.
$1,000.00 – 1,400.00

#440 Pennsylvania comb back Windsor writing arm chair, with drawer under seat. Block brand.
$2,000.00 – 3,000.00

#477 Windsor rocking arm chair. Script branded signature.
$900.00 – 1,300.00

#426 heart & crown arm chair, with rushed seat.
$500.00 – 700.00 (with damaged rush)

#430 roundabout, or corner, arm chair, with rushed seat.
$675.00 – 1,300.00

Also the rarity rule generally applies to arm chairs. That is, because they were more expensive than comparable side chairs, fewer were produced. For example, a #390 New England five-back ladderback side chair cost $45.00 in 1932 while a comparable #490 arm chair cost $66.00. A #364 Carver side chair cost $40.00 while a #464 Carver arm chair cost $60.00. And a #334 Philadelphia fully carved mahogany side chair cost $180.00 while a #434 arm chair cost $240.00. This translates into arm chairs typically costing anywhere from 25% to 50% more than a comparable side chair. Hence the lower overall arm chair production.

#461 country Dutch arm chair, with rushed seat. Block brand. $775.00 – 1,150.00

#464 maple carver arm chair, with rushed seat. Block brand. $850.00 – 1,400.00

#465 maple wild rose arm chair, with rushed seat. Block brand. $950.00 – 1,425.00

#480 Spanish footed baluster arm chair, with rushed seat. Block brand. $1,100.00 – 1,425.00

#490 New England five-back ladderback arm chair, with rushed seat. Block brand. $825.00 – 1,275.00

#492 maple four-back ladderback arm chair, with rushed seat. Block brand. $800.00 – 1,100.00

#493 maple pilgrim arm chair, with rushed seat. Block brand. $850.00 – 1,225.00

#416 pine wing back single panel settle. Seat lifts to open storage area. We are uncertain why this was numbered as an arm chair rather than a settle. Block brand. $925.00 – 1,675.00

#437 Goddard-type Hepplewhite arm chair with carved bird back. Block brand. $1,200.00 – 2,000.00

#471 mahogany Hepplewhite shield back arm chair, with upholstered seat. Block brand. Photo courtesy of the Sharon & Kenny Lacasse collection. $1,125.00 – 1,825.00

#473 Chippendale Martha Washington upholstered arm chair, with matching upholstered stool. Block brand. Photo courtesy of the Sharon & Kenny Lacasse collection. $800.00 – 1,200.00

The 300 – 400 Series: Side Chairs and Arm Chairs

Arm Chair Price Guide

#	Arm Chairs	Low Est.	High Est.	Rarity	1932 List Price
401	Arm chair, New England Windsor (block)	$700.00	$1,050.00	1.00	$40.50
401	Arm chair, New England brace-back Windsor (paper label)	$700.00	$1,050.00	1.00	
401	New England Windsor arm chair, braced (script)	$600.00	$875.00	1.00	$32.00
402	Arm chair, NE comb back (block)	$900.00	$1,400.00	1.33	$45.00
402	Arm chair, New England Windsor, with imposed comb (paper label)	$925.00	$1,550.00	1.33	
402	Arm chair, New England Windsor imposed comb (script)	$750.00	$1,150.00	1.33	$36.00
404	Arm chair, baby's high chair	$1,025.00	$1,775.00	3.33	$33.00
405	Arm chair, bamboo bent rung	$750.00	$1,125.00	2.50	$36.00
406	Arm chair, wainscot	$1,050.00	$1,450.00	3.00	$90.00
407	Arm chair, Windsor, light comb back	$850.00	$1,400.00	1.67	$57.00
408	Arm chair, Windsor, light bow back, carved (block)	$850.00	$1,325.00	1.33	$49.50
408	Arm chair, bow-back bent-arm Windsor (paper label)	$800.00	$1,250.00	1.67	
409	Arm chair, bent-arm Windsor, with very high bow (block)	$800.00	$1,300.00	2.00	
409	Arm chair, very high bow, bent arm Windsor (script)	$725.00	$1,050.00	1.67	$36.00
410	Arm chair, small light comb-back	$800.00	$1,325.00	2.00	
411	Arm chair, great Brewster (block)	$1,050.00	$1,575.00	2.50	$75.00
411	Arm chair, Brewster chair (script)	$725.00	$1,025.00	2.67	$48.00
412	Arm chair, great Penn Windsor comb back (block)	$1,000.00	$1,500.00	2.33	$57.00
412	Arm chair, large Pennsylvania comb back Windsor (paper label)	$1,100.00	$1,950.00	2.67	
412	Arm chair, Large Pennsylvania comb-back chair (script)	$700.00	$1,125.00	2.33	
413	Arm chair, Pennsylvania low back Windsor (block)	$800.00	$1,200.00	2.33	$40.00
413	Arm chair, low-back Pennsylvania Windsor (paper label)	$650.00	$1,075.00	2.00	$45.00
413B	Arm chair, Pennsylvania low back Windsor, smaller	$675.00	$1,025.00	2.33	$36.00
414	Arm chair, Pennsylvania round comb back Windsor	$650.00	$1,075.00	2.50	
415	Arm chair, Windsor Flair comb back (block)	$1000.00	$1,500.00	1.33	$59.00

The 300 – 400 Series: Side Chairs and Arm Chairs

#	Arm Chairs	Low Est.	High Est.	Rarity	1932 List Price
415	Arm chair, comb-back Windsor (paper label)	$925.00	$1,525.00	1.00	
415	Arm chair, comb-back Windsor (script)	$675.00	$1,025.00	1.00	$40.00
415B	Arm chair, Windsor flair comb back, curly back/brace	$975.00	$1,575.00	2.00	$66.00
416	Arm chair, pine wing, panel (block)	$925.00	$1,675.00	3.33	$42.00
416	Arm chair, comb-back, brace-back Windsor (paper label)	$900.00	$1,350.00	1.67	
419	Arm chair, double comb-back (paper label)	$1,100.00	$199.00	3.00	
419	Arm chair, double comb-back (script)	$825.00	$1,150.00	2.67	$44.00
420	Arm chair, Windsor bow back knuckle arm (block)	$950.00	$1,325.00	1.00	$57.00
420	Arm chair, flared bow-back with heavy arm (paper label)	$950.00	$1,500.00	1.00	
420	Arm chair, bow-back Windsor (script)	$650.00	$1,000.00	1.00	$30.00
421	Arm chair, Windsor w/imposed comb, knuckle arm (block)	$1,125.00	$1,500.00	1.67	$63.00
421	Arm chair, tenoned-arm, brace-back, fan back (paper label)	$1,150.00	$1,725.00	2.00	
422	Arm chair, Windsor tenon, fan back with brace (block)	$1,000.00	$1,400.00	1.67	$57.00
422	Arm chair, tenoned-arm fan back (paper label)	$1,000.00	$1,500.00	2.00	
425	Arm chair, Chippendale	$1,350.00	$1,925.00	2.67	$190.00
425B	Arm chair, Queen Anne	$1,225.00	$1,600.00	2.67	$150.00
426	Arm chair, heart & crown (script)	$800.00	$1,125.00	2.67	$40.00
427	Arm chair, bamboo bent rung (block)	$850.00	$1,225.00	3.00	$42.00
427	Arm chair, bamboo Windsor (paper label)	$850.00	$1,225.00	3.00	
427B	Arm chair, bamboo, w/straight rung	$850.00	$1,225.00	3.00	$39.00
430	Arm chair, roundabout, rush seat (block)	$675.00	$1,300.00	3.00	$45.00
430	Writing arm chair, poet's or student writing Windsor, 2-drawer, no candle slide (paper label)	$2,000.00	$3,200.00	3.67	
431	Arm chair, poet's or student writing Windsor, 2-drawer, with ink well	$2,000.00	$2,850.00	3.50	
432	Arm chair, poet's or student writing Windsor, 2-drawer, with candle slide	$2,000.00	$3,250.00	3.50	
433	Arm chair, poet's or student writing Windsor, 2-drawer, with ink well and candle slide	$2,000.00	$3,450.00	3.50	
434	Arm chair, Chippendale, fluted posts	$1,350.00	$2,250.00	4.00	$240.00
436	Arm chair, Sheraton easy chair	$1,425.00	$2,650.00	4.00	$240.00

The 300 – 400 Series: Side Chairs and Arm Chairs

#	Arm Chairs	Low Est.	High Est.	Rarity	1932 List Price
437	Arm chair, Hepplewhite John Goddard	$1,200.00	$2,000.00	3.33	$168.00
438	Arm chair, Hepplewhite, tied reed back	$1,100.00	$2,025.00	3.00	$169.00
438B	Arm chair, Hepplewhite, not carved	$825.00	$1,325.00	3.00	$135.00
439	Arm chair, bamboo Windsor with hub & spoke stretcher	$850.00	$1,250.00	3.33	
440	Arm chair, Pennsylvania writing arm (block)	$2,000.00	$23000.00	3.33	$98.00
440	Arm chair, Pennsylvania writing (paper label)	$2,500.00	$3,500.00	3.33	
441	Arm chair, Pennsylvania, writing with ink well	$2,200.00	$3,225.00	3.33	
442	Arm chair, 5-reed back (block)	$1,500.00	$2,000.00	3.00	$162.00
442	Arm chair, Pennsylvania, writing with candle slide (paper label)	$2,200.00	$3,275.00	3.33	
442B	Arm chair, 5-reed back, no carving	$1,200.00	$1,550.00	3.00	$138.00
443	Arm chair, Chippendale, engraved (block)	$1,750.00	$2,450.00	3.50	$300.00
443	Writing arm chair, Penn, with ink well & candle slide (paper label)	$2,200.00	$3,125.00	3.33	
451	Arm chair, writing arm, taper turned (block)	$2500.00	$3500.00	3.00	$90.00
451	Arm chair, arm, poet's or student Windsor writing (script)	$1,500.00	$2,100.00	3.00	$70.00
452	Arm chair, Sheraton, Martha Washington	$1,350.00	$2,300.00	3.67	$200.00
456	Arm chair, Chippendale, carved, ball & claw	$1,200.00	$1,950.00	3.33	$180.00
456B	Arm chair, Chippendale, carved knee	$1,250.00	$2,050.00	3.67	$195.00
458	Arm chair, Chippendale, fluted leg	$1,200.00	$1,775.00	3.33	$160.00
459	Arm chair, Chippendale, 4 ladders	$1,050.00	$1,450.00	3.00	$156.00
459B	Arm chair, Chippendale, 4 ladder back	$975.00	$1,600.00	3.00	$150.00
460	Arm chair, Cromwellian leather	$825.00	$1,225.00	3.00	$90.00
461	Arm chair, simple Dutch, rush seat	$775.00	$1,150.00	2.67	$39.00
462	Arm chair, Chippendale, 3 ladders	$825.00	$1,300.00	3.00	$110.00
463	Arm chair, Chippendale, straight leg	$925.00	$1,450.00	3.33	$110.00
463B	Arm chair, Chippendale, straight leg, ribbon back	$925.00	$1,450.00	3.33	$115.00
464	Arm chair, carver, rush seat	$850.00	$1,400.00	3.00	$60.00
464	Arm chair, carver, (script)	$775.00	$1,100.00	3.00	$48.00
465	Arm chair, walnut wing	$1,725.00	$2,325.00	4.00	$210.00
465B	Arm chair, wild rose w/ balusters	$950.00	$1,425.00	3.33	$45.00
466	Arm chair, Chippendale wing with stretchers	$1,900.00	$2,775.00	4.00	$231.00
468	Arm chair, Chippendale wing, straight leg	$1,225.00	$1,800.00	3.67	$141.00
468	Arm chair, bent-arm, bow-back Windsor, imposed comb	$1,475.00	$1,475.00	2.67	
468B	Arm chair, Chippendale wing, straight leg with stretchers	$1,350.00	$2,150.00	3.50	$153.00

The 300 – 400 Series: Side Chairs and Arm Chairs

#	Arm Chairs	Low Est.	High Est.	Rarity	1932 List Price
469	Arm chair, Chippendale, French scroll	$1,300.00	$2,125.00	3.00	$240.00
470	Arm chair, rocking, 5-slat	$1,025.00	$1,825.00	3.33	$48.00
471	Arm chair, Hepplewhite, shield back, mahogany	$1,125.00	$1,825.00	3.33	$195.00
473	Arm chair, Chippendale, Martha Washington	$800.00	$1,200.00	3.50	$135.00
474	Arm chair, cane	$1,000.00	$1,450.00	3.67	$150.00
475	Arm chair, Spanish foot, fiddle back	$800.00	$1,150.00	3.00	$78.00
475B	Arm chair, Spanish foot, fiddle back, turned foot	$800.00	$1,175.00	3.33	$72.00
476	Arm chair, flemish, carved	$1,075.00	$1,325.00	3.00	$180.00
476B	Arm chair, flemish, carved panel	$1,200.00	$1,750.00	3.00	$270.00
477	Arm chair, original Windsor rocker (script)	$900.00	$1,300.00	2.67	$38.00
480	Arm chair, Spanish foot, baluster	$1,100.00	$1,425.00	2.67	$105.00
481	Arm chair, leather easy chair	$1,200.00	$1,700.00	3.67	$168.00
490	Arm chair, New England 5-back (block)	$825.00	$1,275.00	1.33	$66.00
490	Arm chair, New England (script)	$700.00	$1,075.00	1.00	$48.00
491	Arm chair, Penn, 6-back, rush seat	$1,000.00	$1,400.00	2.33	$66.00
492	Arm chair, New England 4-back	$800.00	$1,100.00	1.67	$48.00
493	Arm chair, pilgrim 3-back	$850.00	$1,225.00	2.00	$63.00
493B	Arm chair, lighter pilgrim 3-back	$800.00	$1,075.00	2.00	$57.00
494	Arm chair, carved, leather, walnut	$1,275.00	$1,675.00	3.50	$126.00
495	Arm chair, tip and turn leather	$1,100.00	$1,975.00	4.00	$120.00
496	Arm chair, Chippendale, roundabout	$1,125.00	$1,625.00	3.33	$140.00
496B	Arm chair, Chippendale, roundabout, carved knee	$1,300.00	$1,875.00	3.33	$150.00
498	Arm chair, Dutch, plain saddle	$1,075.00	$1,500.00	3.33	$132.00
499	Arm chair, Queen Anne, scroll	$1,350.00	$1,925.00	4.00	$192.00
499C	Arm chair, ball foot, carved knee	$1,575.00	$2,375.00	4.00	$270.00

Set of four #380 Spanish footed baluster side chairs. Block brand. $2,500.00 – 3,500.00/set

Set of four #390 New England five-back ladderback arm chairs. Script brand. $1,500.00 – 2,500.00/set

Sets of Wallace Nutting Chairs: Sets are unusual and will more often than not command a premium price. For example several years ago we were selling a set of four #361 Country Dutch side chairs. We first sold them individually on a tentative-sale basis. Then we re-offered the four chairs as a set, and the auction terms stated that if we received a bid on the set at least comparable to the sum total of the four individual bid prices, we would negate the individual sales and sell the four chairs as a set to the highest bidder on the floor. The set sold for approximately 25% higher than the sum of the individual chairs which suggests that a set of chairs should bring a premium of approximately 25% higher than if the chairs are sold individually.

Summary of Key Points

• Side chairs are the most common form of Wallace Nutting furniture.

• Side chairs are much more common than arm chairs.

• Windsor side chairs were the most popular Wallace Nutting side chair.

• Formal side and arm chairs are quite rare and are extremely desirable to most collectors today.

• In my opinion Wallace Nutting furniture is meant to be used and, if a rushed side or arm chair needs to be re-rushed, that is totally acceptable.

• Sets of Wallace Nutting chairs can command a premium price of approximately 25% higher than if the chairs were sold individually.

Although Wallace Nutting settles, sofas, and settees were produced in more than 40 different styles, relatively few were sold and they are quite scarce today.

Settles: A settle is basically an all-wooden high-back bench which was normally kept near the fireplace during colonial times. It served as cold weather seating for family members who decided to sit near the fire, and its high wooden back helped to retain the fire's heat closer to the hearth instead of allowing it to more readily dissipate throughout the room. Settles were produced in one-panel, two-panel, three-panel, and four-panel backs. They were typically made of pine and maple. More practical during colonial times than in the early twentieth century, their wooden seats and high backs provided relatively little comfort and Nutting apparently sold relatively few settles.

The Goose Chair Quilt, a Nutting interior scene with a girl in a fireside settle.

#589 3-panel wainscot settle. Block brand. $2,000.00 – 2,700.00

#416 single panel settle, with storage compartment. We can't explain why this was numbered in the 400 series. Block brand. $925.00 – 1,675.00

#513 three-panel settle, with storage compartment. Similar to, but larger than the #416. $1,600.00 – 2,000.00

The 500 Series: Settles, Sofas, and Settees

Settle Price Guide

#	Settles	Low Est.	High Est.	Rarity	1932 List Price
513	Settle, pine, 3-panel	$1,600.00	$2,000.00	3.33	$84.00
513B	Settle, pine, 2-panel	$1,375.00	$1,875.00	3.00	$72.00
589	Settle, wainscot	$2,000.00	$2,700.00	3.00	$186.00

#539 Sheraton mahogany sofa, with inlaid and reeded posts. From the 1930 Wallace Nutting furniture catalog. $2,500.00 – 3,600.00

#525 Chippendale four-leg sofa. Block brand. $3,100.00 – 3,800.00

Sofas: Sofas are another unusual Nutting item. You would have expected sofas to be a popular selling form of Wallace Nutting furniture, yet relatively few have come to our attention over the past 30 years. The fact that Wallace Nutting only produced seven different styles of sofas partially accounts for the scarcity of remaining sofas. The high initial cost also contributed to the relatively low sales. But another more common problem is that because the Wallace Nutting brand is often covered by the upholstery, the Wallace Nutting attribution often is overlooked. Which means that there are probably some Wallace Nutting sofas out there still waiting to be discovered.

Sofa Price Guide

#	Sofas	Low Est.	High Est.	Rarity	1932 List Price
525	Sofa, Chippendale, 6-leg	$3,100.00	$3,800.00	4.00	$594.00
525B	Sofa, Chippendale, 4-leg	$1,750.00	$3,000.00	4.00	$420.00
539	Sofa, Sheraton, 22x82"	$2,500.00	$3,600.00	4.00	$465.00
560	Sofa, Jacobean, leather	$2,000.00	$3,250.00	5.00	$420.00
560B	Sofa, Jacobean, pigskin	$2,000.00	$3,250.00	5.00	$450.00
568B	Sofa, Chippendale	$2,750.00	$3,500.00	4.00	$450.00
574	Sofa, flemish carved couch	$2,500.00	$3,500.00	4.00	$300.00

#564 Windsor low back six-leg loveseat (settee), with New England turnings and knuckle arms. Block brand. $1,500.00 – 2,300.00

#533 Windsor low back ten-leg loveseat (settee), with Pennsylvania turnings. Block brand. From the 1930 Wallace Nutting furniture catalog. $2,400.00 – 3,675.00

#550 Windsor tenon-arm six-leg loveseat (settee), with double back, New England turnings, and knuckle arms. Paper label. $2,275.00 – 3,700.00

#515 Windsor triple back, bow back ten-leg settee. Block band. $2,900.00 – 4,175.00

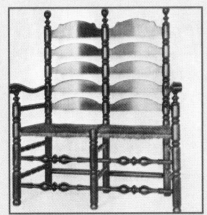

#590 double five-back New England ladderback settee, with rush seat. Block brand. From the 1930 Wallace Nutting furniture catalog. $1,600.00 – 2,175.00

#534 Philadelphia Chippendale mahogany six-leg love seat (settee), fully carved ball & claw feet, knees, and backs. Block brand. From the 1930 Wallace Nutting furniture catalog. $3,375.00 – 4,125.00

The 500 Series: Settles, Sofas, and Settees

#599 Brewster settee. Block brand. Photo courtesy of the Sharon & Kenny Lacasse collection. $3,425.00 – 4,225.00

Settees: Settees, or loveseats, were a much more popular form than Nutting's settles and sofas. Settees came in more than 30 different forms including ladderback, Chippendale, and of course Windsor settees. Windsor settees came in New England and Pennsylvania turnings, six-leg, eight-leg, and ten-leg, high back and low back, along with several other variations.

Settee Price Guide

#	Settees	Low Est.	High Est.	Rarity	1932 List Price
502	Settee, twin bow-back loveseat or courting chair	$2,200.00	$3,175.00	2.67	
503	Settee, comb-back 4-leg courting chair	$2,175.00	$3,100.00	2.67	
505	Settee, twin-bow 5' northern	$1,850.00	$2,500.00	3.00	
514	Settee, New England 10-leg (block)	$2,325.00	$3,225.00	3.33	$162.00
514	Settee, 10-leg low back settee (paper label)	$2,725.00	$3,775.00	3.33	
515	Settee, New England, 10 leg, triple back (block)	$2,900.00	$4,175.00	3.33	$195.00
515	Settee, triple-bow back 10-leg (paper label)	$3,400.00	$4,925.00	3.33	
516	Settee, 8-leg tenoned arm	$2,925.00	$4,500.00	3.33	
517	Settee, 8-leg tenoned arm, brace-back	$2,925.00	$4,500.00	3.33	
528	Settee, Pennsylvania 5' low-back	$2,325.00	$3,575.00	3.67	
532	Settee, Pennsylvania 6' low-back	$2,475.00	$3,675.00	3.67	
533	Settee, Pennsylvania, 10-leg (block)	$2,424.00	$3,675.00	3.33	$162.00
533	Settee, Pennsylvania low back 10-leg (paper label)	$3,000.00	$4,500.00	3.33	
534	Settee, Chippendale, short	$3,375.00	$4,125.00	4.00	$450.00
534B	Settee, Chippendale, short, 3-back	$4,225.00	$5,425.00	4.33	$600.00
538	Settee, Hepplewhite, wheat ear	$3,225.00	$4,175.00	4.00	$450.00
545	Settee, Pennsylvania, 10-leg (block)	$2,675.00	$3,675.00	3.67	$168.00
545	Settee, Pennsylvania comb-back 10-leg (paper label)	$3,175.00	$4,500.00	3.67	
546	Settee, triple bow-back 8-legger	$2,825.00	$4,325.00	3.67	
550	Settee, tenoned-arm loveseat	$2,275.00	$3,700.00	3.67	
551	Settee, tenoned-arm, 5'	$2,400.00	$3,825.00	3.67	
552	Settee, Sheraton loveseat	$4,200.00	$3,825.00	4.00	$294.00

# Settees	Low Est.	High Est.	Rarity	1932 List Price
553 Settee, 10-leg tenoned arm, brace-back	$3,000.00	$4,675.00	4.00	
555 Settee, Pennsylvania 5' comb-back	$2,125.00	$3,425.00	3.67	
556 Settee, Chippendale 3-back	$3,825.00	$5,325.00	4.00	$594.00
559 Settee, 4-ladder back	$4,000.00	$5,250.00	4.00	$594.00
559B Settee, 4-ladder back, not carved	$2,750.00	$3,550.00	4.33	$450.00
564 Settee, Windsor New England loveseat (block)	$1,725.00	$2,375.00	3.67	$90.00
564 Settee, 6-leg loveseat, without comb (paper label)	$1,500.00	$2,300.00	2.67	
565 Settee, Windsor comb back loveseat (block)	$1,725.00	$2,775.00	3.00	$111.00
565 Settee, comb-back 6-leg courting chair (paper label)	$1,925.00	$3,100.00	3.67	
566 Settee, twin bow-back loveseat or courting chair (script)	$1,475.00	$2,325.00	3.33	$80.00
567 Settee, tenoned-arm loveseat, simple comb	$2,000.00	$3,175.00	3.67	
569 Settee, Chippendale, French foot	$3,675.00	$4,675.00	4.33	$600.00
579 Settee, Sheraton	$3,000.00	$4,000.00	4.50	$495.00
590 Settee, 5-back, 6-leg	$1,600.00	$2,175.00	3.67	$110.00
591 Settee, 3-chair back	$2,175.00	$2,700.00	3.67	$150.00
594 Settee, Windsor comb back 10-leg	$2,500.00	$4,175.00	3.67	$180.00
595 Settee, Windsor comb back 8-leg	$3,250.00	$4,750.00	4.00	$145.00
598 Settee, walnut	$3,350.00	$4,250.00	4.00	$430.00
599 Settee, Dutch, 3-back	$3,425.00	$4,225.00	4.00	$525.00
599B Settee, Dutch, 3-back, carved	$3,825.00	$4,675.00	4.00	$660.00

Summary of Key Points

• Wallace Nutting settles are unusual and are quite desirable to collectors today.

• Wallace Nutting sofas are also quite unusual. Their high initial cost kept production low and we suspect that upholstery might be covering the Wallace Nutting brand on many undiscovered sofas.

• Wallace Nutting settees and loveseats were sold in much greater numbers than either settles or sofas. Certain windsor settees seem to have been pulled from production and were replaced by the much higher-priced formal Chippendale and Sheraton settees.

#603 splay-leg drop leaf table. Block brand. $1,325.00 – 1,825.00

#609 Windsor ogee top table, with New England turnings. Block brand. $850.00 – 1,150.00

#613 ball turned tavern table. Block brand. $1,200.00 – 1,775.00

#614 trestle table, pine top with maple base. Block brand. $725.00 – 950.00

#616 single folding gateleg (or tuckaway) table (closed). Block brand. $1,175.00 – 1,825.00

#616 single folding gateleg (or tuckaway) table (extended).

The 600 Series: Tables, Stands, Sideboards, and Lowboys

#620 maple gateleg table, with Spanish foot.
Block brand. $1,825.00 – 2,825.00

#623 maple butterfly table.
Block brand. $1,500.00 – 2,825.00

#621 maple four-gate gateleg table, with one-drawer (closed).
Block brand. $1,825.00 – 2,300.00

#621 maple four-gate gateleg table (extended)

#625 maple butterfly trestle table (closed).
Block brand. $1,075.00 – 1,725.00

#625 maple butterfly trestle table (extended)

The 600 Series: Tables, Stands, Sideboards, and Lowboys

#628 mahogany Pembroke table, with one-drawer.
Block brand. $1,825.00 – 2,500.00

#637 maple library table, with one-drawer.
Block brand. $1,600.00 – 2,000.00

#644 mahogany Hepplewhite tilt top table.
Block brand. $1,775.00 – 2,625.00.

#650 Chippendale hall or side table, fully carved. Block brand.
Sharon & Ken Lacasse collection. $5,100.00 – 6,900.00

#650 Chippendale hall or side table (close-up apron carving)

#650 Chippendale hall or side table
(close-up knee carving)

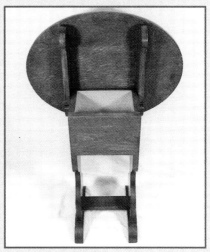

#654 pine hutch table (closed). Block brand. $875.00 – 1,325.00

#654 pine hutch table (extended)

#660 tavern table, with one-drawer, pine top and maple base.
Paper label. $1,000.00 – 1,600.00

#664 mahogany pie crust tilt top table.
Block brand. $2,100.00 – 3,375.00

#670 mahogany Hepplewhite three-part banquet table (closed).
$4,000.00 – 5,800.00

#670 mahogany Hepplewhite three-part banquet table (extended)

The 600 Series: Tables, Stands, Sideboards, and Lowboys

#670 mahogany Hepplewhite three-part banquet table (in three sections)

#693-B Chippendale pie crust tilt top table, fully carved.
Block brand. $3,750.00 – 5,000.00

#695 dished top tilt top table.
Block brand. $2,225.00 – 3,100.00

#697 Queen Anne card table. Block brand.
Sold at our June 2003 auction for $6,600.00.

Mahogany swivel top table (closed).
Paper label. $1,200.00 – 1,600.00

Mahogany swivel top table (extended)

The 600 Series: Tables, Stands, Sideboards, and Lowboys

Sheraton three-part banquet table (closed). Photo courtesy of the Sharon & Kenny Lacasse collection. $4,000.00 – 6,000.00

Sheraton three-part banquet table (extended)

Sheraton three-part banquet table (in 3 sections)

Tables: If people purchased more Wallace Nutting chairs than any other furniture form, they must have also needed tables because tables were seemingly Wallace Nutting's second bestselling furniture form. His 1930 furniture catalog lists nearly 120 different table types including Windsor tables, refractory tables, drop leaf tables, Porringer tables, trestle tables, tavern tables, gateleg tables, crane bracket tables, butterfly tables, Pembroke tables, tilt top tables, library tables, Dutch dining tables, card tables, dressing tables, serving tables, banquet tables, and Lazy Susans. The 600 Series also included stands, sideboards, and lowboys as well. Periods ranged from early Pilgrim Century to Queen Anne, Hepplewhite, Chippendale, and Sheraton.

Table Price Guide

#	Tables	Low Est.	High Est.	Rarity	1932 List Price
601	Table, refractory, heavy	$1,200.00	$1,675.00	3.67	$144.00
601A	Table, refractory, heavy, with middle stretcher	$1,300.00	$1,900.00	3.67	$144.00
602	Table, refractory, carved (block)	$2,475.00	$3,275.00	4.00	$240.00
602	Table, splay leg, drop leaf (script)	$1,250.00	$1,650.00	3.50	$70.00
603	Table, drop leaf, splayed leg	$1,325.00	$1,825.00	3.00	$105.00
604	Table, Dutch porringer	$1,775.00	$2,225.00	4.00	$59.00
605	Table, Windsor 3-leg (block)	$675.00	$1,100.00	2.00	$17.00
605	Table, Windsor tripod (paper label)	$675.00	$1,100.00	2.00	
605	Table, tripod (script)	$450.00	$625.00	2.33	$14.00
607	Table, oak refractory, 6 leg	$1,700.00	$2,200.00	4.00	$240.00

The 600 Series: Tables, Stands, Sideboards, and Lowboys

#	Tables	Low Est.	High Est.	Rarity	1932 List Price
607B	Table, oak refractory, 6 leg, carved	$2,225.00	$2,825.00	4.00	$444.00
607C	Table, oak refractory, 6 leg, 36x156"	$2,675.00	$3,675.00	4.00	$510.00
609	Table, Windsor ogee-top with stretcher (paper label)	$850.00	$1,150.00	1.67	
609	Table, Windsor ogee-top (script)	$700.00	$1,025.00	1.67	$20.00
609B	Table, trestle, pine top, 36x72"	$925.00	$1,475.00	1.33	$99.00
609C	Table, trestle, pine top, 30x60"	$775.00	$1,275.00	1.33	$72.00
610	Table, trestle, oak, 36x72"	$1,100.00	$1,600.00	2.33	$117.00
610B	Table, trestle, oak, 36x84"	$1,225.00	$1,850.00	3.00	$120.00
610C	Table, trestle, pine, 36x96"	$1,375.00	$2,000.00	3.00	$129.00
611	Table, trestle, pine, 30x108"	$1,325.00	$2,000.00	3.00	$117.00
611B	Table, trestle, pine, 36x108"	$1,400.00	$2,250.00	3.50	$126.00
612	Table, trestle, pine, 36x120"	$1,650.00	$2,350.00	4.00	$144.00
612B	Table, trestle, pine, 36x132"	$2,175.00	$3,025.00	4.00	$147.00
613	Table, ball turned tavern (block)	$1,200.00	$1,775.00	3.00	$72.00
613	Table ball turned tavern (script)	$775.00	$1,050.00	2.50	$32.00
614	Table, trestle, pine	$725.00	$950.00	2.00	$36.00
614B	Table, trestle, pine, 40"l	$700.00	$850.00	2.00	$45.00
615	Table, trestle, pine, 30x50"	$900.00	$1,400.00	3.00	$72.00
615B	Table, trestle, oak, 30x60"	$950.00	$1,450.00	3.50	$81.00
615C	Table, trestle, pine, 30x60"	$950.00	$1,450.00	3.00	$75.00
616	Table, single folding gateleg (block)	$1,175.00	$1,825.00	3.00	$42.00
616	Table, tuckaway (script)	$725.00	$1,250.00	3.00	$40.00
617	Table, Swedish vase trestle	$1,300.00	$1,775.00	3.67	$105.00
618	Table, knoll trestle, oak, 108" (block)	$2,500.00	$3,500.00	4.00	$330.00
618	Table, Pennsylvania ogee (paper label)	$1,500.00	$2,025.00	3.00	
618B	Table, knoll trestle, oak, 41x96"	$1,425.00	$2,450.00	3.33	$291.00
618C	Table, knoll trestle, oak, 14 ft.	$1,700.00	$2,850.00	3.33	$570.00
619	Table, crane bracket (block)	$1,600.00	$2,125.00	3.33	$114.00
619	Table, turned crane bracket (script)	$1,050.00	$1,475.00	2.67	$56.00
620	Table, gateleg, Spanish foot, 48x59"	$1,825.00	$2,825.00	3.33	$180.00
621	Table, gateleg, 4-gate, 48x59"	$1,825.00	$2,300.00	3.00	$180.00
622	Table, gateleg, 4-gate, 60x70"	$2,125.00	$2,650.00	3.33	$221.00
622B	Table, gateleg, Spanish foot	$2,425.00	$2,900.00	3.67	$312.00
623	Table, butterfly, 28x36" (block)	$1,500.00	$1,950.00	3.00	$57.00
623	Table, four-gate (script)	$1,475.00	$2,000.00	2.67	$90.00
624	Table, butterfly, 30x40" (block)	$1,250.00	$1,725.00	2.67	$69.00
624	Table, butterfly (script)	$525.00	$1,000.00	2.50	$50.00
625	Table, butterfly trestle	$1,075.00	$1,725.00	2.33	$49.00
626	Table, trumpet, X stretcher	$2,525.00	$3,200.00	4.00	$111.00
627	Table, lazy susan	$1,775.00	$2,750.00	4.00	$99.00
627B	Table, lazy susan, carved	$2,500.00	$3,900.00	4.00	$170.00
628	Table, Pembroke, mahogany, 36" sq.	$1,825.00	$2,500.00	3.50	$96.00
628B	Table, Pembroke, mahogany, vertical stretcher	$1,825.00	$2,650.00	3.50	$105.00
629	Table, Pembroke, Hepplewhite, maple	$1,825.00	$2,425.00	3.67	$57.00

The 600 Series: Tables, Stands, Sideboards, and Lowboys

#	Tables	Low Est.	High Est.	Rarity	1932 List Price
629B	Table, Pembroke, Hepplewhite, inlaid, mahogany	$1,925.00	$2,800.00	3.67	$90.00
630	Table, Chippendale torchere, ball & claw	$1,175.00	$1,925.00	4.00	$72.00
631	Table, gateleg, 2-gate, 60x70"	$2,250.00	$3,250.00	3.50	$210.00
632	Table, gateleg, plain, 2-gate, 48x59"	$2,000.00	$2,825.00	3.33	$135.00
634	Table, Chippendale card table	$2,625.00	$3,525.00	3.33	$276.00
635	Table, Chippendale Pembroke, fine	$2,300.00	$3,200.00	3.33	$138.00
636	Table, gateleg, heavy 4-gate	$3,000.00	$4,175.00	3.67	$400.00
636B	Table, gateleg, heavy 4-gate, walnut	$4,000.00	$5,425.00	3.33	$420.00
637	Table, library, maple (block)	$1,600.00	$2,000.00	3.00	$108.00
637	Table, library or refractory (script)	$1,000.00	$1,425.00	3.00	$70.00
637B	Table, library, walnut	$1,350.00	$1,825.00	3.50	$111.00
638	Table, library, oak, 6-leg	$2,825.00	$4,000.00	4.00	$450.00
640	Table, library, mahogany, ball & claw	$2,175.00	$3,025.00	3.67	$249.00
640B	Table, library, carved	$2,675.00	$3,675.00	3.67	$375.00
641B	Table, dressing	$2,175.00	$2,975.00	3.33	$321.00
642	Table, Chippendale, mahogany	$1,400.00	$2,200.00	3.00	$90.00
642B	Table, square leaf	$1,400.00	$2,375.00	3.00	$114.00
644	Table, Hepplewhite, tripod, inlaid	$1,775.00	$2,625.00	3.33	$66.00
646	Table, Hepplewhite mahogany, tip, oval	$1,800.00	$2,400.00	3.50	$39.00
647	Table, Dutch, round, dished	$1,400.00	$2,000.00	3.00	$42.00
647B	Table, Dutch, round, dished, tip, 24"h	$1,525.00	$2,425.00	3.00	$39.00
647C	Table, Dutch, round, dished, plain top	$1,475.00	$2,375.00	3.00	$33.00
648	Table, Dining, Dutch, round	$2,325.00	$2,925.00	3.33	$117.00
648B	Table, Chippendale, ball & claw	$2,500.00	$3,200.00	3.50	$144.00
649	Table, serving, mahogany, 1-drawer	$2,675.00	$2,575.00	3.00	$129.00
650	Table, Chippendale, hall or side	$5,100.00	$6,900.00	4.33	$750.00
650B	Table, carved legs only	$4,000.00	$6,000.00	4.00	$345.00
653	Table, turned, splayed (script)	$625.00	$800.00	3.00	$42.00
654	Table, hutch, pine (block)	$875.00	$1,325.00	3.33	$36.00
654	Table, pine work (script)	$600.00	$875.00	3.50	$24.00
655	Table, high tavern, w/stretcher	$1,200.00	$1,800.00	3.00	$90.99
656	Table, dressing, adapted	$2,325.00	$2,925.00	3.67	$135.00
658	Table, card, mahogany, fluted	$2,175.00	$3,175.00	3.33	$174.00
659	Table, mahogany, square, fluted	$1,400.00	$2,000.00	3.33	$117.00
660	Table, tavern, 1-drawer, maple with pine top	$1,000.00	$1,600.00	3.00	$63.00
661	Table, Hepplewhite card, inlaid	$2,150.00	$3,325.00	3.67	$150.00
662	Table, coffee, pine top	$1,000.00	$1,375.00	3.00	$28.50
663	Table, piecrust, carved foot	$1,500.00	$2,575.00	3.33	$66.00
664	Table, piecrust, carved foot, all carved	$2,100.00	$3,375.00	3.33	$78.00
668	Table, Sheraton card	$2,925.00	$3,675.00	4.00	$150.00
669	Table, dressing, small plain	$1,700.00	$2,675.00	3.67	$66.00
669B	Table, dressing, reeded, mahogany	$2,000.00	$2,925.00	3.67	$72.00
670	Table, Hepplewhite, 3-part, inlaid	$4,000.00	$5,800.00	4.00	$390.00
671	Table, Hepplewhite, #670 center only, inlaid	$1,600.00	$2,025.00	3.67	$171.00

The 600 Series: Tables, Stands, Sideboards, and Lowboys

#	Tables	Low Est.	High Est.	Rarity	1932 List Price
672	Table, Hepplewhite, #670 end only, inlaid	$1,425.00	$1,975.00	3.67	$114.00
673	Table, Sheraton, 3-part	$3,175.00	$4,875.00	4.00	$375.00
674	Table, Sheraton, #673 center only	$1,600.00	$2,025.00	3.67	$171.00
675	Table, Sheraton, #673 end only	$1,425.00	$1,975.00	3.67	$114.00
676	Table, Sheraton 2-part	$2,675.00	$4,000.00	3.67	$294.00
678	Table, dressing, arched	$2,325.00	$3,325.00	3.67	$135.00
680	Table, Chippendale, 3-part	$4,325.00	$6,325.00	4.33	$570.00
680B	Table, Dutch dining, 3-part	$3,850.00	$4,900.00	4.50	$476.00
681	Table, Duncan Phyfe, 3-part	$3,675.00	$5,600.00	4.33	$474.00
681B	Table, Duncan Phyfe, 3-part, Plain	$3,775.00	$5,100.00	4.33	$456.00
684	Table, Duncan Phyfe drop leaf	$2,725.00	$4,475.00	4.00	$234.00
684B	Table, Duncan Phyfe drop leaf, no carving	$2,500.00	$3,675.00	3.50	$153.00
685	Table, serving, plain Hepplewhite	$2,075.00	$3,275.00	3.50	$72.00
693	Table, Chippendale pie crust	$2,825.00	$4,000.00	3.67	$270.00
693B	Table, Chippendale pie crust, fully carved	$3,750.00	$5,000.00	4.00	$369.00
694	Table, Dutch tea table, dished	$2,225.00	$2,825.00	3.33	$162.00
695	Table, with tray top, curly maple	$2,225.00	$3,100.00	3.33	$145.00
696	Table, Dutch, curly maple, 18"	$1,825.00	$2,500.00	3.33	$36.00
697	Table, walnut card table	$2,325.00	$3,425.00	3.67	$120.00
698	Table, Dutch serving table, walnut	$2,925.00	$4,075.00	4.00	$177.00

Pair of #643 Sheraton four-leg stands. Block brand. Photo courtesy of the Sharon & Kenny Lacasse collection. $1,575.00 – 2,275.00

#608 mahogany two-drawer stand. Block brand. Photo courtesy of the Sharon & Kenny Lacasse collection. $1,275.00 – 2,175.00

Stands: Nutting produced relatively few different stands and they are quite rare today. Their petite size and overall rarity makes them quite desirable to most collectors.

Stand Price Guide

#	Stands	Low Est.	High Est.	Rarity	1932 List Price
606	Stand, high Hepplewhite	$700.00	$1,200.00	3.33	$32.00
608	Stand, 2-drawer, mahogany or maple	$1,275.00	$2,175.00	3.33	$66.00
608C	Stand, 2-drawer, curly maple	$1,375.00	$2,175.00	3.33	$72.00
633	Stand, Hepplewhite octagon	$1,100.00	$1,975.00	3.00	$27.00
639	Stand, bedside, 4-leg	$1,075.00	$1,900.00	3.67	$48.00
643	Stand, Sheraton, 4-leg	$1,575.00	$2,275.00	3.33	$54.00
643B	Stand, Sheraton, 4-leg, curly and mahogany	$2,250.00	$2,800.00	3.50	$60.00
653	Stand, colonial all-turned	$600.00	$775.00	3.50	$42.00

#692 mahogany savery school lowboy, fully carved. Block brand. Photo courtesy of the Sharon & Kenny Lacasse collection.
$5,000.00 – 6,625.00

Sideboards and Lowboys: Although sideboards and lowboys are more closely akin to case and cabinet pieces than tables, Nutting apparently felt that their tabletop space allowed them to be classified as tables. The fact that Nutting produced relatively few different styles and their higher initial cost, means that sideboards and lowboys are quite rare today and generally highly sought after by collectors.

Sideboard Price Guide

#	Sideboard	Low Est.	High Est.	Rarity	1932 List Price
641	Sideboard, arched	$2,500.00	$3,900.00	3.67	$327.00
665	Sideboard, Chippendale, mahogany	$3,675.00	$6,175.00	4.00	$270.00
665B	Sideboard, Gadroon	$3,875.00	$7,125.00	4.33	$315.00
665C	Sideboard, Gadroon, fully carved	$5,500.00	$7,676.00	4.33	$480.00
667	Sideboard, Dutch	$3,676.00	$4,675.00	4.00	$270.00
682	Sideboard, Sheraton	$4,500.00	$6,925.00	4.33	$600.00
682B	Sideboard, Sheraton, carved	$5,000.00	$8,175.00	4.33	$650.00
683	Sideboard, Hepplewhite, plain	$4,675.00	$6,225.00	4.33	$420.00
683B	Sideboard, Hepplewhite, plain, vaneered	$5,075.00	$7,400.00	4.33	$759.00
683C	Sideboard, Hepplewhite, small plain	$3,900.00	$5,725.00	4.33	$285.00

The 600 Series: Tables, Stands, Sideboards, and Lowboys

Lowboy Price Guide

#	Lowboy	Low Est.	High Est.	Rarity	1932 List Price
689	Lowboy, like #989	$4,000.00	$5,625.00	4.00	$252.00
691	Lowboy, maple	$3,325.00	$4,125.00	4.00	$180.00
691B	Lowboy, mahogany	$3,700.00	$5,200.00	4.00	$186.00
692	Lowboy, mahogany	$5,000.00	$6,625.00	4.67	$450.00
699	Lowboy, William & Mary, walnut	$3,500.00	$5,675.00	4.00	$222.00
699B	Lowboy, veneered	$4,500.00	$5,675.00	4.33	$360.00

Summary of Key Points

• Wallace Nutting probably produced more tables than any other form besides chairs.

• Some Wallace Nutting tables are fairly modestly priced and fairly common.

• Other tables are quite rare and could require a considerable outlay to acquire.

• Wallace Nutting stands are fairly uncommon and are desirable to most collectors.

• Wallace Nutting sideboards and lowboys are more typical of case pieces than tables but he assigned them table furniture design numbers because of their utilitarian use.

• Sideboards and lowboys are quite rare and difficult to obtain.

#700B open oak slant front desk, on maple tavern base. Block brand. From the 1937 furniture catalog. $1,225.00 – 2,175.00

#705 mahogany desk on carved frame. Block brand. $2,000.00 – 3,000.00

#701 open slant front desk, one drawer with stretcher (closed). Block brand. $2,100.00 – 3,375.00

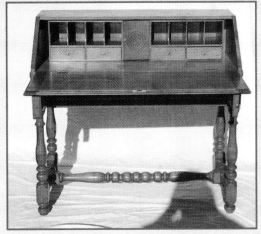

#701 open slant front desk (open)

#727 open tiger maple slant front desk, one drawer and trumpet turnings (closed). Block brand. Photo courtesy of the Bill & Gretchen Hamann collection. $4,000.00 – 6,175.00

#727 open tiger maple slant front desk

The 700 Series: Desks and Mirrors

The 700 Series consisted of two distinctly different furniture forms: desks and mirrors.

Desks: Although Wallace Nutting desks came in more than 40 different styles, they are fairly unusual today and typically come in four distinct categories: open bottom, slant front, secretary, and office adaptation desks. Desks came in a variety of styles (Chippendale, Tambour, Trumpet, etc.) and in a variety of woods (mahogany, maple, tiger maple, etc.). Desk prices varied between $84.00 for a #700 small, plain oak desk with no drawer, to $1,800.00 for Nutting's finest #733 Goddard block front nine-shell secretary desk. High end or low end, Wallace Nutting desks are difficult to locate today and can bring strong prices if in good condition.

Open Bottoms Desks: Nutting offered several different open-bottom desks. Probably his most popular desk was the #701 slant front open bottom desk which opened to four small drawers, eight cubbyholes, and one small door which was usually hand carved. This desk was produced as a paper label, script brand, and block brand piece. Several other open-bottom desks were also offered including a trumpet desk, a small oak tavern-type desk, and a desk-on-frame, among others.

#703C mahogany tambour desk. Block brand. From the 1937 furniture catalog. $10,500.00 – 17,000.00

#730 tiger maple Chippendale slant front desk, with four graduated drawers. Block brand. $4,300.00 – 6,000.00

Mahogany slant-front desk, with three graduated drawers. Block brand. $4,000.00 – 6,000.00.

Slant Front Desks: Nutting's slant front desks were exceptionally well built and came in several different forms. One of Nutting's finest slant front desks was his #729 mahogany Chippendale slant front desk. This piece has four graduated drawers and a slant front which opened to reveal four small drawers, four small cubbyholes, and three small shell-carved doors. The #734 block front slant front desk with six shell carvings cost $1,000.00, or a top portion could be added to make it a #733 secretary desk for an additional $800.00.

#731 tiger maple secretary desk, with two-raised panel top doors and four graduated lower drawers. Block brand. 1937 furniture catalog. $11,000.00 – 15,000.00

#703B tambour secretary desk. Contrast this with the #703C tambour desk pictured earlier, without the upper portion. Block brand. From the 1930 furniture catalog. $6,800.00 – 10,000.00

#733 Goddard supreme block front secretary desk, with nine shell carvings and three graduated lower drawers. This piece set the current Wallace Nutting auction record when it sold for $36,750.00 in 2002. Photo courtesy of the Sharon & Kenny Lacasse collection. $28,325.00 – 43,325.00

#733 Goddard supreme block front secretary desk, with Sharon Lacasse standing by the open top.

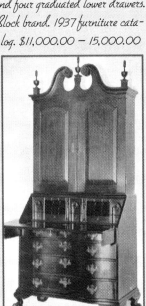

#740B ox bow secretary desk, with ball & claw feet, four graduated ox bow front drawers, two raised panel upper doors, three finials & two rosette carvings, and a slant front that opens to reveal two small drawers, six cubbyholes, and three small doors having shell carvings. Block brand. From the 1937 furniture catalog. $14,000.00 – 18,000.00

#708 mahogany seven-drawer leather top desk. From the 1937 furniture catalog. $1,500.00 – 2,000.00

The 700 Series: Desks and Mirrors

Secretary Desks: Although these might be more accurately described as case or cabinet pieces, secretary desks represent several of Nutting's finest and most costly reproduction pieces. There were only approximately five secretary desk designs and extremely few of each were ever produced. For example, we know from documented correspondence that Wallace Nutting only produced seven #733 Goddard block front secretary desks. He might have produced even fewer of the other secretary desks.

#735 mahogany Chippendale-style seven-drawer executive desk. From the 1937 furniture catalog. $6,500.00 – 9,175.00

Office Adaptations: Office adaptations were typically custom-built reproduction desks which had a colonial or traditional look but which were especially functional and specially built for successful, image-conscious executives such as bank presidents, insurance company executives, board of directors rooms, etc. Nutting claimed that he knew of only one authentic antique flat top desk and, in order to satisfy a perceived market need, he created several different desk models that had no true antique precedent but which offered the proper look. Nutting also offered a series of secretarial and typists office adaptation desks as well.

Desk Price Guide

#	Desks	Low Est.	High Est.	Rarity	1932 List Price
700	Desk, small oak, no drawer	$1,025.00	$1,950.00	4.00	$84.00
700B	Desk, small oak, 1-drawer	$1,225.00	$2,175.00	4.00	$115.00
701	Desk, large turned with stretcher (block)	$2,100.00	$3,375.00	3.00	$205.00
701	Desk middle stretcher, turned frame (script)	$1,100.00	$1,500.00	3.00	$100.00
701B	Desk, large turned with stretcher, walnut	$2,000.00	$2,900.00	2.67	$208.00
703	Desk, tambour, curly maple and mahogany	$7,000.00	$9,825.00	4.67	$456.00
703B	Desk, tambour, mahogany	$6,825.00	$10,000.00	4.67	$456.00
703C	Desk, tambour, secretary	$10,500.00	$17,000.00	5.00	$840.00
704	Desk, secretary, Milton	$9,500.00	$16,500.00	4.50	$900.00
706	Desk, Cabriole, Dutch foot	$3,825.00	$5,675.00	4.00	$330.00
707	Desk, small mahogany, 1-drawer	$2,750.00	$3,750.00	3.50	$162.00
707B	Desk, small mahogany, no drawer	$2,750.00	$3,750.00	3.50	$156.00
710	Desk, Washington	$6,000.00	$8,500.00	5.00	$512.00
716	Desk, walnut ball foot	$5,750.00	$10,250.00	4.50	$442.00
717	Desk, secretary, walnut ball foot	$6,000.00	$10,500.00	4.50	$590.00
726	Desk, trumpet, turned, plain	$3,250.00	$4,750.00	4.00	$180.00
727	Desk, trumpet, turned, curly maple	$4,000.00	$6,175.00	4.33	$250.00
729	Desk, fine cabinet, mahogany,	$5,000.00	$6,825.00	4.33	$330.00
730	Desk, fine cabinet, maple	$4,300.00	$6,000.00	4.33	$315.00

#	Desks	Low Est.	High Est.	Rarity	1932 List Price
730B	Desk, fine cabinet, curly maple	$5,500.00	$7,750.00	4.50	$330.00
731	Desk, secretary with square top, maple	$7,825.00	$11,325.00	4.33	$450.00
731B	Desk, secretary with square top, curly maple	$11,000.00	$15,000.00	4.50	$594.00
732	Desk, secretary w/ scroll top, maple	$9,275.00	$12,675.00	4.67	$590.00
733	Desk, secretary, all block, supreme	$28,325.00	$43,325.00	5.00	$1,800.00
734	Desk, secretary, all block, lower portion of #733 only	$11,750.00	$15,000.00	4.67	$1,000.00
735	Desk, flat top, ogee, mahogany	$6,500.00	$9,175.00	4.67	$450.00
735B	Desk, flat top, ogee, mahogany, smaller, 8-panel	$6,175.00	$8,675.00	4.67	$420.00
735C	Desk, flat top, ogee, any wood, carved	$9,000.00	$12,325.00	4.67	$750.00
735D	Desk, flat top, ogee, any wood, plain	$8,000.00	$10,675.00	4.67	$525.00
736	Desk, typist, like #735	$6,175.00	$8,000.00	4.33	$300.00
737	Desk, Chippendale, adapted	$5,000.00	$6,500.00	4.50	$400.00
738	Desk, typist, like #737	$3,500.00	$4,500.00	4.50	$300.00
738B	Desk, single typist	$4,600.00	$6,075.00	4.33	$220.00
739	Desk, ox bow, ball & claw	$7,000.00	$10,000.00	4.67	$405.00
739B	Desk, ox bow, bracket foot	$5,675.00	$8,000.00	4.67	$295.00
740	Desk, secretary, ox bow, bracket	$14,000.00	$18,000.00	5.00	$594.00
745	Desk, flat top, turned	$6,250.00	$8,250.00	4.50	$615.00
746	Desk, standing check desk	$2,250.00	$3,250.00	4.00	$135.00
747	Desk, chest style, oak, flat	$3,500.00	$4,250.00	4.00	$420.00
747B	Desk, chest style, oak, flat, 30x60"	$3,825.00	$4,825.00	4.33	$390.00
748	Desk, typewriter desk	$3,000.00	$4,000.00	4.00	$270.00
749	Desk, typewriter desk, single tier	$2,750.00	$3,750.00	4.00	$240.00

#772 walnut mirror, with scrolled top. Block brand. $600.00 – 1,000.00

#774 walnut Chippendale mirror, with scrolled top. Block brand. $700.00 – 1,100.00

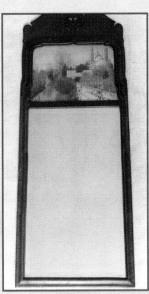

#755 walnut mirror, having a carved top and containing a Wallace Nutting hand-tinted photo. Block brand. $1,000.00 – 1,525.00

The 700 Series: Desks and Mirrors

#761 maple gold feather mirror. Punched brand. $1,000.00 – 1,675.00

The same #761 gold feather mirror, but in mahogany. Block brand. $1,000.00 – 1,500.00

Unusually large carved maple mirror. Block brand. $2,000.00 – 3,000.00

#765 mahogany Chippendale mirror, inlaid, with carved gold eagle and small rosettes. Block brand. 1930 furniture catalog. $2,400.00 – 3,500.00

#757 mahogany Georgian mirror, with gilded trim and bird ornamentation. Block brand. 1930 furniture catalog. $2,900.00 – 4,300.00

#769 mahogany Hepplewhite filigree mirror, inlaid, and having wheat ears, flowers, urn, rosettes, and swag. Block brand. From the 1930 furniture catalog. $3,000.00 – 4,300.00

Mirrors: Wallace Nutting's mirrors covered #750 – 799 in the 700 Series and came in nearly 30 different styles, ranging from relatively basic and simple carved walnut mirrors to highly elaborate carved and gilded mirrors having exotic ornamentation. Two styles of mirrors were also available with one or two Wallace Nutting hand-colored pictures. 1932 List prices from 1932 ranged between $12.00 for a small, plain mirror to $450.00 for the richest Georgian mirror. Mirrors are very popular with collectors today and have been bringing extremely strong prices if in grade 4.0 condition or better.

Mirror Price Guide

#	Mirrors	Low Est.	High Est.	Rarity	1932 List Price
750	Mirror, Elizabethan, carved (block)	$1,575.00	$2,375.00	3.00	$60.00
750	Mirror, Elizabethan hand carved oak (script)	$1,100.00	$1,825.00	3.50	$42.00
751	Mirror, heavy walnut	$1,000.00	$1,625.00	2.33	$69.00
753	Mirror, gold mantle	$3,000.00	$4,500.00	4.33	$300.00
754	Mirror, Chippendale, maple or mahogany	$1,100.00	$1,900.00	2.33	$36.00
755	Mirror, walnut, with Wallace Nutting hand-colored picture	$1,000.00	$1,525.00	2.33	$72.00
756	Mirror, walnut, with two Wallace Nutting hand-colored pictures	$1,400.00	$1,800.00	2.50	$72.00
757	Mirror, richest Georgian	$2,900.00	$4,300.00	4.33	$450.00
758	Mirror, mantle, Empire, curly	$1,500.00	$2,125.00	4.00	$90.00
758B	Mirror, mantle, Empire, curly, without balls	$1,350.00	$1,950.00	4.00	$60.00
760	Mirror, Queen Anne, curly or mahogany	$1,125.00	$1,925.00	2.00	$72.00
761	Mirror, 3-feather, mahogany	$1,000.00	$1,675.00	2.00	$42.00
762	Mirror, pine carved	$1,075.00	$1,475.00	3.00	$54.00
762B	Mirror, pine carved, gilded	$1,400.00	$1,900.00	3.00	$72.00
763	Mirror, walnut, carved, gold	$1,200.00	$1,725.00	2.67	$63.00
764	Mirror, carved bird	$1,475.00	$2,200.00	2.33	$72.00
765	Mirror, gold bird, mahogany	$2,400.00	$3,500.00	3.00	$115.00
766	Mirror, Chippendale mantle, scrolled	$1,200.00	$1,775.00	3.33	$75.00
767	Mirror, courting, small	$1,050.00	$1,750.00	3.00	$51.00
768	Mirror, Queen Anne, small	$550.00	$850.00	3.00	$10.00
769	Mirror, Hepplewhite filigree	$3,000.00	$4,300.00	4.33	$294.00
770	Mirror, shaving mirror, curly maple or mahogany	$1,200.00	$1,825.00	3.67	$69.00
771	Mirror, Hepplewhite shaving	$1,100.00	$1,475.00	3.67	$48.00
772	Mirror, small plain	$700.00	$1,000.00	2.67	$12.00
773	Mirror, love bird	$1,400.00	$2,125.00	2.67	$72.00
774	Mirror, simple scroll, small	$700.00	$1,100.00	2.33	$18.00
775	Mirror, large courting mirror	$1,475.00	$2,025.00	3.67	$90.00
776	Mirror, Georgian, medium	$3,025.00	$3,925.00	4.33	$394.00
777	Mirror, Sheraton, with gilded balls	$1,800.00	$2,400.00	3.50	$75.00
777B	Mirror, Sheraton, mahogany	$1,400.00	$2,250.00	3.50	$37.50

Summary of Key Points

• Wallace Nutting desks came in open bottom, slant front, secretary, and office adaptation models and are fairly unusual and especially desirable to today's collectors.

• Most examples of Wallace Nutting's office adaptations come in desks and chairs and were frequently produced for executive or corporate offices.

• Wallace Nutting secretary desks are one of the most desirable forms of Wallace Nutting furniture and can be extremely difficult to locate and expensive to acquire.

• Wallace Nutting mirrors came in nearly 30 different styles, ranging from plain and simple mirrors to extremely rich and elaborate mirrors.

A Wallace Nutting maple bedroom, where all furniture, including the rug, was made by Wallace Nutting. From the 1937 Wallace Nutting furniture catalog.

Another Nutting bedroom scene where all furniture, including the mirror and ironwork, was made by Wallace Nutting. From the 1930 Wallace Nutting furniture catalog.

#809 maple low post bed with urn top. $725.00 – 1,200.00

#846-B mahogany Sheraton reeded four-post bed. Paper label. $1,600.00 – 2,675.00

#825 rushed Pennsylvania day bed. Block brand. $2,225.00 – 3,175.00

The 800 Series: Beds, Box Springs, Mattresses, and Bedding

#828 maple eight-leg chaise lounge with swing head. From the 1930
Wallace Nutting furniture catalog. $2,075.00 – 3,000.00

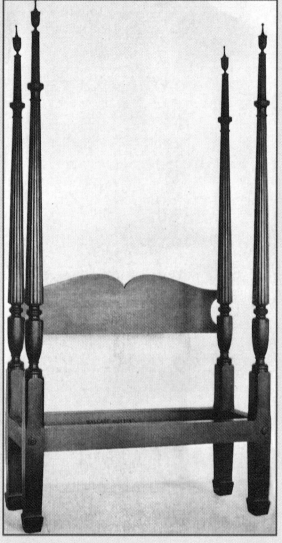

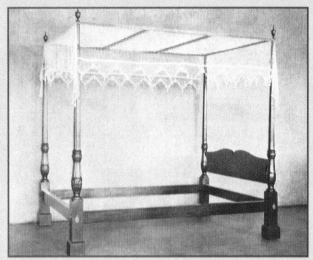

#832 carved mahogany four-post bed with canopy. Block brand. From
the 1930 Wallace Nutting furniture catalog. $1,775.00 – 2,575.00

#848 Hepplewhite mahogany four-post bed, having reeded
posts and tapered legs. Block brand. From the 1930
Wallace Nutting furniture catalog. $1,500.00 – 2,400.00

#810 child's walnut crib. Block crand. $1,300.00 – 2,275.00

The 800 Series: Beds, Box Springs, Mattresses, and Bedding

Beds: Wallace Nutting beds were produced in nearly 50 different styles ranging from a simple #809 maple low post, urn top bed ($49.00) to an exquisite #806-b mahogany tall four-post bed having highly carved knees and posts ($450.00). Child's cribs and bassinets were also produced. Nutting manufactured mahogany, oak, maple, curly maple, walnut, and pine beds, in styles ranging from early Pilgrim and Brewster to Chippendale, Hepplewhite, Sheraton, and Queen Anne styles. Nutting even produced child's cribs, chaise lounges, and day beds as well. Beds included low posts, medium posts, and tall posts, with your choice of plain posts, reeded posts, and carved posts.

Beds came in three basic sizes: single (39"x82"), narrow double (54"x82"), and wide double (60"x82"). Beds of special sizes could be built at no additional charge.

Single beds had head and foot boards built as a single unit with only four bolts needed to hold the bed together. Double beds were almost always capable of being "knocked down," that is, with the posts separating from the head and foot boards to enable easier transportation and storage. Double beds required eight bolts to hold them together.

All beds came with special brass bolt caps that were included in the basic price of the bed.

Bed Price Guide

#	Beds	Low Est.	High Est.	Rarity	1932 List Price
806	Bed, mahogany with carved knee	$1,725.00	$2,475.00	3.33	$360.00
806	Bed, twin-bow double	$1,150.00	$2,000.00	3.00	
806B	Bed, mahogany with carved knee and 4 carved posts	$2,600.00	$3,400.00	3.67	$450.00
807	Bed, urn top, medium	$775.00	$1,200.00	2.67	$54.00
808	Bed, hired man's bed, acorn	$775.00	$1,225.00	2.67	$51.00
809	Bed, low post urn top, maple	$725.00	$1,200.00	2.00	$49.00
809B	Bed, low post urn top, head and foot same	$600.00	$1,050.00	1.50	$51.00
810	Bed, Dutch walnut crib	$1,300.00	$2,275.00	4.00	$114.00
811	Bed, oak brewster	$1,400.00	$2,125.00	3.33	$120.00
812	Bed, carved and turned	$1,700.00	$2,475.00	4.00	$183.00
813	Bed, turned foot	$1,450.00	$1,475.00	3.50	$114.00
814	Bed, Pennsylvania Windsor, braced-bow	$1,100.00	$1,575.00	3.67	$90.00
815	Bed, maples, fluted & turned	$975.00	$1,525.00	3.00	$120.00
821	Bed, Hepplewhite with taper feet, light	$1,300.00	$2,150.00	3.00	$99.00
821B	Bed, Hepplewhite, reeded, light	$1,475.00	$2,425.00	3.33	$112.00
821C	Bed, Hepplewhite, reeded, mahogany, light	$1,300.00	$1,275.00	3.00	$115.00
822	Bed, Chippendale, plain, fluted	$1,050.00	$1,700.00	3.00	$90.00
823	Bed, mahogany with 2 carved posts	$1,700.00	$2,500.00	3.00	$195.00
823B	Bed, mahogany with 4 carved posts	$1,900.00	$2,800.00	3.50	$213.00
824	Bed, chaise lounge, ball & claw	$2,200.00	$2,850.00	3.50	$330.00
825	Bed, Pennsylvania day bed, rushed	$2,225.00	$3,175.00	3.67	$135.00
826	Bed, Sheraton, mahogany, carved	$2,075.00	$2,875.00	4.00	$300.00
826B	Bed, Sheraton, mahogany, carved, ½ high	$1,475.00	$2,325.00	3.00	$231.00
827	Bed, maple, fluted	$1,600.00	$2,425.00	3.00	$180.00
828	Bed, day, 8-leg, swing head, rush	$2,075.00	$3,000.00	3.67	$225.00
829	Bed, day, Dutch, 8-leg	$2,000.00	$2,825.00	3.67	$240.00

The 800 Series: Beds, Box Springs, Mattresses, and Bedding

#	Beds	Low Est.	High Est.	Rarity	1932 List Price
831	Bed, Pilgrim with post & foot rail	$1,050.00	$1,750.00	3.00	$108.00
832	Bed, with 2 carved posts	$1,775.00	$2,575.00	3.33	$180.00
832B	Bed, with 4 carved posts	$2,075.00	$2,925.00	3.67	$249.00
834	Bed, New York, single, 71x26x30"	$650.00	$1,100.00	3.00	
835	Bed, light turned daybed	$1,700.00	$2,675.00	3.33	$270.00
836	Bed, Sheraton, mahogany, light	$1,275.00	$2,000.00	3.00	$78.00
836B	Bed, Sheraton, mahogany, turned, curly maple	$1,250.00	$1,900.00	2.50	$93.00
836C	Bed, Sheraton, mahogany, plain maple	$1,050.00	$1,600.00	2.50	$66.00
837	Bed, Sheraton, reeded, light	$1,300.00	$2,000.00	2.50	$96.00
839	Bed, ½ high, turned feet	$1,125.00	$1,700.00	3.00	$78.00
839B	Bed, ½ high, turned feet, small	$1,125.00	$1,700.00	3.00	$57.00
840	Bed, 2-carved posts, mahogany	$1,825.00	$2,675.00	3.00	$330.00
840B	Bed, 4-carved posts, mahogany	$1,900.00	$3,250.00	2.00	$420.00
841	Bed, 2 carved posts, mahogany	$1,825.00	$2,525.00	3.00	$330.00
841B	Bed, 4 carved posts, mahogany	$2,150.00	$3,250.00	2.00	$426.00
842	Bed, ball top, ½ high, foot rail	$900.00	$1,475.00	3.00	$72.00
843	Bed, canopy, curly maple	$2,000.00	$3,000.00	3.00	$195.00
844	Bed, curly maple, no canopy	$1,700.00	$2,400.00	3.33	$174.00
845	Bed, Queen Anne, 2-shaped posts	$1,500.00	$2,100.00	3.00	$174.00
845B	Bed, Queen Anne, 4-shaped posts	$1,825.00	$2,825.00	3.33	$204.00
845C	Bed, Queen Anne, shell on 2-shaped posts	$1,650.00	$2,500.00	2.50	$195.00
846	Bed, urn turned, maple	$1,225.00	$2,025.00	3.00	$99.00
846A	Bed, urn turned, curly maple	$1,500.00	$2,550.00	3.00	$108.00
846B	Bed, Sheraton, reeded posts, mahogany or curly maple	$1,600.00	$2,675.00	2.67	$115.00
847	Bed, acorn top, very light	$1,200.00	$2,100.00	3.00	$60.00
847B	Bed, acorn top, very light, low posts	$900.00	$1,500.00	3.00	$54.00
848	Bed, Hepplewhite, reeded w/taper	$1,500.00	$2,400.00	3.33	$108.00
848B	Bed, Hepplewhite, reeded with taper, mahogany	$1,350.00	$2,250.00	3.00	$115.00
849	Bed, New York, 71x24x30"	$1,500.00	$2,500.00	4.00	
850	Bed, like F.T. 7504–5	$2,500.00	$3,500.00	5.00	$330.00
850B	Bed, fully carved	$2,500.00	$3,500.00	5.00	$450.00

Box Springs, Mattresses, and Bedding: Most of Nutting's beds followed the mid-eighteenth century low bed rail style which allowed for a 9" deep upholstered box spring which sat 4" below the rail and 5" above the rail. The upper part of the box spring extended out over the full width of the bed rail which provided added width and comfort. The box springs offered by Nutting even included special corner cut-outs which fit around the rounded corner posts. The cost of Nutting's specially-made box springs in 1930 were as follows: single, 39"x 82": $48.00; narrow double, 54"x 82": $54.00; and wide double, 60"x 82": $57.00. As far as we know Wallace Nutting box springs were never branded or marked.

Nutting also supplies high grade hair mattresses, also with the special corner cut-outs required by his beds. The 1930 mattress costs were single, $66.00; narrow double, $90.00; and wide double, $102.00. As far as we know Nutting's mattresses were never marked.

The 800 Series: Beds, Box Springs, Mattresses, and Bedding

Wallace Nutting even supplied bedding to go along with his beds, box springs, and mattresses. He offered a #804 choice live goose pillow for $6.00, with a larger 22" x 28" #804-b live goose pillow selling for $7.20. A #805 feather and down pillow was $7.50, with a larger 22" x 28" #805 size selling for $9.00. Nutting's best #805-b feather and down pillow sold for $9.00, and a similar larger size pillow sold for $11.40. As far as we know Nutting's pillows were never marked.

Box Springs, Mattresses, and Bedding

#	*Box Springs, Mattresses, and Bedding*	*1932 List Price*
801	Box spring, upholstered, 39x82"	$48.00
802	Box spring, upholstered, 54x82"	$54.00
803	Box spring, upholstered, 60x82"	$57.00
801B	Mattress, single, 39x82"	$54.00
802B	Mattress, double, 54x82"	$90.00
803B	Mattress, double, 60x82"	$102.00
804	Pillow, choice live goose	$6.00
804B	Pillow, choice live goose, 22x28"	$7.20
805	Pillow, feather & down	$7.50
805A	Pillow, feather & down, 22x28"	$9.00
805B	Pillow, best feather & down	$9.00
805C	Pillow, best feather & down, 22x28"	$11.40
818	Tester frame, ogee only	$19.00
818B	Tester frame, ogee pointed	$21.00
819	Tester frame, plain oval	$21.00
817	Canopy frame, flat top	$15.00
820	Canopy frame, rounded top	$21.00

Summary of Key Points

• Wallace Nutting beds were produced in nearly 50 different styles, including cribs and bassinets.

• Wallace Nutting beds came in three basic sizes, but special sizes could also be special ordered.

• Wallace Nutting also offered box springs, mattresses, and bedding specially created to fit Wallace Nutting beds.

Just as Mercedes has its S Series and BMW has its 7 Series, Wallace Nutting had his 900 Series. Although he never marketed it as such, the "900 Series" is what basically every collector is looking for today, Aside from a few especially desirable items found in other series (e.g., 700 Series secretary desks and 600 Series sideboards and lowboys), the majority of Wallace Nutting's most desirable furniture pieces are found within the 900 Series. Many of these items represent some of Nutting's most expensive pieces and, based upon the rarity rule, their high cost meant that extremely few of the best-of-the-best case and cabinet pieces were ever produced. And unfortunately for collectors, prices can go sky high when they appear in a competitive bidding situation.

Minor 900 Series Pieces: For lack of a better term I call a limited number of items found within the 900 Series "minor pieces." This is not meant to degrade them, but rather to differentiate them from the majority of case and cabinet pieces found within this series. This would include wooden boxes, wall shelves, a spoon rack, a pipe box, and a Chinese Chippendale lantern. These items initially sold for $15.00 – 90.00 each and, although fairly unusual today, they don't represent the rarity or high value of some of the other larger pieces found within this series.

900 Series Minor Piece Price Guide

#	*Minor 900 Series Items*	*Low Est.*	*High Est.*	*Rarity*	*1932 List Price*
900	Box, oak carved	$1,225.00	$1,925.00	4.67	$66.00
901	Box, Hadley, initialed	$1,225.00	$1,925.00	4.67	$69.00
903	Spoon rack, carved	$800.00	$1,325.00	4.00	$27.00
905	Pipe box, scalloped	$800.00	$1,325.00	4.00	$30.00
906	Wall shelf, pine, open back	$525.00	$875.00	3.00	$15.00
907	Wall shelf, pine w/ back	$875.00	$1,375.00	3.00	$37.50
939	Lantern, Chippendale, Chinese	$900.00	$1,375.00	4.50	$90.00

#903 carved spoon rack, in original red paint.
Unsigned. $800.00 – 1,325.00

#906 open back pine shelf. Block brand. $525.00 – 875.00

#935 oak Hadley chest. From the Wallace Nutting furniture catalog. $6,825.00 – 9,500.00

#944 pine open scroll one-door corner cupboard. From the Wallace Nutting furniture catalog. $3,100.00 – 4,500.00

#909 oak one-drawer chest, dark finish. Block brand. $2,675.00 – 4,325.00

#909 oak one-drawer chest, black ornaments on light finish. Block brand. $2,675.00 – 4,325.00

Wallace Nutting

The 900 Series: Cases and Cabinet Pieces

#913 pine chest of drawers. Block brand. Sold at our
November 2002 auction for $3,410.00

#916 curly maple chest of drawers. Block brand. Sold at our
March 2001 auction for $5,610.00

#918 mahogany block front chest of drawers. Block brand.
$5,000.00 – 7,000.00

#918 maple block front chest of drawers. Block brand.
$3,500.00 – 5,500.00

Case and Cabinet Pieces: Most 900 Series case and cabinet pieces are extremely difficult to locate. The 1932 furniture catalog lists more than 50 different types of case and cabinet pieces including dressers, chest of drawers, lift-top chests, court cupboards, hanging cupboards, bureau tables, Welsh dressers, corner cupboards, highboys, and chest-on-chests. The finest woods were used including Cuban mahogany, tiger and curly maple, oak, walnut, and, of course regular maple and pine. Elaborate carvings and wood inlays were not uncommon. List prices from 1932 ranged from $27.00 for a #943 pine hanging cupboard to $1,230.00 for a #992 carved Savery highboy. When you review the 1932 list prices within the 900 Series you will understand why so few pieces were ever produced and why they are so highly desirable to collectors today. In my opinion a 900 Series case piece just may be the first piece of Wallace Nutting furniture to reach the $50,000.00 or $100,000.00 level.

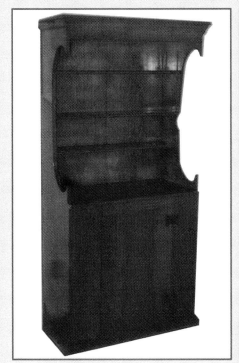

#927 pine one-door bookcase. Block brand.
$3,650.00 – 5,000.00

#991 maple highboy, with two shell carvings.
Block brand. Photo courtesy of the Sharon and
Kenny Lacasse collection.
$9,675.00 – 13, 675.00

Maple chest on chest. Block brand.
Photo courtesy of the Sharon and Kenny
Lacasse collection. $8,000.00 – 12,000.00

900 Series Cabinet Piece Price Guide

#	900 Series Cabinet Pieces	Low Est.	High Est.	Rarity	1932 List Price
909	Chest, oak, 1-drawer (block)	$2,675.00	$4,325.00	4.00	$195.00
909	Chest, oak (script)	$1,200.00	$1,775.00	3.67	$160.00
910	Court cupboard, Sudbury, oak	$9,675.00	$15,675.00	4.67	$645.00
911	Court cupboard, oak	$10,000.00	$16,675.00	4.67	$720.00
912	Sideboard, oak, 6-leg	$4,675.00	$5,675.00	4.33	$234.00
912B	Sideboard, oak, 6-leg, no ornaments	$4,350.00	$5,250.00	4.00	$210.00
915	Chest of drawers, pine	$2,925.00	$4,175.00	4.33	$99.00
915B	Chest of drawers, curly maple, dovetailed	$3,750.00	$6,250.00	4.50	$210.00
916	Chest of drawers, maple	$4,000.00	$5,675.00	4.00	$148.00
916B	Chest of drawers, curly maple	$4,400.00	$6,500.00	4.00	$195.00
917	Chest of drawers, mahogany	$3,850.00	$5,000.00	4.00	$153.00
918	Chest of drawers, block front	$5,000.00	$7,000.00	4.33	$265.00
919	Chest of drawers, oxbow, mahogany	$4,675.00	$6,500.00	4.00	$261.00
919B	Chest of drawers, oxbow, mahogany, bracket foot	$4,500.00	$6,000.00	4.00	$251.00
920	Chest on frame, oak	$2,575.00	$3,925.00	4.00	$150.00
921	Chest on chest, maple	$5,750.00	$7,700.00	4.00	$288.00
922	Welsh dresser, oak	$5,500.00	$9,500.00	4.00	$300.00

The 900 Series: Cases and Cabinet Pieces

#	900 Series Cabinet Pieces	Low Est.	High Est.	Rarity	1932 List Price
922	Arched panel dresser	$2,500.00	$3,900.00	4.00	$150.00
923	Chest of drawers, scrolled pine dresser	$2,825.00	$4,175.00	3.67	$78.00
924	Chest of drawers, simple	$2,900.00	$3,750.00	4.00	$96.00
924B	Chest of drawers, curly maple	$2,075.00	$4,350.00	4.00	$111.00
925	Corner cupboard, pine	$8,675.00	$13,675.00	5.00	$480.00
926	Hanging cupboard	$1,175.00	$1,800.00	4.00	$54.00
927	Bookcase-dresser, pine	$3,650.00	$5,000.00	4.00	$78.00
928	Bookcase-dresser, pine, wider, carved top	$4,250.00	$6,500.00	4.00	$129.00
929B	Cupboard, pine, arched	$2,925.00	$4,075.00	3.67	$66.00
930	Chest, name not lined	$2,100.00	$2,900.00	4.00	$78.00
931	Chest, sunflower, Connecticut	$5,000.00	$7,825.00	4.00	$375.00
931	Chest, Connecticut sunflower	$2,775.00	$4,300.00	4.00	$250.00
933	Chest, Norman tooth	$4,675.00	$7,175.00	4.67	$246.00
934	Chest of drawers, Sheraton, inlaid	$5,175.00	$7,325.00	4.00	$297.00
934B	Chest of drawers, Sheraton, line inlay	$4,000.00	$6,500.00	4.00	$198.00
935	Chest, Hadley, carved	$6,825.00	$9,500.00	5.00	$375.00
936	Chest of drawers, oak	$4,325.00	$9,500.00	4.67	$240.00
937	Chest of drawers, oak, inlaid	$4,175.00	$6,500.00	4.67	$258.00
937	Chest of drawers, oak	$1,300.00	$1,850.00	4.00	$130.00
938	Chest, Pennsylvania painted	$6,175.00	$8,000.00	4.67	$294.00
940	Corner cupboard, mahogany	$4,800.00	$6,400.00	4.50	$219.00
941	Chest of drawers, mahogany, quarter column	$4,275.00	$5,925.00	4.00	$240.00
942	Dresser, New England pine	$3,325.00	$6,500.00	4.00	$198.00
943	Hanging cupboard, pine	$775.00	$1,400.00	3.33	$27.00
944	Cupboard, open scroll	$3,100.00	$4,500.00	4.00	$78.00
945	Cupboard, pine fluted	$4,675.00	$7,325.00	5.00	$180.00
945B	Cupboard, pine fluted w/ arched door	$5,175.00	$7,500.00	5.00	$228.00
947	Dresser, pine scrolled	$4,750.00	$6,500.00	4.50	$285.00
952	Bureau table, knee hole	$6,325.00	$10,675.00	4.67	$534.00
979	Chest of drawers, ball & claw	$5,500.00	$8,100.00	5.00	$375.00
980	Cupboard, Sheraton	$5,500.00	$8,750.00	4.50	$450.00
989	Highboy, flames	$14,000.00	$19,675.00	5.00	$600.00
991	Highboy, sunrise, maple	$9,675.00	$13,675.00	4.67	$375.00
992	Highboy, Savery, carved	$17,675.00	$27,325.00	5.00	$1,230.00
996	Highboy, bonnet top, maple	$10,000.00	$19,000.00	5.00	$610.00
999	Highboy, walnut	$10,825.00	$15,675.00	5.00	$480.00
999B	Highboy, walnut veneered	$13,325.00	$18,000.00	5.00	$720.00
1000	Chest on chest	$19,000.00	$28,325.00	5.00	$990.00

Our Wish List of Wallace Nutting Furniture Pieces

What follows here is my personal wish list of my favorite Wallace Nutting furniture pieces. Not listed in any particular order, each of these items represents a piece of Wallace Nutting furniture that I have never had the opportunity to own, and something that I probably never will have the opportunity to own (but wish that I could).

#932 Closed Pennsylvania 20-Light Cupboard: As far as I know the only catalog where this item appeared was in the 1937 *Wallace Nutting Furniture Catalog, Final Edition*. It could be purchased in pine for $250.00 or in walnut for $265.00. Although far from being Nutting's most expensive piece, its late introduction makes it extremely rare and I'm partial to the Pennsylvania design.

#988 Philadelphia Highboy: This was Wallace Nutting's richest mahogany highboy and was only made to order. It was copied from an original piece owned by the Metropolitan Museum of Art in New York and cost $1,350.00 in 1930.

#992 Carved Savery Highboy: This was another of Nutting's finest mahogany highboys. Its extensive carving contributed to this piece's $875.00 list price in 1930 which made it prohibitively expensive to most households.

#932 closed Pennsylvania 20-light cupboard

#988 Philadelphia highboy

#992 carved Savery highboy

The 900 Series: Cases and Cabinet Pieces

#989 mahogany highboy

#925 corner cupboard with
carved shell top

#925 corner cupboard, with
18-light door

#1000 Goddard type block & shell
chest-on-chest

#989 Mahogany Highboy: With two shell carvings and three flame finials, this represents another of Nutting's finest highboys. It cost $500.00 in 1930 which was considerably less than the two highboys mentioned before. If the buyer chose to eliminate the carved quarter columns and substitute Dutch pad feet for the more highly carved ball and claw feet, $50.00 – 75.00 could also be knocked off the price.

#925 Corner Cupboard with Carved Shell Top: This rare corner cupboard included a lower door having four raised panels and a massive shell carving sitting atop three scalloped shelves. It could be ordered with or without an 18-light arched door. In 1930 it cost $425.00.

#1000 Goddard Type Block & Shell Chest-On-Chest: At #1000 this was Nutting's only design number beyond #999, and it is still considered to be within the 900 Series. The lower portion includes two massive block-front drawers beneath a smaller drawer having three exquisite shell carvings. The bonnet-top upper portion includes four graduated drawers beneath two smaller drawers and a single center drawer featuring a fourth shell carving. Gorgeous and massive, it cost $775.00 in 1930.

#922 oak Welsh dresser

#942 New England pine dresser

#922 Oak Welsh Dresser: I am only aware of the existence of one of these oak Welsh dressers and it has always been one of my favorites. Although costing only $200.00 in 1930, this is an absolutely beautiful and very desirable piece of furniture. Its two arched, raised panel lower doors are flanked by four raised-panel drawers. It has three shelves within its upper portion. Approximately 15 years ago I purchased a Welsh dresser, based upon a photograph, assuming it was oak. I paid to have it shipped back east from California and only when it arrived did I learn that it wasn't oak, but maple, and painted in a green wash. This mistake taught me to always ask the right questions, I never made that mistake again.

#942 New England Pine Dresser: Although similar to the #922 Welsh dresser, this New England pine dresser has three graduated center drawers flanked by two full-sized vertical raised-panel drawers. The upper portion has scalloped edging bordering three upper shelves. With a 1930 cost of only $145.00, it is still quite rare and one that I have never seen.

The 900 Series: Cases and Cabinet Pieces

#945 Pine Corner Cupboard: At $130.00 in 1930, this represents the lowest original list price of all of my favorite items within the 900 Series. But I'm partial to corner cupboards and always have wished I could find one for sale. This 15-light cupboard features fluted upper and lower pilasters and a single lower door.

#938 Pennsylvania Painted 3-Panel Chest: Last, but not least, I have always dreamed of owning a Wallace Nutting painted chest. Wallace Nutting rarely painted his furniture but, in keeping with the Pennsylvania style, this wonderful lift-top chest included three painted front panels standing over two painted lower drawers. Rare, but with a $200.00 list price in 1930, it was not all that expensive compared to many of his other pieces.

#945 pine corner cupboard

#938 Pennsylvania painted two-drawer chest

Summary of Key Points

• Although there are several smaller non-cabinet pieces found within the 900 Series, most items within this group are larger cabinet-type pieces.

• Wallace Nutting's case and cabinet pieces, the 900 Series, include many of Wallace Nutting's most highly sought-after items.

• Although there were more than 50 different 900 Series designs, most are quite difficult to locate and rarely come inexpensively.

• I predict that a piece from the 900 Series just may become the first piece of Wallace Nutting furniture to hit the $50,000.00 or $100,000.00 mark.

Wallace Nutting furniture at a typical Michael Ivankovich auction

Michael Ivankovich, the auctioneer

What follows is a listing of Wallace Nutting furniture that sold through Michael Ivankovich Auction Company auctions between 1998 and 2003. We have sorted these items by furniture design number to better help you better evaluate prices.

There are several things you should keep in mind when evaluating these prices:

• These are not estimated values. The are actual auction prices of items that were sold in a competitive bidding situation in a well-advertised, nationally-attended auction.

• Our auction attendees are generally the most knowledgeable in the country and rarely does a sleeper go unnoticed. Therefore most prices here reflect, in our opinion, a realistic estimate of what each particular piece was worth on that given day.

• Prices differences for similar or comparable items can most likely be attributed to differences in condition, woods, overall quality, or the date and/or time of sale.

• These prices reflect nearly six years of auction results. As prices have been rising over the past several years, those 1998 – 2000 prices might be somewhat low by today's price levels, but they do reflect actual auction sales.

And although these are actual auction prices, the price you might achieve if your item were sold either through our auction company, or through another auction company, might be higher or lower than the numbers reported here.

Listing of Recent Auction Prices

Description	Amount	Date
Ironwork		
#I-61 Wallace Nutting Wrought Iron Candlestand.		
Impressed "Wallace Nutting."	$2,970.00	November 1998
Smalls		
Pair of #2 Treenware Frames		
both of which include a WN Silhouette Label.	$231.00	March 2001
Pair of #2 Treenware Frames. Curly Maple.	$198.00	November 2001
#17 Windsor Tripod Candlestand. Tiger Maple.		
Paper Label.	$1,238.00	March 2003
#17 Windsor Tripod Candlestand. Punched #17.	$660.00	June 2000
#17 Windsor Tripod Candlestand. Paper Label.	$495.00	June 2002
#17 Windsor Tripod Candlestand. Script Brand.	$495.00	November 1999
#17 Windsor Tripod Candlestand. Punched #17.	$467.50	June 1998
#17 Windsor Tripod Candlestand. Script Brand.	$357.50	June 2001
#22 Maple Cross Base Candlestand. Block Brand.	$577.50	November 2000
#22 Maple Cross Base Candlestand. Block Brand.	$412.50	November 2000
#22 Maple Cross Base Candlestand. Unsigned.	$143.00	June 1999
#24 Costumer/Coat Rack. Block Brand.	$330.00	June 1998
#40 Spinning Wheel Hat Rack. Block Brand.	$798.00	November 2002
#40 Spinning Wheel Hat Rack. Block Brand.	$605.00	June 2001
Stools		
#101 Windsor Round Stool. Paper Label.	$523.00	June 2002
#102 Windsor Oval Stool. Paper Label.	$413.00	November 2002
#102 Windsor Oval Stool. Block Brand.	$358.00	June 2002
#102 Windsor Oval Stool. Paper Label.	$275.00	March 1999
#102 Windsor Oval Stool. Script Brand.	$220.00	November 2001
#143 Windsor Stool, Pennsylvania Turnings. Ogee Top.		
Punched #143.	$385.00	June 1999
#153 Pennsylvania Windsor Oval Stool. Block Brand.	$319.00	November 1999
#161-c Joint Stool, 24". Block Brand.	$577.00	June 1998
#164 Brewster 3-Legged Stool. Block Brand.	$660.00	November 2002
#165 Maple Joined Stool, 15". Block Brand.	$825.00	November 2002
#165 Maple Joint Stool, 15". Block Brand.	$660.00	June 1998
#171 Jacobean Stool. Block Brand.	$798.00	March 2003
#290 Maple 6-Leg Bench. Block Brand.	$1,320.00	June 2002
#292 Gothic Stool. Block Brand.	$495.00	June 2002
#292 Gothic Stool. Block Brand.	$143.00	March 2000
Child's Chairs		
#210 Child's Windsor High Chair. Partial Paper Label.	$1,430.00	June 2001
#211 Windsor Fan Cack Child's Chair. Block Brand.	$2,970.00	March 2003
#211 Child's Comb Back Arm Chair. Block Brand.	$1,705.00	June 2001
Child's High Chair with Liftable Food Tray. Block Brand.	$2,310.00	November 2001

Description	Amount	Date
Side Chairs		
#301 Windsor Braced Back Side Chair. Block Brand.	$660.00	November 2002
#301 Windsor Braced Back Side Chair. Script Brand.	$660.00	March 2001
#301 Windsor Braced Back Side Chair. Block Brand.	$605.00	June 2002
#301 Windsor Braced Back Side Chair. Block Brand.	$495.00	June 2002
#301 Windsor Braced Back Side Chair. Script Brand.	$319.00	June 2001
#305 Bent Rung Windsor Side Chair. Block Brand.	$742.50	March 2001
#310 Windsor Fan Back Side Chair. Block Brand.	$825.00	March 2003
#311 Fan Back Windsor Side Chair, with Imposed Comb. Block Brand.	$1,210.00	March 1999
#311 Fan Back Windsor Side Chair, with Imposed Comb. Block Brand.	$1,072.50	March 1998
#311 Fan Back Windsor Side Chair, with Imposed Comb. Punched #311 and Paper Label.	$825.00	June 2001
#326 Windsor Fan Back Side Chair. Block Brand.	$852.00	March 2000
#326 Windsor Fan Back Side Chair. Block Brand.	$660.00	June 2002
#326 Windsor Fan Back Side Chair. Unmarked.	$660.00	June 2003
#326 Windsor Fan Back Side Chair. Paper Label.	$578.00	June 2002
#326 Windsor Fan Back Side Chair. Paper Label.	$550.00	June 2002
#326 Windsor Fan Back Side Chair. Unmarked.	$385.00	November 2002
#326 Windsor Fan Back Side Chair. Punched "Wallace Nutting."	$247.50	June 2001
#329 Windsor Swivel Chair. Block Brand.	$743.00	June 2003
#329 Windsor Swivel Chair. Block Brand.	$330.00	March 2002
#349 Windsor Slipper Side Chair. Block Brand and Paper Label.	$385.00	June 2001
#365 Wild Rose Side Chair. Block Brand.	$450.00	March 2000
#365 Wild Rose Side Chair. Block Brand.	$440.00	March 2001
#365 Wild Rose Side Chair. Block Brand.	$440.00	June 2001
#365 Wild Rose Side Chair. Block Brand.	$440.00	March 2000
#365 Wild Rose Side Chair. Block Brand.	$420.00	March 2000
#365 Wild Rose Side Chair. Block Brand.	$193.00	March 2000
#374 Maple Side Chair, Rush Seat. Block Brand.	$577.00	June 1999
#377 Maple Side Chair, Rush Seat. Block Brand.	$385.00	June 1999
Set of 4 #390 New England 5-Back Ladderback Side Chairs. Unsigned.	$1,100.00	November 1998
#390 New England 5-Back Ladderback Side Chair. Block Brand.	$385.00	November 2001
#392 4-Back Ladderback Side Chair, Rushed Seat. Block Brand.	$385.00	November 2000
#392 4-Back Ladderback Side Chair, Rushed Seat. Block Brand.	$330.00	March 1999
#392 4-Back Ladderback Side Chair, Rushed Seat. Block Brand.	$165.00	November 2000
#393 Pilgrim Side Chair. Block Brand.	$715.00	March 2002
#393 Pilgrim Side Chair. Block Brand.	$522.50	June 2001
#393 Pilgrim Side Chair. Block Brand.	$275.00	November 2000

Wallace Nutting

Listing of Recent Auction Prices

Description	Amount	Date
Side Chairs		
#393 Pilgrim Side Chair. Unsigned, with #3840 Metal Bank Tag.	$247.50	June 1998
Arm Chairs		
#402 Windsor Continuous Arm Chair. Script Brand and Impressed #402.	$770.00	November 1998
#408 Windsor Bow Back Knuckle Arm Chair. Block Branded Signature.	$1,320.00	June 2002
#408 Windsor Bow Back Knuckle Arm Chair. Paper Label and Punched #408.	$935.00	November 1999
#408 Windsor Bow Back Knuckle Arm Chair. Paper Label.	$825.00	November 2002
#408 Windsor Bow Back Knuckle Arm Chair. Block Branded Signature.	$825.00	November 2001
#408 Windsor Bow Back Knuckle Arm Chair. Block Branded Signature.	$550.00	June 1998
#412 Pennsylvania Comb Back Windsor Arm Chair. Partial Label and Punched #412.	$1,045.00	November 1999
#413 Windsor Low Back Arm Chair. Block Branded Signature.	$853.00	November 2002
#415 Comb Back Windsor Knuckle Arm Chair. Block Brand and Paper Label.	$1,155.00	March 1999
#415 Comb Back Windsor Knuckle Arm Chair. Paper Label.	$880.00	June 2001
#415 Comb Back Windsor Knuckle Arm Chair. Unmarked.	$770.00	March 2003
#420 Windsor Bow Back Knuckle Arm Chair. Block Brand and Paper Label.	$660.00	March 1998
#420 Windsor Bow Back Knuckle Arm Chair. Paper Label.	$550.00	March 1999
#422 Windsor Tenon Arm Chair. Block Brand.	$1,650.00	June 2003
#422 Windsor Tenon Arm Chair. Block Brand.	$1,155.00	November 1998
#422 Windsor Tenon Arm Chair. Block Brand.	$1,155.00	June 1998
#430 Maple Corner Arm Chair. Block Brand.	$633.00	November 2002
#437 Hepplewhite John Goddard-type Mahogany Block Brand.	$742.50	March 1998
#440 Windsor Writing Arm Chair, Pennsylvania Turnings. Block Brand.	$2,145.00	November 2001
#451 Windsor Writing Arm Chair, New England Turnings. Block Brand.	$1,760.00	March 1999
#461 Set of 4 Country Dutch Arm Chairs. Block Brand.	$1,870.00	November 2002
#461 Country Dutch Maple Arm Chair. Block Brand.	$825.00	March 1999
#464 Carver Arm Chair. Unsigned.	$963.00	November 1999
#464 Carver Arm Chair. Unsigned, Letter of Authenticity.	$715.00	March 1999
#464 Carver Arm Chair. Script Brand.	$550.00	November 2001
#473 Upholstered Chippendale Martha Washington Arm Chair. Block Brand.	$550.00	March 1998
#476 Flemish Carved Arm Chair. Block Brand.	$1,155.00	November 2001
#476 Flemish Carved Arm Chair. Block Brand.	$935.00	March 2002
#477 Windsor Rocking Chair. Script Brand.	$770.00	June 2003

Description	Amount	Date
#490 New England 5-Back Side Chair. Block Brand.	$990.00	June 2000
#490 New England 5-Back Side Chair. Block Brand.	$907.50	November 2000
#490 New England 5-Back Side Chair. Block Brand.	$825.00	November 2000
#490 New England 5-Back Side Chair. Block Brand.	$797.50	June 2000
#490 New England Ladderback Arm Chair. Unsigned.	$742.50	September 1998
#490 New England 5-Back Side Chair. Block Brand.	$742.50	June 2000
#490 New England 5-Back Side Chair. Block Brand.	$715.00	June 2000
#490 New England 5-Back Side Chair. Block Brand.	$687.50	June 2000
#490 New England 5-Back Side Chair. Block Brand.	$660.00	June 2000
#490 New England Ladderback Arm Chair. Unsigned.	$522.50	September 1998
#490 New England 5-Back Side Chair. Block Brand.	$522.50	June 2000
#490 New England 5-Back Side Chair. Block Brand.	$330.00	March 2002
#492 New England 4-Back Ladderback Arm Chair. Block Brand.	$770.00	March 2000
#493 Pilgrim Arm Chair. Block Brand.	$1,073.00	March 2000
#493 Pilgrim Arm Chair. Block Brand.	$1,018.00	March 2000
#493 Pilgrim Arm Chair. Block Brand.	$850.00	March 2000

Settles, Sofa, Settees

Description	Amount	Date
#550 Tenon-Arm Love Seat. Partial Paper Label.	$2,860.00	June 2001
#564 Maple Low Back Settee. Block Brand.	$2,420.00	March 2002
#589 Maple Wainscot Settle. Block Brand.	$2,200.00	March 2002
Mahogany Vanity Bench. Block Brand.	$247.50	March 1998

Tables

Description	Amount	Date
#601 Oak Refractory Table. Block Brand.	$1,705.00	November 2002
#603 Maple Drop-Leaf Table. Block Brand.	$1,155.00	March 2001
#603 Maple Drop-Leaf Table. Block Brand.	$1,045.00	March 1999
#605 3-Leg Windsor Stand. Script Brand.	$660.00	March 1999
#609 Windsor Ogee-Top Table. Block Brand.	$687.50	November 2000
#609 Windsor Ogee-Top Table. Unsigned.	$687.50	June 2000
#613 Maple Tavern Table. Paper Label.	$1,375.00	June 2002
#613 Maple Tavern Table. Unsigned.	$522.50	June 1998
#614 Maple Trestle Table with Pine Top. Block Brand.	$715.00	November 1998
#614 Maple Trestle Table with Pine Top. Block Brand.	$605.00	June 2003
#614 Maple Trestle Table with Pine Top. Block Brand.	$385.00	June 1999
#615 Maple Trestle Table. Block Brand.	$550.00	June 1998
#616 Maple Tuckaway Gateleg Table. Block Brand.	$2,090.00	June 1999
#620 Maple Drop Leaf Table, Spanish Feet, 1-Drawer. Block Brand.	$2,090.00	March 1999
#621 Maple Gate Leg Table. Block Brand.	$3,520.00	November 1998
#621 Maple Gate Leg Table. Block Brand.	$1,650.00	March 2002
#623 Maple Butterfly Table. Block Brand.	$2,090.00	June 2003
#623 Maple Butterfly Table. Block Brand.	$2,090.00	June 2003
#625 Trestle Butterfly Table. Block Brand.	$2,420.00	November 2000
#628 Mahogany Pembroke Table, 1-Drawer. Block Brand.	$1,760.00	June 1999
#628-b Mahogany Pembroke Table. Block Brand.	$1,485.00	November 1999
#637 Maple Library Table, 1-Drawer. Unsigned.	$1,595.00	November 1998

Listing of Recent Auction Prices

Description	Amount	Date
#639 Maple Library Table. Block Brand.	$1,430.00	June 1998
#653 4-Leg Table Stand. Partial Paper Label.	$550.00	March 2003
#653 4-Leg Table Stand. Partial Paper Label.	$550.00	March 2003
#660 Maple Tavern Table, 1-Drawer. Block Brand.	$770.00	November 1998
#660 Maple Tavern Table, 1-Drawer. Block Brand.	$660.00	March 1999
#664 Carved Mahogany Pie Crust Tilt Top Table. Block Brand.	$3,410.00	November 1998
#689 Mahogany Lowboy. Block Brand.	$3,650.00	March 1998
#697 Walnut Queen Anne Card Table. Block Brand.	$6,600.00	June 2003

Desks

Description	Amount	Date
#701 Open Bottom Slant Front Desk. Script Brand.	$1,375.00	June 2001
#701 Open Bottom Slant Front Desk. Block Brand.	$1,210.00	March 1999
#729 Mahogany Slant Front Desk. Block Brand.	$9,900.00	March 1998
#730 Slant Front Desk, Tiger Maple. Block Brand.	$5,060.00	June 1998

Mirrors

Description	Amount	Date
#751 Walnut Mirror. Block Brand.	$688.00	November 2002
#754 Carved Chippendale Mirror. Block Brand.	$907.50	June 1998
#761 Maple 3-Feather Mirror. Block Brand.	$1,870.00	March 2002
#761 Maple 3-Feather Mirror. Punch Brand.	$688.00	June 2003
#764 Mahogany Queen Anne Mirror with Phoenix Bird. Block Brand.	$2,640.00	June 2001
#764 Mahogany Queen Anne Mirror with Phoenix Bird. Block Brand.	$2,035.00	November 2002
#774 Walnut Mirror. Block Brand.	$1,375.00	March 2002
Mahogany Mirror, Gold Shell Carving. Block Brand.	$577.50	June 1998

Beds

Description	Amount	Date
#810 Child's Walnut Crib with Block Brand.	$1,540.00	March 2001
#823-b Mahogany 4-Poster Bed. Block Brand.	$2,860.00	June 2003
#825 Maple Day Bed. Block Brand.	$1,210.00	June 2002
#846 Light Maple 4-Poster Sheraton Bed. Block Brand.	$1,705.00	June 2001
#848 Hepplewhite Bed. Block Brand.	$1,870.00	June 2002
Mahogany 4-Poster Bed. Block Brand.	$2,090.00	June 1998

Case Pieces

Description	Amount	Date
#906 Pine Hanging Shelf. Block Brand.	$880.00	June 2002
#907 Pine Hanging Wall Shelf. Block Brand.	$1,430.00	June 1999
#909 1-Drawer Oak Chest. Paper Label.	$1,760.00	March 1999
#913 Pine Chest of Drawers. Block Brand.	$3,410.00	November 2002
#916 Curly Maple Chest of Drawers. Block Brand.	$5,610.00	March 2001
#918 Mahogany Block Front Chest of Drawers. Block Brand.	$4,510.00	June 1998
#923 Pine Stepback Cupboard. Block Brand.	$4,290.00	November 1999
#931 Oak 2-Drawer Sunflower Chest. Script Brand.	$990.00	March 1998

Michael Ivankovich has been collecting Wallace Nutting pictures since 1974 and has been collecting Wallace Nutting furniture for nearly as long. Today he is generally considered to be the country's leading authority of Wallace Nutting pictures, books, furniture, and memorabilia.

This specialization in Wallace Nutting led to his first book in 1984, *The Price Guide to Wallace Nutting Pictures* First Edition. Three additional editions of that book were released between 1986 and 1991. He has also authored three other books relating to Wallace Nutting including: *The Alphabetical & Numerical Index to Wallace Nutting Pictures* (1988), *The Guide to Wallace Nutting Furniture* (1990), and *The Guide to Wallace Nutting-Like Photographers of the Early Twentieth Century* (1992). He has also published three additional books on Wallace Nutting: *The Wallace Nutting Expansible Catalog*, *Wallace Nutting: The Great American Idea*, and *Wallace Nutting Windsors: Correct Windsor Furniture*.

Michael Ivankovich

In 1997 his *Collector's Guide to Wallace Nutting Pictures: Identification & Value* was published by Collector Books and is generally considered to be the #1 book for Wallace Nutting picture collectors.

In 1998 he published *The Collector's Guide to Popular Early Twentieth Century Prints* which is actually eight individual prices guides, with separate value chapters on Wallace Nutting, David Davidson, Fred Thompson, Charles Sawyer, Maxfield Parrish, Bessie Pease Gutmann, R. Atkinson Fox, and a separate catch-all chapter on all of the lesser-known photographers.

Mr. Ivankovich conducted the first all-Wallace Nutting catalog auction in 1988. The enthusiasm generated by this auction has led to 60 more Wallace Nutting catalog auctions between 1988 and 2004, with quarterly auctions taking place each year throughout the New England and Mid-Atlantic states. Mr. Ivankovich's auctions now also appear on eBay Live Auctions.

These auctions have now become the national center of Wallace Nutting collecting. They provide buyers with the opportunity to compete for a wide variety of Wallace Nutting pictures and furniture ranging from common scenes to the best and rarest items in the country. These live catalog auctions also provide sellers and dealers with the opportunity to place their consignments in front of the country's leading and most knowledgeable collectors.

A frequent lecturer, Mr. Ivankovich has written articles for most major trade papers, has appeared on various radio and television programs, provides appraisal services, and is frequently consulted by antique columnists from throughout the country. His *Exploring Early Twentieth Century Prints* column appears in 12 trade papers and publications around the country.

Mr. Ivankovich is a licensed auctioneer in Pennsylvania and New Hampshire. He is a member of the National Auctioneers Association, the Pennsylvania Auctioneers Association, and has served as the president of the Lehigh Valley Society

A typical Michael Ivankovich Auction Co. auction

of Auctioneers. He is also a member of the Bucks County Antiques Dealers' Association. In 2004, the Pennsylvania Auctioneer's Association named Mr. Ivankovich as its 2004 Actioneer of the Year.

Michael and his wife Susan live in Doylestown, Pennsylvania, and have five children (Jenna, Lindsey, Megan, Nash, and son-in-law Jake), and two grandchildren (Jake and Kayla). They personally designed and maintain their seven websites which are all accessible through www.michaelivankovich.com (Sue operates her own web design business and has co-authored four cookbooks as well). You can either e-mail them at: ivankovich@wnutting.com Or you can write them at: PO Box 1536, Doylestown, PA 18901.

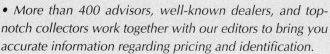